高等院校"财会"专业系列教材

会 计 英 语

刘建华 主 编
白 鸥 黑 岚 副主编

清华大学出版社
北 京

内 容 简 介

我国加入 WTO 后，随着我国经济的快速发展，社会呼唤、企业需要、市场急需大批精通会计英语的专门人才，这也正是本书出版的目的和意义。本书以企业财会活动为主线，深入浅出地介绍会计英语的制单、记账、核算、会计业务、财务管理及审计等知识技能；并以实际工作需要为核心，突出高职教育的特点，采用了单元制模块写法，具体形式包括：学习目标、对话、阅读、常用语句、口语练习、自测练习等环节。

由于本书具有内容翔实、贴近实际、实用性强，且采取新颖统一的格式化体例设计，因此不仅适用于高等院校会计、财务管理、审计、经济管理等专业的教学，也可以作为广大财会从业者的在岗培训教材，对于广大社会读者也是一本有益的专业读物。

本书封面贴有清华大学出版社防伪标签，无标签者不得销售。
版权所有，侵权必究。举报：010-62782989，beiqinquan@tup.tsinghua.edu.cn。

图书在版编目(CIP)数据

会计英语/刘建华主编；白鸥，黑岚副主编. —北京：清华大学出版社，2009.7(2021.1重印)
(高等院校"财会"专业系列教材)
ISBN 978-7-302-20383-4

Ⅰ.①会… Ⅱ.①刘… ②白… ③黑… Ⅲ.①会计—英语—高等学校—教材 Ⅳ.①H31

中国版本图书馆 CIP 数据核字(2009)第 101102 号

责任编辑：	章忆文　葛小莉			
装帧设计：	杨玉兰			
责任校对：	李玉萍			
责任印制：	宋　林			
出版发行：	清华大学出版社		地　址：	北京清华大学学研大厦A座
	http://www.tup.com.cn		邮　编：	100084
	社 总 机：010-62770175		邮　购：	010-62786544
	投稿与读者服务：010-62776969，c-service@tup.tsinghua.edu.cn			
	质量反馈：010-62772015，zhiliang@tup.tsinghua.edu.cn			
印 装 者：	三河市君旺印务有限公司			
经　　销：	全国新华书店			
开　　本：	185mm×260mm	印　张：18	字　数：	434千字
版　　次：	2009年7月第1版		印　次：	2021年1月第20次印刷
定　　价：	49.00元			

产品编号：026788-03

编委会

主　　任：牟惟仲

副 主 任：王纪平　吴江江　冀俊杰　赵志远　郝建忠　储祥银
　　　　　　鲁瑞清　丁建忠　周　平　王茹琴　王　松　米淑兰
　　　　　　宁雪娟　李大军

编　　委 (排名不分先后)：

　　　　宋承敏　仲万生　孟震彪　冯仁华　林　亚　王伟光
　　　　高光敏　阚晓芒　马爱杰　李贵保　白文祥　栾茂茹
　　　　卫停战　张惠欣　梁　露　孟乃奇　李书胜　李敬锁
　　　　付绪昌　盛定宇　孟繁昌　赵　茜　程旭阳　刘雅娟
　　　　赵立群　葛文芳　严晓红　赵春萍　朱学军　贾　晖
　　　　黄世一　卜晓铃　杨文杰　刘建华　王群建　李　洁
　　　　王桂霞　李爱华　白　鸥　吴　霞　王景香　李东辉

总　　编：李大军

副总编：梁　露　宁雪娟　武信奎　车亚军　程旭阳　刘雅娟

丛书序

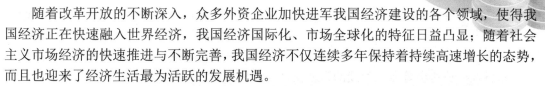

随着改革开放的不断深入,众多外资企业加快进军我国经济建设的各个领域,使得我国经济正在快速融入世界经济,我国经济国际化、市场全球化的特征日益凸显;随着社会主义市场经济的快速推进与不断完善,我国经济不仅连续多年保持着持续高速增长的态势,而且也迎来了经济生活最为活跃的发展机遇。

为此,国家需要不断地加大税制改革、调整财政与会计政策,以适应搞活经营、拉动内需、活跃市场、发展经济和与国际经济接轨的需要;为了稳步推动我国经济和社会全面、协调、可持续发展,国家财政部颁布和实施了新的《企业会计准则》,以促进我国会计理论与实践发生重大变革。会计是企业的管家,会计规章管理制度是企业合法经营的基本保障,企业会计准则与财务管理制度在发展经济、改善民生、构建和谐社会等方面发挥着极其重要的作用,财会政策体现了国家经济发展的主导性。

竞争与效益既是市场经济的核心,也是市场经济永恒的主题。企业要在激烈的市场竞争环境中求生存,寻发展,就必须不断提高经营效益、不断减少成本支出,就必须加强会计核算,强化财务管理。当前,面对激烈的市场竞争,面对经济的快速发展,面对就业上岗的压力,更新观念,学习新会计制度,调整业务知识结构,掌握新会计核算技能以及加强会计职业从业人员的技能培训与综合业务素质培养已成为目前亟待解决的问题。高等院校"财会"系列教材的出版,旨在培养大量财会专业人才,解决各行各业发展对既掌握财务理论知识又懂得会计实际业务的专业技能型人才的急需,对提高在岗从业人员业务素质,提升服务质量,促进会计工作规范化具有十分重要的意义。

本套教材是我们全面贯彻教育部关于"加强职业教育"的精神,严格按照高等职业教育教学必须"强化实践实训,突出技能培养"的要求,根据企业用人与就业岗位的真实需要,结合高职高专院校"财会"专业教学计划和"创新"课程设置与调整的实际情况,组织北京物资学院、北京联合大学、北方工业大学、北京财贸职业学院、首钢工学院、北京青年政治学院、北京石景山社区学院、北京城市学院、北京西城社区学院、北京朝阳社区学院、北京宣武社区学院及黑龙江、湖北、广西等全国30多所高校"财会"专业多年在一线从事教学的主讲教师和具有丰富实践经验的企业人士共同编写的。

针对我国高职教育"财会"专业存在的重理论轻实践、教材陈旧、知识老化、数据案例过时、缺乏创新、缺乏贴近行业企业实际而沿袭简化"克隆"写法等问题,本系列教材自觉地以科学发展观为统领,严守统一的创新型格式化设计,注重基础性、通俗性、实用性、注重校企结合、注重职业岗位要求与基本操作技能培训,遵循国家财政部颁布施行的新《企业会计准则》及其他规章制度,以培养实践技能和加强应用能力为主线。正是由于具有定位准确、理论适中、知识系统、内容翔实、案例丰富、贴近实际、突出实用性、适用范围宽泛及通俗易懂、便于学习和掌握等特点,因此本套教材不仅适合高职高专财会、财税及经管类各专业的教学，也可作为工商企业与经济公司财会及税务人员职业教育的岗位培训用书，对广大社会自学者也是非常有益的读物。在编写过程中，我们参考借鉴了大量有关会计核算和财务管理方面的书刊资料及管理制度与法规文件，并得到企业、院校、会计事务及行业协会等专家教授的帮助支持与具体指导，在此一并致谢。由于作者水平有限，书中难免有疏漏和不足，恳请同行和读者批评指正。

　　本书习题答案及电子课件下载服务网址：http://www.wenyuan.com.cn。

高等院校"财会"专业系列教材编委会

前　　言

随着我国改革开放进程的加快和社会主义市场经济的快速推进，随着我国加入 WTO 和中国经济的国际化发展，不仅有众多外资企业快速涌入，我国企业也在加速迈出国门参与国际市场竞争。为培养大批急需的具有会计英语专业知识与操作技能的专业人才，我们组织长期从事会计英语教学与实践活动的主讲教师及具有丰富经验的企业人士共同编写此教材，旨在迅速提高大学生和会计从业者的专业素质，更好地掌握会计英语，更好地服务于我国经济建设。本教材的出版，对帮助学生尽快熟悉外资企业会计操作规程与业务管理，对帮助学生顺利就业具有特殊意义。

全书共 10 个单元，以企业财会活动为主线，深入浅出地介绍会计英语的制单、记账、核算、会计业务、财务管理及财务审计等知识技能；并以实际工作需要为核心，突出高职教育特点，采用单元制模块写法，在每个单元中包括学习目标、词汇词组表、对话、阅读、常用语句、补充阅读材料、口语练习、自测练习等环节，有利于组织教学。

为了适应会计专业英语教学改革的需要，本书在编写上遵循如下原则。

第一，注重内容表达精确。本书参考了最新版本的多种会计英语教材，从实际出发，注意把握教学的深度和难度，采用简练的语言，注重表述的精确性和实用性。

第二，注重突出英语在会计业务中的具体运用。全书包括：常用专业英语词汇、日常主要经济业务的英文描述、各个会计业务过程的英语表述、会计报表的英文表现形式和会计工作中常用的英语表达方式和词汇等，注重英语语言和西方会计知识两者兼顾，并安排相应的课后实务练习，重在培养学生用英语处理日常会计业务的能力。

第三，体例新颖，紧跟时代。本书依据财政部最新颁布的会计准则和管理制度及法规，注意内容编排的创新，案例及例题均紧贴企业会计的真实业务，在对话设计中涵盖了日常会计业务交流的主要场景，通过相应的练习能够有效提高读者的会计英语交际能力，对现实财会工作具有较强的指导性。

第四，注重英语语法的强化。为了突出会计专业英语复合句的特点，在课文内容编写中特别选择了一些具有典型意义的句型，以使读者在学习专业会计英语的同时，能够有效地巩固已学英语的语法知识。

本书作为财会专业学历教育和职业培训的特色教材，注重知识体系的完整，突出会计英语实践能力和应用技能的培养，并注意教学内容和教材结构的创新。由于本书具有知识系统、内容翔实、案例丰富、贴近实际、突出实用性、通俗易懂、便于学习等特点，因此本书不仅适用于高职高专财务会计、审计等财经管理类专业的教学，也可作为企业财会从业人员的在职岗位培训教材，对于广大社会读者也是一本有益的读物。

本教材由李大军进行总体方案的策划和具体组织，刘建华主编和统稿，白鸥和黑岚担任副主编，最终由北京中瑞岳华会计师事务所黄峰注册会计师审定。编者分工：刘建华(第 1 单元、第 8 单元)，白鸥(第 2 单元、第 4 单元和第 7 单元)，李克红(第 2 单元、第 7 单元

和附录2),黄中军(第3单元),黑岚(第5单元和第9单元),牟章(第6单元),宋晓星和李康(第10单元和附录4),郭琦妮(附录1、附录3和附录5);李瑶和马瑞奇等人协助有关单元的资料查找和编写,李晓新负责本教材课件的制作。

在编写过程中,我们参考了大量有关会计英语的最新书刊资料和财政部新出台的会计准则及财务管理规章制度,并得到业内专家教授的具体指导,在此一并致谢。因编写时间紧,作者水平有限,书中难免存在疏漏和不足,恳请同行和读者批评指正。

编 者

目 录

Unit 1　Basic Knowledge of Accounting .. 1
- Dialogue 1
- Section 1　What is accounting 5
- Section 2　Accounting Elements & Accounting Equation 6
- Section 3　T account & Double-entry System 7
- Section 4　The Ledger and Chart of Accounts 8
- Section 5　Journalizing and Posting Entries 13
- 应用专栏 17
  - Useful Expressions 17
  - Additional Reading Material 19
  - Oral Practices 20
  - Self-test Exercises 20
- 参考译文 23

Unit 2　Current Assets 34
- Dialogue：Cash Management 34
- Section 1　Cash and Cash Equivalents 37
- Section 2　Accounts Receivable 37
- Section 3　Inventory 39
- Section 4　Short- term Investment 40
- 应用专栏 42
  - Useful Expressions 42
  - Additional Reading Material 43
  - Oral practices 44
  - Self-test Exercises 45
- 参考译文 48

Unit 3　Long-term Assets 53
- Dialogue 53
- Section 1　Fixed Assets 56
- Section 2　Depreciation of Fixed Assets 56

- Section 3　Intangible Assets 60
- 应用专栏 62
  - Useful Expressions 62
  - Additional Reading Material 65
  - Oral Practices 66
  - Self-test Exercises 66
- 参考译文 69

Unit 4　Liabilities 74
- Dialogue 74
- Section 1　Current Liabilities 77
- Section 2　Long-term Liabilities 79
- 应用专栏 81
  - Useful　Expressions 81
  - Additional Reading Material 82
  - Oral Practices 83
  - Self-test Exercises 83
- 参考译文 84

Unit 5　Owner's Equity 89
- Dialogue：The accounting of Owner's Equity 89
- Section 1　Ownerships of Business Entities 91
- Section 2　Sole Proprietorship and Partnerships Accounting 92
- Section 3　Rights and Privilege of Shareholders 94
- Section 4　Capital vs. Retained Earnings 95
- Section 5　Issuance of Shares 96
- Section 6　Retained Earnings 97
- 应用专栏 102
  - Useful Expressions 102
  - Additional Reading Material 105
  - Oral Practices 108

Self-Test Exercises 109
参考译文 112

Unit 6　Revenue & Expense 122

Dialogue 122
Section 1　Revenue 124
Section 2　Expenses 126
应用专栏 127
　　Useful Expressions 127
　　Additional Reading Material 128
　　Oral Practices 128
　　Self-test exercises 129
参考译文 130

Unit 7　Financial Statements 132

Dialogue：What is Balance Sheet 132
Section 1　Balance Sheet 134
Section 2　the Income Statement 135
Section 3　Cash Flow Statement 137
应用专栏 140
　　Useful Expressions 140
　　Additional Reading Material 141
　　Oral Practices 142
　　Self-test Exercises 143
参考译文 145

Unit 8　Interpretations of financial statements 150

Dialogue 150
Section 1　Introduction to Financial Analysis 155
Section 2　Limitations of financial ratio analysis 158
应用专栏 159
　　Useful Expressions 159

Additional Reading Material 161
Oral Practices 161
Self-test Exercises 163
参考译文 164

Unit 9　Cost Accounting and Management Accounting 167

Dialogue 167
Section 1　Cost Elements 169
Section 2　Cost Accounting—A Concept Emphasis 171
Section 3　Management Accounting ... 174
Section 4　Cost-Volume-Profit Analysis 176
应用专栏 179
　　Useful Expressions 179
　　Additional Reading Material 181
　　Oral Practices 182
　　Self-Test exercises 183
参考译文 184

Unit 10　Auditing 191

Dialogue 191
Section 1　Introduction of Modern Auditing 194
Section 2　the Process of Auditing 196
Section 3　Audit Report 198
应用专栏 199
　　Useful Expressions 199
　　Additional Reading Material 201
　　Oral Practices 206
　　Self-test Exercises 207
参考译文 210

附录 A　常用词汇汇编 215
附录 B　会计报表汇编 235

附录 C　财务比率术语英文详解..............249

附录 D　企业会计准则——基本准则
　　　　中英文对照.....................251

附录 E　原版英文求职信：
　　　　应聘会计师事务所.....................263

参考答案.....................264

参考文献.....................274

Unit 1 Basic Knowledge of Accounting

Objectives

- In Dialogue, students should understand the meaning of each accounting principle.
- In Section 2, students should understand the meaning of the accounting elements and the accounting equation.
- In Section 3, T account and double-entry system are demonstrated. Students should know the structure of T account and understand how to make correct entries based on double-entry system.
- In Section 4 and Section 5, students should learn to make entries in the ledger accounts, journalize transactions and post them to the ledgers.

Dialogue

1. GAAP

John: Have you seen or heard of the abbreviation GAAP?

Mary: I've seen it before, but I only know that GAAP is the initial of "Generally Accepted Accounting Principles". I don't know what principles are included in it.

John: GAAP consists of a series of concepts, assumptions and principles.

Mary: GAAP could include concepts and assumptions?

John: Yes. The major concept is the concept of accounting entity; of course, it can also be called an assumption. The other assumptions are the going concern assumption, the accounting period assumption, and the stable money unit assumption.

Mary: Does the accounting entity refer to an organization accounting serves?

John: Yes. An accounting entity is any economic organization which controls resources and engages in economic activities. Accounting for every entity should be independent.

Mary: I guess the accounting period refers to a time period like a year or a month, right?

John: Right. The account entity is assumed to continue in operation for a period of time sufficient to carry out its commitments and realize its objectives. It's what we call the going concern assumption. But in order to make it more convenient to measure, we divide the life of a business into time periods of equal length, like a year, a quarter, or a month. The time periods are what we call accounting periods.

Mary: Then what does the stable money unit assumption refer to?

John: It requires that money be used as the basic measuring unit for financial reporting. According to this assumption, accounting recording generally doesn't consider the effect of inflation, that is, the purchasing power remains unchanged.

Mary: I think it's a shortcoming, for it can't reflect true values of the product or service at different time.

John: It's true. However, in periods of low inflation, this assumption doesn't cause serious problems. If the effects of inflation are too great, you can explain it by preparing supplementary information upon financial statements.

Mary: That's a good idea.

译文： 公认会计原则

约翰： 见到过或听到过GAAP这个缩写吗？

玛丽： 以前见过。但我只知道GAAP是公认会计原则的英文首字母缩写。公认会计准则到底有哪些，我就不知道了。

约翰： 公认会计原则是由一系列的概念、假设和原则构成的。

玛丽： 公认会计原则居然还包括概念和假设？

约翰： 是的。主要的概念是会计主体概念，当然这也可以说成是一种假设。其他的假设有持续经营假设、会计期间假设和稳定货币单位假设。

玛丽： 会计主体是指会计为之服务的组织吧？

约翰： 是的。会计主体是指任何一个掌握资源并从事经济活动的经济组织。每一个主体的会计都应独立。

玛丽： 我猜想，会计期间是指一年或一个月这样的时间段，对吗？

约翰： 对。会计主体都被假设为能存续足够长的时间以履行其职责，实现其目标，我们称为持续经营假设。但为了便于计量，我们把企业的整个生存期划分为相等长度的期间，如一年、一个季度或一个月，这就是会计期间。

玛丽： 那么，稳定货币单位假设指的是什么呢？

约翰： 它要求用货币单位作为财务报告的基本计量单位。根据该项假设，会计记录中一般不考虑通货膨胀的影响，即假设购买力保持不变。

玛丽： 我觉得这是个缺点，因为它不能真实地反映商品和服务在不同时期的真正价值。

约翰： 是的。但在低通货膨胀时期，这个假设一般不会产生什么严重问题。如果影响较大，可在编制财务报表时，编制补充信息予以说明。

玛丽： 这个主意不错。

2. Major Principles

Mary: Besides the four assumptions you mentioned, what principles does the GAAP include?

John: Major principles include the objective principle, the materiality principle, the consistency principle, the conservatism principle, the accrual basis accounting principle, the adequate disclosure, the matching principle, the realization principle, and the cost principle.

Mary: Oh, so many. But for some principles, I can tell the meaning from its name. For example, the objective principle may mean that accounting should reflect the transactions truly and objectively, right?

John: Quite right. Then, please guess the meaning of the consistency principle and the conservatism principle.

Mary: I guess the consistency principle means that accounting data can't be changed and the conservatism principle requires that accountants not be too optimistic of transactions, right?

John: The consistency principle means that accounting methods should be consistent from one period to the other and shouldn't be arbitrarily changed. The conservatism principle does require accountants not be too optimistic, but its fundamental meaning is like this: Accountants should be conservative in choosing the one that has the least favorable impact on net income when there are two or more alternative accounting methods.

Mary: Thank you for your instruction. Does the adequate disclosure principle require that accountants report as much accounting information as possible when they prepare financial statements?

John: You're quite right there. But when they disclose the information, they should obey the regulations of the law, the industry, and the company, and the information should be focused on certain aspects. Yes, the materiality requires accountants pay more attention to the important items of the financial statements. Of course, there are no definite criteria by which to judge whether an item is important. It is subject to the judgment of the account in practice. Besides, the matching principle is to compare the revenue with the expenses of the same period and work out the net income or net loss of that period. In most cases, the realization principle indicates that the revenue should be recognized at the time goods are sold or services are rendered. At this point, the business has essentially completed the earning process and the sales value of the goods or services can be measured objectively. At any time prior to sale, the ultimate sales values of the goods or services sold can only be

estimated. As for the cost principle, both the balance sheet and the income statement are affected by it. Assets are initially recorded in the accounts at cost, and no adjustment is made to the evaluation in later periods.

Mary: What does the accrual basis accounting principle mean then?

John: The accrual basis and the cash basis are two different accounting principles. According to the accrual basis principle, whenever a transaction happens, the accountant should enter it into the journal, whether or not cash has been received or paid. But under the cash basis accounting, the entry is done only when cash is received or paid. In comparison, the accrual basis accounting is more justifiable, for it provides more complete information.

Mary: It is very practical.

译文：主要的会计原则

玛丽：公认会计原则除你所说的四个假设外，还有哪些原则？

约翰：主要有客观性原则、重要性原则、一致性原则、稳健性原则、权责发生制原则、充分披露原则、配比原则、实现原则和成本原则。

玛丽：哦，这么多。但有些原则，我能根据名称猜出意思来。比如客观性原则，可能是指会计工作应真实、客观地反映经济业务，对吗？

约翰：非常对。那你猜猜一致性原则和稳健性原则。

玛丽：我想一致性原则是指会计数据不能改动，稳健性原则要求会计师不能对经济业务过分乐观，是吗？

约翰：一致性原则是指会计处理方法前后各期应当保持一致，不能随意变更。稳健性原则确实是要求会计师不能过分乐观，但其根本的意思是说，当有两种或两种以上的会计方法可以选择时，会计师应稳健地选择一种可以使净收益最低的方法。

玛丽：谢谢你的指教。充分披露原则是不是要求会计师在编制财务报表时，尽量多地报告会计信息？

约翰：说得非常对。但在披露信息时，应遵守法律规定以及行业和公司规定，要有所侧重。对了，重要性原则要求会计师关注财务报表中的重要项目。当然，一个项目是否重要，并没有明确的标准，这需要会计师在实践中加以判断。另外，配比原则就是将收入与当期的费用进行比较，计算出当期的净损益。实现原则在大多数情况下是指收入应该在销售商品和提供劳务的那一刻确认。这时，企业已经基本完成了盈利过程并且商品或劳务的销售价值可以被客观地计量。在销售以前的任何时刻，销售商品或提供劳务的基本价值只是个估计。至于成本原则，资产负债表和收益表都要受其影响。资产最初是按成本记账的，以后期间不对资产估算作调整。

Unit 1 Basic Knowledge of Accounting

玛丽：那么，权责发生制原则又是什么意思呢？

约翰：权责发生制和现金收付制是两种不同的会计原则。根据权责发生制原则，会计师在交易发生时，不论现金是否收到或付出，都应马上在日记账中予以记录。而在现金收付制下，仅当有实际的现金收付才予以记录。相比之下，权责发生制更为合理，因为它提供的是更加完整的信息。

玛丽：这个原则非常实用。

Tips：The Securities and Exchange Commission took an important step toward what many hope will eventually lead to a global accounting standard, dropping a requirement that non-U.S. companies with U.S. listings reconcile their results to U. S. rules.

美国证券交易委员会(Securities and Exchange Commission，简称SEC)取消了在美国上市的外国企业所提交的财务报告必须符合美国公认会计原则(GAAP)的规定，许多人希望此举能为全球会计准则的最终形成带来重要推动。

Section 1 What is accounting

Accounting contains elements both of science and art. The important thing is that it is not merely a collection of arithmetical techniques but a set of complex processes depending on and prepared for people. The human aspect, which many people, especially accountants, forget, arises because:

1. Most accounting reports of any significance depend, to a greater or lesser extent, on people's opinions and estimates.

2. Accounting reports are prepared in order to help people make decisions.

3. Accounting reports are based on activities which have been carried out by people.

But what specifically is accounting? It is very difficult to find a pithy definition that is all-inclusive but we can say that accounting is concerned with:

The provision of information in financial terms that will help in decisions concerning resource allocation, and the preparation of reports in financial terms describing the effects of past resource allocation decisions.

Examples of resource allocation decisions are:

Should an investor buy or sell shares?

Should a bank manager lend money to a firm?

How much tax should a company pay?

Which collective farm should get the extra tractor?

As you can see, accounting is needed in any society requiring resource allocation and its usefulness is not confined to "capitalize" or "mixed" economies.

An accountant is concerned with the provision and interpretation of financial information. He does not, as an accountant, make decisions. Many accountants do of course get directly involved in decision making but when they do they are performing a different function.

Accounting is also concerned with reporting on the effects of past decisions. But one should consider whether this is done for its own sake or whether it is done in order to provide information which it is hoped will prove helpful in current and future decision. We contend that knowledge of the past is relevant only if it can be used to help in making current and future decisions, for we can hope that we shall be able to influence the future by making appropriate decisions but we cannot redo the past. Thus the measurement of past results is a subsidiary role, but because of the historical development of accounting and, perhaps, because of the limitations of the present state of the art, " backward looking" accounting sometimes appears to be an end in itself and not as a means that will help in achieving a more fundamental objective.

Section 2 Accounting Elements & Accounting Equation

Financial accounting is intended to provide information both for managers and for the outsiders such as shareholders, banks, government agencies, the general public, etc. Accounting elements include assets, liabilities, owner's equity, revenue, expenses, and profits of a business during a certain accounting period.

Assets are, in general, the properties or economic resources that are owned by the business. Assets include such things as cash, accounts receivable, inventory, supplies, equipment, buildings, land, etc.

Liabilities are debts of a business, including such obligations as notes payable, accounts payable, tax payable, salaries payable, etc.

Owner's equity means the net assets of a business. It is the owner's interest in the business. When a business is owned by one person, the owner's equity is shown as "capital". But when it is owned by shareholders, it is shown as "shareholders' equity".

Revenue is the increase in owner's equity resulting from the sales of goods or services by the business. In amount, the revenue is equal to the cash, bank deposit and receivables gained in compensation for the goods or services rendered. Please note that a cash receipt qualifies as revenue only when it helps to increase owner's equity. Thus, borrowing cash from a bank does not belong to revenue; it simply belongs to liability.

Expenses are the decrease in owner's equity caused by the business's revenue-producing operations. In amount, the expense is equal to the value of goods and services used up in gaining revenue. Please also note that a cash payment can be regarded as an expense only if it decreases owner's equity.

Unit 1 Basic Knowledge of Accounting

Profit is also the increase in owner's equity resulting from profitable operation of a business. It is the excess of revenue over expenses for the accounting period.

The **accounting equation** shows the basic financial position of a business. It is represented by the relationship of assets to liabilities and owner's equity. Thus the accounting equation is:

$$\text{Assets} = \text{Liabilities} + \text{Owner's equity}$$

Assume that a business owns assets of \$1,000,000, borrows from creditor \$200,000, and the owner invests \$800,000. The entries made in the accounting equation would be:

Assets	=	Liabilities	+	Owner's equity
\$1,000,000	=	\$200,000	+	\$800,000

Suppose that \$5,000 in cash has been used to pay for a debt, the changed equation would then be:

Assets	=	Liabilities	+	Owner's equity
\$995,000	=	\$195,000	+	\$800,000

Suppose again that the business has received \$6,000 as an income; the accounting equation is as follows:

Assets	=	Liabilities	+	Owner's equity
\$1,001,000	=	\$195,000	+	\$806,000

Any business event that alters the amount of the accounting elements is called a **transaction**.

Section 3 T account & Double-entry System

T account is the simplest form of the account. It is so called because it resembles the letter "T". On top of the T account there is the account title and the account number. Below on each side of the vertical line are the debit which is on the left side and the credit which is on the right side. Often the debit and credit are abbreviated as Dr. and Cr. When an amount is placed on the left side of the account, the account is said to be debited. If the amount is entered on the right side, the account is credited. The difference between the debit and the credit side is called the balance of the account.

Table 1-1 T account

Account Title	
Debit	Credit

Whether an account is to be debited or credited depends on the accounting elements. By convention, increases in assets and expenses are recorded as debits, whereas increases in liability,

owner's equity, revenue and profit are recorded as credits. Asset and expense decreases are recorded as credits, whereas liability, owner's equity, revenue and profit decreases are recorded as debits.

Table 1-2   Entries in the T account

Assets and Expenses		Liability, Owner's Equity, Revenue and Profit	
Dr.	Cr.	Dr.	Cr.
+	−	−	+
(Increases)	(Decreases)	(Decreases)	(Increases)

In double-entry system, there are equal debit and credit entries for every transaction. Where there only two accounts affected, the debit and credit amounts are equal. If more than two accounts are affected, the total of the debit entries must equal the total of the credit entries. This rule helps when we need to find a mistake in our records. If the total debits do not equal total credits, there must be a mistake.

Section 4   The Ledger and Chart of Accounts

The actual accounts can differ depending on different accounting systems. In an accounting system, a separate account is designated for each asset, each liability, and each component of owner's equity, including revenues and expenses. That's to say, accounts are grouped according to accounting elements. These groups of accounts are called the **ledger**. As most businesses today, even the smallest, use computerized accounting systems, the accountants must establish the ledger accounts that can be easily and quickly referred to.

The emplacement of accounts and the number of accounts depend on the size and operations of a business. A small business may get by with as few as 20 or 30 accounts, while a large company may need several thousand. Therefore, it is desirable to establish a systematic method of identifying and locating each account in the ledger by means of chart of accounts.

The **chart of accounts** is a listing of the accounts by title and number. Businesses assign the numbers to different accounts for identification in an orderly manner. Usually they would use a three or four digital code that is useful in tracking down the accounts and adequately flexible for future expansion without revising the basic system. The following are the numerical designations for the ledger accounts under two three-digital code systems.

Table 1-3 Two Kinds of Three-digital Code Systems of Chart of Accounts

Account Group	Account Name	Account Number	Account Number
1.Assets	Cash	101	111
	Notes Receivable	105	113
	Accounts Receivable	106	114
	Supplies	125	116
	Prepaid Insurance	128	118
	Furniture	130	120
	Equipment	167	146
2.Liabilities	Notes Payable	201	211
	Accounts Payable	202	212
	Salaries Payable	205	213
	Unearned Revenue	236	214
3.Owner's equity	T. Lott, Capital	301	311
	T. Lott, Withdrawals	302	312
4.Revenue	Service Fees Earned	401	411
5.Expenses	Rent Expenses	501	511
	Salaries Expenses	502	512
	Supplies Expenses	504	513
	Utilities Expenses	506	518

Asset and liability accounts are arranged according to their liquidity. While income, expense and owner's equity accounts are listed according to their importance.

Let us show you how the accountant makes a meaningful record of a series of transactions step by step with the double entry system in the ledger accounts.

Example 1.1

During the month of January, Ted Lott, a lawyer

(1) invested $8,000 to open his practice.

(2) bought office supplies (stationery, forms, pencils, and so on) for cash, $700.

(3) bought several pieces of office furniture from Ferraro Furniture Company on account, $2,000.

(4) received $3,500 in service fees earned during the month.

(5) paid office rent for January, $600.

(6) paid salary for part-time help, $800.

(7) paid $1,600 to Ferraro Furniture Company on account.

(8) after taking inventory at the end of the month, Lott found that he had used $200 worth of supplies.

(9) withdrew $470 for personal use.

These transactions might be analyzed and recorded in the accounts as follow.

Transaction (1) — Invested $8,000 to open his practice. The two accounts affected are Cash and Capital. Remember that an increase in an asset (cash) is debited, whereas an increase in owner's equity (capital) is credited.

Cash		Capital	
Dr.	Cr.	Dr.	Cr.
+	−	−	+
(1) 8,000			(1) 8,000

Transaction (2) — Bought office supplies for cash, $700. Here we are substituting one asset (cash) for another asset (supplies). We debit Supplies because we are receiving more supplies. We credit Cash because we are paying out cash.

Cash		Supplies	
Dr.	Cr.	Dr.	Cr.
+	−	+	−
8,000	(2) 700	(2) 700	

Transaction (3) — Bought office furniture from Ferraro Furniture Company on account, $2,000. We are receiving an asset (equipment) and, therefore, debit Furniture to show the increase. We are not paying cash but creating a new liability, thereby increasing the liability account (Accounts Payable).

Furniture		Accounts Payable	
Dr.	Cr.	Dr.	Cr.
+	−	−	+
(3) 2,000			(3) 2,000

Transaction (4) — Received $3,500 in service fees earned during the month. In this case, we are increasing the asset account Cash, since we have received $3,500. Therefore, we debit it. We are increasing the owner's equity, yet we do not credit Capital. We contemporarily separate the revenue from the owner's equity (capital) and create a new account, Fees Income.

Unit 1 Basic Knowledge of Accounting

Cash		Fees Income	
Dr.	Cr.	Dr.	Cr.
+	−	−	+
8,000	700		(4) 3,500
(4) 3,500			

Transaction (5) — Paid office rent for January, $600. We must decrease the asset account Cash because we are paying out money. Therefore, we credit it for $600. Expenses are also separated from the owner's equity. Therefore, a new account for the expense, Rent Expense is opened. The $600 is entered on the left side of Rent Expense since expense decreases capital.

Cash		Rent Expense	
Dr.	Cr.	Dr.	Cr.
+	−	+	−
8,000	700	(5) 600	
3,500	(5) 600		

Transaction (6) — Paid salary for part-time help, $800. Again, we must reduce our asset account Cash because we are paying out money. Therefore, we credit it. Lott's capital was reduced by an expense, and we open another account, Salaries Expense. A debit to this account shows the decrease in capital, an increase in expense.

Cash		Salaries Expense	
Dr.	Cr.	Dr.	Cr.
+	−	+	−
8,000	700	(6) 800	
3,500	600		
	(6) 800		

Transaction (7) — Paid $1,600 to Ferraro Furniture Company on account. This transaction reduced our asset account Cash since we are paying out money. We therefore credit Cash. We also reduce our liability account Accounts Payable by $1,600; we now owe that much less. Thus, we debit Accounts Payable.

Cash		Accounts Payable	
Dr.	Cr.	Dr.	Cr.
+	−	−	+
8,000	700	(7) 1,600	2,000
3,500	600		
	800		
	(7) 1,600		

Transaction (8) — **After taking inventory at the end of the month, Lott found that he had used $200 worth of supplies.** We must reduce the asset account Supplies by crediting it for $200. Supplies Expense is debited for the decrease in capital. This is computed as follows: Beginning inventory of $700, less supplies on hand at the end of the month $500, indicates that $200 have been used during the month.

Supplies		Supplies Expense	
Dr.	Cr.	Dr.	Cr.
+	−	+	−
700	(8) 200	(8) 200	

Transaction (9) — **Withdrew $470 for personal use.** The withdrawal of cash means that there is a reduction in the asset account Cash. Therefore, it is credited. The amount in the owner's equity (capital) account is also $470 less. We must open the account Withdrawals, which is debited to show the decrease in capital.

Cash		Withdrawals	
Dr.	Cr.	Dr.	Cr.
+	−	+	−
8,000	700	(9) 470	
3,500	600		
	800		
	1,600		
	(9) 470		

An account has a **debit balance** when the sum of its debits exceeds the sum of its credits; it has a credit balance when the sum of the credits is greater.

Section 5 Journalizing and Posting Entries

In the accounting cycle, journalizing is the second step after analyzing the transactions and business documents. **Journalizing** is the process to record transactions in a journal. The merits of journalizing are: providing a chronological record of transactions, helping locate errors in recording, simplifying the ledger entries, and enabling division of labor. A journal can be broken into two kinds: the general journal (or journal) and special journal.

1. General journal

For illustration of the general journal, let's take the transaction data in Example 1.1 for example.

Example 1.2

Journal   J-1   (page)

Date Year 2007		Account Titles and Explanation	P.R.	Debit($)	Credit($)
Jan.	4	Cash	101	8,000	
		T. Lott, Capital	301		8,000
		Investment in law practice			
	4	Supplies	125	700	
		Cash	101		700
		Bought supplies for cash			
	4	Furniture	130	2,000	
		Accounts Payable	201		2,000
		Bought from Ferraro Furniture Co. on account			
	29	Cash	101	3,500	
		Fees Income	401		3,500
		Receive service fees			
	30	Rent Expense	501	600	
		Cash	101		600

Date Year 2007		Account Titles and Explanation	P.R.	Debit($)	Credit($)
		Paid rent for month			
	30	Salaries Expense	502	800	
		Cash	101		800
		Paid salaries of part-time help			
	31	Accounts Payable	201	1,600	
		Cash	101		1,600
		Paid Ferraro Furniture Company on account			
	31	Supplies Expense	504	200	
		Supplies	125		200
		Adjustment of supplies used			
	31	T. Lott, Withdrawals	302	470	
		Cash	101		470
		Personal withdrawal			

Posting entries for the above general journal

Copying journal entries from the journal to the ledger for purpose of summarizing is called posting which is ordinarily carried out in the following steps: ①Copy the Date and amount (debit an credit) to the ledger accounts. ②Copy the journal page number(s) and account numbers for cross-reference in the P.R. columns.

Assets		=	Liabilities		+	Owner's Equity	
Cash		101	Accounts Payable	201		T. Lott, Capital	301
Jan.4	8,000		Jan.4	2,000		Jan.4	8,000
4		700	31 1,600				
29	3,500					T. Lott, Withdrawals	302
30		600				Jan.31 470	
30		800					
31		1,600				Fees Income	401
31		470				Jan.29	3,500

Supplies	125		Rent Expense	501
Jan.4 700			Jan.30 600	
Jan.31	200			

			Salaries Expense	502
			Jan.30 800	

Furniture	130		Supplies Expense	504
Jan.4 2,000			Jan.31 200	

2. Special journal

It is time-consuming and wasteful if transactions are First recorded in the general journal and then posted to the relevant general ledger. If special journals are used in this case, the recording and posting process would be much simpler and more efficient.

A special journal is designed to record a specific group of repetitive transactions, for instance, payrolls, cash receipts, cash disbursements, sales on account, purchases on account, etc. When special journals are used, the general journal is used only for adjusting and closing entries and for recording transactions that do not fit well in any special journal.

The design and number of a special journal will vary depending on the needs of a particular business. The special journals used in a typical firm are as follows.

Name of Special Journal	Journal No.	Type of Transaction
Cash Receipts Journal	CR-	All cash received
Cash Disbursements Journal	CD-	All cash paid out
Sales Journal	S-	All sales on account
Purchases Journal	P-	All purchases on account

Example 1.3

For illustration of the special journal, let's again take the cash disbursement transactions in Example 1.1 for example.

Cash Disbursements Journal   CD-1

Date	Description	P.R.	Check No.	Cash Cr.	Acc.Pay. Dr.	Sundry Dr.
Jan.4	Purchase supplies	125	1	700		700
30	Rent Expense	501	2	600		600
30	Salaries Expense	502	3	800		800
31	Ferraro Furniture Company	√	4	1,600	1,600	
31	Personal Withdrawal	302	5	470		470
				4,170	1,600	2,570
				(101)	(201)	(√)

Posting entries for the above special journal

1. The cash credit column ($4,170) is posted in total to the general ledger at the end of the month.

2. Debits to Accounts Payable represent cash paid to creditors. These individual amounts will be posted to of the creditors' accounts in the accounts payable subsidiary ledger. At the end of the month, the total of the accounts payable column is posted to the general ledger.

3. The Sundry column is used to record debits for any account that cannot be entered in the other special columns. They would include purchases of equipment, inventory, payment of expense, and cash withdrawals. Each item is posted separately to the general ledger at the time they are incurred. The total of the Sunday column (2,570) is NOT posted.

General Ledger

Assets		=	Liabilities		+	Owner's Equity	
Cash	101		Accounts Payable	201		T. Lott, Capital	301
Jan.4 8,000			Jan.4	2,000		Jan.4	8,000
29 3,500			31 1,600				
31	4,170			400		T. Lott, Withdrawals	302
7,330						Jan.31 470	
						Fees Income	401
						Jan.29	3,500
Supplies	125					Rent Expense	501
Jan.4 700						Jan.30 600	
Jan.31	200						
						Salaries Expense	502
						Jan.30 800	
Furniture	130					Supplies Expense	504
Jan.4 2,000						Jan.31 200	

Accounts Payable Subsidiary Ledger

Creditors' Accounts

Ferraro Furniture Company	
Jan.4	2,000
Jan.31 1,600	
	400
	(201)

应用专栏

Useful Expressions

accounting principle	会计准则
accounting element	会计要素
accounting equation	会计方程式(会计等式)
shareholder *n.*	股东
asset *n.*	资产
liability *n.*	负债
owner's equity	所有者权益
revenue *n.*	收益，收入
expense *n.*	费用
accounting period	会计期间
cash *n.*	现金
accounts receivable	应收账款
inventory *n.*	存货
notes payable	应付票据
accounts payable	应付账款
salaries payable	应付工资
shareholders' equity	股东权益
capital *n.*	资本
ledger *n.*	总分类账
chart of accounts	会计科目表
ledger account	总账账户
prepaid insurance	预付保险费
bank deposit	银行存款
cash receipt	现金收入
financial position	财务状况
creditor *n.*	债权人
creditors' account	债权人账户
transaction *n.*	经济业务
T account	丁字账户
account number	账户编号

debit *n. & vt.*	借方；借记
credit *n. & vt.*	贷方；贷记
enter *vt.*	登录，记账
double-entry *a.*	复式的，复式记账的
entry *n.*	分录
supplies expense	物资费用
debit balance	借方余额
credit balance	贷方余额
miscellaneous expense	其他费用，杂项费用
notes payable	应付票据
posting *n.*	过账
accounting cycle	会计循环，会计周期
journal *n.*	日记账
general journal	普通日记账
journalizing *n.*	登日记账
general ledger	总账
payroll *n.*	工资表
cash receipts	现金收入
cash disbursements	现金支出
sales on account	赊销
purchases on account	赊购
adjusting and closing entries	调整及结账分录

1. An accounting entity is an organization or a section of an organization that stands apart from other organizations and individuals as a separate economic unit.

会计主体是独立于其他企业的某一企业或团体，或某一企业的部门，以及作为独立经济单位的个人。

2. Under the going concern or continuity concept, accountants assume that the business will continue operating for the foreseeable future.

在持续经营假设下，会计人员假定企业在可以预见的将来持续经营。

3. In all business firms, revenues and expenses may be measured either on cash basis or accrual basis.

所有企业的收入和费用可以按收付实现制或权责发生制计量入账。

4. One of the principles of accounting is that information is provided to a clearly defined accounting entity.

会计的一个原则是会计信息应向某一特定的会计主体提供。

5. The cost principle is derived, in large part, from the principle of objectivity.

Unit 1 Basic Knowledge of Accounting

成本原则主要是在客观性原则的基础上发展而来的。

6. The principle of consistency implies that a particular accounting method, once adopted, will not be changed from period.

一致性原则的含义是，一旦采用某种会计方法，以后各期就不能改变。

7. The relationship among assets, liabilities, and owner's equity can be expressed in the accounting equation.

资产、负债和所有者权益之间的关系可以用会计等式表示。

8. The total figure for assets always equals the total figure for liabilities and owner's equity.

资产总额总是与负债和所有者权益总额相等。

9. For an account, the left side is the debit side and the right side is the credit side.

账户的左边是借方，右边的是贷方。

10. Asset and expense increases are recorded as debit.

资产或费用增加记为借项。

Additional Reading Material

Accounting is a system of gathering, summarizing, and communicating financial information for a business firm, government, or other organizations. Accounting, also called accountancy, enables decision makers to interpret financial information and use the results in planning for the future. For example, such data tell executives which products or departments are doing well and which poorly.

Business people often call accounting the "Language of Business" because they use accounting data in communicating about a firm's activities. Information provided by accountants helps managers and other executives understand the results of business transactions and interpret the financial status of their organization. With this knowledge, managers can make decisions about such matters as production, marketing, and financing. Charities, churches, colleges, government agencies, and other nonprofit organizations also use accounting to keep track of their financial situation.

Persons with little knowledge of accounting may fail to understand the difference between accounting and bookkeeping. Bookkeeping means the recording of transactions, the record making phase of accounting. The recording of transactions tends to be mechanical and repetitive, it is only a small part of field of accounting and probably the simplest part. Accounting includes not only the maintenance of accounting records, but also the design of efficient accounting systems, the performance of audits, the development of forecasts. A person might become a reasonably proficient bookkeeper in a few weeks or months; however, to become a professional accountant requires several years of study and experience.

Oral Practices

Directions: *Steven meets Tony after he has taken the financial accounting course. Read the conversation and answer the questions.*

Tony: Hi, Steven. How are you getting on with your lessons?

Steven: I am still struggling with my Accounting Principle course.

Tony: Oh, don't get discouraged. Not everyone can do as well as you.

Steven: Thanks. Tony, can you give me an example of an entity?

Tony: General Motors Corporation is a good case in point. It is an enormous entity that encompasses many smaller entities such as the Chevrolet Division and the Buick Division. In turn, Chevrolet encompasses many smaller entities such as a Michigan Assembly Plant and an Ohio Assembly Plant.

Steven: Why is the entity concept important?

Tony: Because it helps the accountant relate events to a clearly defined area of accountability.

Steven: Can you make it more specific?

Tony: For example, the business entity should not be confused with personal entity. A purchase of groceries for merchandise inventory is an accounting transaction of a grocer's store, which is the business entity, but the store owner's purchase of a stereo set with a personal check is a transaction of the owner, which is the personal entity.

Steven: I begin to understand. I think I need to do a lot of study today.

Tony: Keep up. Steven, you will make it.

Questions:

1. What is an entity?
2. What examples can you tell Steven to help him understand what an entity is?

Self-test Exercises

Section 2 & Section 3

Fill in the following blanks.

1. The accounting elements include _____, _____, _____, _____, _____, and _____.
2. Liabilities are _____ of a business.
3. Borrowing cash from a bank does not belong to _____; it simply belongs to liability.
4. Expenses are the decrease in owner's equity caused by the business's _____ operations.

Unit 1 Basic Knowledge of Accounting

5. Profit is the _____ of revenue over expenses for the accounting period.
6. The accounting equation is: _____ = _____ + _____ .
7. The debit side is on the _____ of the vertical line. The credit side is on the _____ of the account.
8. "Dr." stands for _____, while "Cr." is the abbreviation for _____ .
9. If an amount is recorded on the debit, account is said to be _____ .
10. Liability, owner's equity, revenue and profit decreases are recorded as _____ .

Section 4

Fill in the following blanks.

1. All owner's equity account numbers begin with the number _____ .
2. All revenue accounts begin with _____ , whereas expense account numbers begin with _____ .
3. Below is a list of accounts. Rearrange them as they would appear in the ledger by assigning a numerical designation for each one from these numbers: 107, 202, 302, 509, 102, 501, 401, 101, 201, 301.

    Accounts Payable   (   )
    Accounts Receivable   (   )
    Capital   (   )
    Cash   (   )
    Drawing   (   )
    Equipment   (   )
    Service Income   (   )
    Miscellaneous Expense   (   )
    Notes Payable   (   )
    Rent Expense   (   )

4. Record each transaction in the accompanying account of L & T Co.
(a) Bought supplies on account for $600.
(b) Bought equipment for $2,700, paying one third down and owing the balance.
(c) Gave a note in settlement of transaction (b).
(d) Received $500 as an income.

(a) _____Supplies_____   _____Cash_____   _____Accounts Payable_____
                                 Balance 2,000

(b) _____Equipment_____   _____Cash_____   _____Accounts Payable_____
                                 Balance 2,000

(c)	Accounts Payable		Cash		Notes Payble
	1,800	Balance 2,000			

(d)	Cash	Service Fees Income

Section 5

Fill in the following blanks.

1. Journalizing is the process to record transactions in a _____.

2. A _____ is designed to record a specific group of repetitive transactions, for instance, payrolls, cash receipts, cash disbursements, sales on account, purchases on account, etc.

3. When special journals are used, the general journal is used only for _____ entries and for recording transactions that do not fit well in any special journal.

4. The total of the Sundry column is _____.

5. Record the following entries in the general journal for Stephens Cleaning Company.

(a) Invested $10,000 cash in the business.

(b) Paid $2,000 for office furniture.

(c) Bought equipment costing $6,000 on account.

(d) Received $2,200 in cleaning income.

(e) Paid a quarter of the amount owed on the equipment.

		Dr.	Cr.
(a)			
(b)			
(c)			
(d)			
(e)			

6. For each of the following transactions, indicate with a check mark the special journal in

which it should be recorded.

(a) Sale of merchandise to M. Simpson on account, $680.
(b) Sale of merchandise to Andrea Co. for cash, $2,345.
(c) Cash returned to Andrea Co. for goods returned.
(d) Purchase materials on account, $3,000.
(e) M. Simpson returned part of merchandise sold, $35.

	Sales Journal	General Journal	Cash Journal	Purchases Journal
(a)				
(b)				
(c)				
(d)				
(e)				

参 考 译 文

第一节 什么是会计

会计既是科学，也是艺术。重要的是，它不仅仅是一项算术技术，而且是一套复杂的程序(因编制信息的人和信息使用者不同而有所不同)。会计中人的因素为许多人，尤其被会计人员所忽略，其产生的原因是：

(1) 大多数会计报告(无论多么重要)都或多或少地依赖于人的意见和估计。
(2) 编制会计报告是为了帮助人作决策。
(3) 会计报告以人们已经完成的活动为基础。

但是，会计究竟是什么？很难找到一个简练而全面的定义，但是我们可以说，会计是关于：

从财务角度提供有助于作出关于资源分配决策的信息，并从财务角度编制用来描述过去资源分配决策影响的报告。

资源分配决策的例子：
投资者应该买或卖股票吗？
银行经理应该将钱借给某家企业吗？
公司应该付给多少税？
哪家集体农场应该得到额外的拖拉机？

正如你所看到的，任何要求资源分配的社会都需要会计，其用处不限于资本主义经济或混合经济。

会计师的职责是提供和解释财务信息。作为会计师,他不作决策。当然,许多会计师直接参与决策,但是他们这样做时是在执行不同的职能。

会计的职能也包括对过去决策影响的报告。但是人们应该考虑的是这样做是为了例行公事还是为了提供可能有助于当前和未来决策的信息。我们认为,过去的知识只有当它有助于当前和未来决策时才是相关的,因为我们只能希望通过正确的决策以影响未来,但我们无法改变过去。因此,对过去结果的计量是次要的,但是因为会计的历史发展以及或许因为目前会计水平的局限性,"向后看"的会计有时似乎本身就是一个目标,而不是一种有助于达到更基本目标的手段。

第二节 会计要素和会计等式

财务会计是为内部管理层和股东,以及银行、政府机构、公众等外部人士提供信息的。会计要素包括资产、负债、所有者权益和一定会计期间的收入、费用和利润。

资产通常是指企业所拥有的财产或经济资源。资产包括现金、应收账款、存货、物资、设备、建筑物和土地等。

负债是企业的债务,包括应付票据、应付账款、应交税费和应付工资等。

所有者权益是指企业的净资产,是企业所有者的利益。当企业只由一个人拥有时,所有者权益被称为"资本"。但当企业由许多股东拥有时,则称为"股东权益"。

收入是企业销售商品或提供劳务而引起的所有者权益的增加。数量上,收入等于为补偿所提供的商品或劳务而获得的现金、银行存款和应收款项。请注意,收到现金只有在能增加所有者权益时才是收入。因此,从银行借入的现金不属于收入,它只属于负债。

费用是指由于企业产生收入的经营活动而导致的所有者权益的减少。数量上,费用等于获得收入时所耗费的商品和劳务的价值。也请注意,支出现金只有在减少所有者权益时才称为费用。

利润也是由于企业的盈利性活动而导致的所有者权益的增加。它是会计期间内收入超过费用的差额。

会计等式表示企业的基本财务状况。它表示资产和负债、所有者权益之间的关系。因此,会计等式是:

$$资产 = 负债 + 所有者权益$$

假设一家企业拥有$1 000 000资产,借入$200 000,所有者投入$800 000。代入会计等式就是:

资产　　　＝　　负债　＋　所有者权益
$1 000 000 ＝ $200 000 ＋ $800 000

假设有$5 000现金用于偿债,等式就变为:

资产　　　＝　　负债　＋　所有者权益
$995 000　＝　$195 000 ＋　$800 000

假如企业收到$6 000,会计等式如下:

$$资产 = 负债 + 所有者权益$$
$$\$1\,001\,000 = \$195\,000 + \$806\,000$$

任何改变会计要素金额的企业行为称为一项经济业务。

第三节 丁字账户和复式记账

丁字账户是最简单的账户形式。之所以这么称呼是由于它像字母"T"。丁字账户的顶部是账户名称和账户编号。竖线下左方称为借方,右方称为贷方。常缩写为 Dr. 和 Cr.。当一笔金额计入一个账户的左边时,这个账户被认为是借记。当一笔金额计入右边时,这个账户被认为是贷记。借方与贷方之间的差额被称为账户余额。

表 1-1 丁字账户

账户名称	
借	贷

一个账户是借记还是贷记取决于会计要素。按照惯例,资产和费用的增加记入借方,而负债、所有者权益、收入和利润的增加记入贷方。资产和费用的减少记入贷方,而负债、所有者权益、收入和利润的减少记入借方。

表 1-2 丁字账户中的记账

资产和费用		负债、所有者权益、收入和利润	
借	贷	借	贷
+	−	−	+
(增加)	(减少)	(减少)	(增加)

在复式记账法中,每笔交易都有相等的借贷方。当只涉及两个账户时,借贷双方金额相等。如果涉及超过两个账户,借方总额必定与贷方总额相等。这一规则有助于找出我们记账的错误。如果借方总额与贷方总额不相等,必定出现了错误。

第四节 分类账和会计科目表

不同的会计系统会有不同的账户。一个会计系统中,每一个资产、每一个负债项目以及所有者权益中的每一部分,包括收入和费用,都分配有一个单独的科目。也就是说,科目是根据会计要素来分类的。这些不同的账户种类被称为分类账。如今的大多数企业,即使是最小的企业,都应用电算化会计系统,会计人员必须建立能轻松快速查找的分类账科目。

账户的定位和编号取决于企业的规模和经营情况。小企业可能设置20~30个账户就够了，而大型公司可能需要设定数千个账户。因而，就有必要建立一种通过科目表在分类账中对每个账户进行识别和定位的系统方法。

会计科目表是一张列示所有账户名称和编号的一览表。企业以一定的秩序给不同的账户分配编号用于账户识别。通常用到三位或四位数字代码，这在查找账户时十分有用，而且在将来扩充账户时不用改变其基本系统，可以保持足够灵活性。以下就是在分类账目中两种三位数字代码的数字分配。

表 1-3　两种三位数字代码会计科目表系统

账户类别	账户名称	账户编号	账户编号
1. 资产	现金	101	111
	应收票据	105	113
	应收账款	106	114
	物资	125	116
	预付保险	128	118
	家具	130	120
	设备	167	146
2. 负债	应付票据	201	211
	应付账款	202	212
	应付工资	205	213
	预收收入	236	214
3. 所有者权益	特德·罗特，资本	301	311
	特德·罗特，提款	302	312
4. 收入	服务收入	401	411
5. 费用	租金	501	511
	工资费用	502	512
	物资费用	504	513
	公共事业费用	506	518

资产和负债项目是按其流动性顺序排列的。收入、费用和所有者权益项目是按重要性顺序排列的。

下面将展示会计师是如何在分类账账户中用复式记账法逐步对一系列经济业务进行记录的。

> **例 1.1**
>
> 在 1 月份，律师特德·罗特
>
> (1) 投资 8 000 美元开业；
> (2) 花费 700 美元现金购买办公设备(文具、表格和铅笔等)；
> (3) 从费雷罗家具公司赊购几件办公家具，价值 2 000 美元；
> (4) 收到 3 500 美元服务费用；

(5) 支付1月份办公室租金600美元;

(6) 为兼职者支付薪水800美元;

(7) 支付费雷罗家具公司1 600美元;

(8) 月底盘存后,罗特发现耗费了200美元物资;

(9) 从企业中提款470美元用于个人花销。

这些经济业务分析记账如下。

经济业务(1)投资8 000美元开业。涉及的两个账户是现金账户和资本账户。请记住,资产(现金)增加记在借方,所有者权益(资本)增加记在贷方。

现金		资本	
借	贷	借	贷
+	−	−	+
(1) 8 000			(1) 8 000

经济业务(2)购买办公设备,支付现金$700。在这里,一项资产(现金)转换为另一项资产(办公设备)。应借记办公设备,因为办公设备增加,贷记现金,因为支付了现金。

现金		办公设备	
借	贷	借	贷
+	−	+	−
8 000	(2) 700	(2) 700	

经济业务(3)从费雷罗家具公司赊购办公家具,价值2 000美元。收到一项资产(设备),借记家具账户表示增加。未支付现金产生一项新的负债,因此增加负债账户(应付账款)。

家具		应付账款	
借	贷	借	贷
+	−	−	+
(3) 2 000			(3) 2 000

经济业务(4)收到本月3 500美元服务费。在此情况下,因为收到3 500美元,增加了资产账户现金,所以借记现金。所有者权益增加,然而并不贷记资本账户。现在我们将收入从所有者权益(资本)中分离出来设立一个新账户:收入账户。

现金		收入	
借	贷	借	贷
+	−	−	+
8 000	700		(4) 3 500
(4) 3 500			

经济业务(5)支付1月份办公室租金600美元。付钱应减少资产账户现金,所以贷记600美元。费用也要从所有者权益中分开。应设立一个新的费用账户:租金费用账户。由于费用的发生减少了资本,所以600美元记入租金费用账户的左边。

现金		租金费用	
借	贷	借	贷
+	−	+	−
8 000	700		
3 500	(5) 600	(5) 600	

经济业务(6)支付兼职人员工资800美元。支付工资,我们应再次减少资产账户现金。所以贷记现金账户。费用的发生减少了罗特的资本,应开设另一个账户:工资费用。借记该账户表示资本减少,费用增加。

现金		工资费用	
借	贷	借	贷
+	−	+	−
8 000	700	(6) 800	
3 500	600		
	(6) 800		

经济业务(7)支付费雷罗家具公司1 600美元。付出钱,资产账户现金减少,因而贷记现金账户。负债账户应付账款也减少了1 600美元。现在欠款少了很多。所以借记应付账款账户。

现金		应付账款	
借	贷	借	贷
+	−	−	+
8 000	700	(7) 1600	2000
3 500	600		
	800		
	(7) 1 600		

经济业务(8)月末盘存后,罗特发现用了200美元的物资。应贷记资产账户——物资$200,因为资本减少,借记物资费用账户。计算如下:期初存货700美元,减去期末存货500美元,显示本月花销了200美元的存货。

Unit 1 Basic Knowledge of Accounting

物资		物资费用	
借	贷	借	贷
+	−	+	−
700	(8) 200	(8) 200	

经济业务(9)提取 470 美元个人使用。提取现金意味着资产账户现金减少，所以要贷记现金账户。所有者权益(资本)账户金额也减少了 470 美元。应设立提款账户，借记该账户表示资本减少。

现金		提款	
借	贷	借	贷
+	−	+	−
8 000	700	(9) 470	
3 500	600		
	800		
	1 600		
	(9) 470		

一个账户的借方金额大于贷方金额时，该账户有借方余额；当贷方金额更大时，该账户有贷方余额。

第五节　登记日记账和过账

在会计循环中，登记日记账是分析经济业务和营业单据后的第二步。登记日记账是在日记账中记录经济业务的过程。登记日记账的优点有：对经济业务进行序时的记录；帮助在记录时确定差错之处；简化分类账的分录；容许分工。日记账分为两类：普通日记账(或日记账)和特种日记账。

1. 普通日记账

以下以例 1.1 中的经济业务数据为例，来阐述普通日记账。

例 1.2

日记账 J-1 (页)

日　期 2007 年		账户名称及摘要	备　查	借　方	贷　方
1 月	4 日	现金	101	8 000	
		特德·罗特，资本	301		8 000

续表

日　期	账户名称及摘要	备　查	借　方	贷　方
2007年				
	投资开业			
4日	物资	125	700	
	现金	101		700
	用现金购买物资			
4日	家具	130	2 000	
	应付账款	201		2 000
	从费雷罗家具公司赊购办公家具			
29日	现金	101	3 500	
	收入	401		3 500
	收到服务费			
30日	租金	501	600	
	现金	101		600
	支付当月租金			
30日	工资费用	502	800	
	现金	101		800
	支付兼职人员工资			
31日	应付账款	201	1 600	
	现金	101		1 600
	支付赊购费雷罗家具公司办公家具款项			
31日	物资费用	504	200	
	物资	125		200
	已用物资调整			
31日	特德·罗特，提款	302	470	
	现金	101		470
	个人提款			

将分录过入上述普通日记账

为了汇总而将日记账中的分录过入分类账中称为过账，通常包括下列步骤：①将日期和金额(借方和贷方)记入分类账账户中；②在备查栏中记下日记账页数和账户编号以便核对。

资产	=	负债	+	所有者权益	
现金	101	应付账款	201	特德·罗特，资本	301
1月4日 8 000		1月4日	2 000	1月4日	8 000
4日	700	31日 1 600			
29日 3 500				特德·罗特，提款	302
30日	600			1月31日 470	
30日	800				
31日	1 600			收入	401
31日	470			1月29日	3 500
物资	125			租金	501
1月4日 700				1月30日 600	
1月31日	200				
				工资费用	502
				1月30日 800	
家具	130			物资费用	504
1月4日 2 000				1月31日 200	

2. 特种日记账

如果先将经济业务记入普通日记账，然后再过账到相关总分类账中，这会花费不少时间。这种情况下，如果使用特种日记账，则记账和过账程序会简单得多，并且更加有效。

特种日记账旨在记录某一重复发生的特定类别的经济业务，如员工薪水册、现金收入、现金支出、赊销和赊购等。当使用特种日记账时，普通日记账就只用于登记调整分录和结账分录，以及不适合使用特种日记账进行记录的经济业务。

出于特定业务的需要，特种日记账的种类和编号也是不同的。典型的企业会用到下列特种日记账：

特种日记账的名称	日记账编号	经济业务类型
现金收入日记账	CR-	现金收入
现金支出日记账	CD-	现金支出
销货日记账	S-	赊销
购买日记账	P-	赊购

例 1.3

下面，我们再次以例 1.1 中的现金支出业务为例来阐述特种日记账。

现金支出日记账　　　　　　　　　　　　　　　现付-1

日期	摘要	备查	支票号码	现金贷方	应付账款借方	杂项栏借方
1月4日	购买物资	125	1	700		700
30日	租金费用	501	2	600		600
30日	工资费用	502	3	800		800
31日	费雷罗家具公司	√	4	1 600	1 600	
31日	个人提款	302	5	470		470
				4 170	1 600	2 570
				(101)	(201)	(√)

将分录过入上述特种日记账。

1. 将现金贷方栏($4 170)总额月末过入总分类账。

2. 借记应付账款表示应付给债权人的现金。这些单个的金额将过入应付账款明细分类账的债权账户中。月末，应付账款栏的总额过入总分类账。

3. 杂项栏用于登记不能记入其他专门栏目的借方账户。这包括购买设备、存货、支付费用和现金提款。每一项在发生时单独过入总分类账。杂项栏的总金额(2 570)没有过账。

总分类账

资产　　＝　　负债　　＋　　所有者权益

现金		101
1月4日	8 000	
29日	3 500	
31日		4 170
	7 330	

应付账款		201
1月4日		2 000
31日	1 600	
		400

特德·罗特，资本		301
1月4日		8 000

特德·罗特，提款		302
1月31日	470	

收入		401
1月29日		3 500

物资		125
1月4日	700	
31日		200

租金费用		501
1月30日	600	

工资费用		502
1月30日	800	

家具		130
1月4日	2 000	

物资费用		504
1月31日	200	

Unit 1 Basic Knowledge of Accounting

应付账款明细分类账	
债权人账户	
费雷罗家具公司	
1月4日	2 000
1月31日 1 600	
	400
	(201)

Unit 2 Current Assets

Objectives

- In Section 1, students should understand the importance of cash and the accounting treatment of cash.
- In Section 2, students ought to learn the treatment of bad debt and how to make an allowance for doubtful accounts.
- In Section 3, students should understand the categories of inventories and learn to use the inventory valuation method.
- In Section 4, students must understand the meaning of short-term investments and learn the accounting treatment of short-term investments.

Dialogue: Cash Management

John: The business should establish a cash account, right?

Mary: Generally more than one. By its definition in the accounting, the cash not only includes paper money and coins the business holds, but also bank deposits and highly liquid instruments like checks and money orders. Therefore, the business usually has a cash on hand account and some bank deposit accounts. If the business has checking accounts with several banks, then it will maintain a separate ledger account for each bank account.

John: Accountants play a very important role in cash management, don't they?

Mary: Yes. Their responsibilities in cash management are really important.

John: I think accountants should provide accurate accounting for cash receipts, cash disbursements, and cash balances.

Mary: More than that. They should ensure that the business has sufficient cash for operations and meanwhile they should make good use of the cash and create some income.

John: By depositing the cash with the bank?

Mary: No. Generally, bank deposits don't generate income, so they should invest the idle cash, for example, by purchasing some marketable securities that may increase in value.

John: Then accountants should make a comprehensive cash plan for the business.

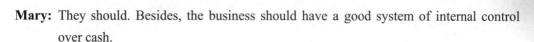

Mary: They should. Besides, the business should have a good system of internal control over cash.

John: What specific things should the system include?

Mary: First, cash handling should be separated from cash recording. Employees who handle cash should not have access to the accounting records, and accounting personnel should not have access to cash.

John: In this way, a good mechanism of controlling each other can be ensured.

Mary: Yes. Each department of the business should have a practical and feasible cash budget so that the business will not run short of cash or have too much excessive cash. Of course, all cash receipts should be deposited in the bank in order to prevent the cash from being stolen. In addition, all major payments should be made by check.

John: Besides, the validity of every expenditure should be verified before a check is issued in payment, right?

Mary: Right. Also, accountants should reconcile bank statements with the accounting records and prepare a statement of bank reconciliation.

John: Why is the reconciliation necessary?

Mary: Usually the balance in the bank statement is different from that in the cash account of the business. Some transactions recorded by the business may not have been recorded by the bank. For example, checks have been issued and recorded by the business but not yet presented to the bank for payment. Of course, the bank statement doesn't have such checking payments.

John: Is it possible that some transactions recorded in the bank statement are not recorded in the cash account of the business?

Mary: It's possible. Collections by the bank for the company, NSF checks and relevant charges are just cases in point.

John: NSF checks?

Mary: NSF is the abbreviation of " Not Sufficient Funds". When the company deposits a check issued by his client in a bank account, the bank will immediately credit the company's account for the amount of the check. On occasions, the check proves to be un-collectible because the maker of the check does not have sufficient funds in his account. In such case, the bank will debit the company's account for the amount of the check and return the check to the company marked " NSF ".

John: Then this check cannot be considered cash, can it?

Mary: No. This check can only be regarded as an account receivable.

译文：现金管理

约翰： 公司都应该设立现金账户，对吧？

玛丽： 一般还不止一个现金账户。根据会计中的定义，现金不仅包括公司拥有的纸钞和硬币，还有银行存款和高流动性票据，比如支票和汇票。因此，公司应当有一个现金账户和若干银行存款账户。如果公司在几家银行都有支票账户，应该给每个银行的账户分别设立分类账。

约翰： 在现金管理中，会计人员扮演着非常重要的角色，是吧？

玛丽： 对，他们对现金管理的责任实在是太重要了。

约翰： 我认为，无论是现金收入、现金支出，还是现金余额，会计人员都应该进行准确无误的记账。

玛丽： 不止如此。会计人员应该确保公司有足够的现金用于运营。同时，还应当很好地使用现金并取得收益。

约翰： 是靠把现金存入银行吗？

玛丽： 不是。一般来说，银行存款不产生收益，所以应该用闲置资金进行投资。比如，购买可能升值的有价证券。

约翰： 那么，会计人员就要为公司做一个详尽的现金计划了。

玛丽： 是的。而且，公司应该有一套良好的现金内部控制系统。

约翰： 这样的系统都包括什么特殊的东西呢？

玛丽： 首先，掌管现金和记录现金账目应该分开。掌管现金的人不能去为现金做会计记录。反过来，记账人员也不能够掌管现金。

约翰： 这样的话，就确保了互相控制的良好机制。

玛丽： 是的。公司的每一个部门都应该有切实可行的现金预算，以使公司不至于出现现金短缺或者是现金大量闲置。当然，所有的现金收入都应该存入银行，以免发生现金被盗。此外，所有重要的支付项目都应通过支票完成。

约翰： 还有，在签支票付款之前，是不是每一笔开支的有效性都要得到证实？

玛丽： 对，而且会计人员应当确保银行对账单和会计记录一致，并填制银行存款调节表。

约翰： 为什么必须要做调节表？

玛丽： 一般来说，银行对账单的余额和公司现金账户的余额都会有差异。有些经济业务被公司做了账，但可能银行没有做记录。比如，公司已经签发支票并做了账，但支票还没有到银行手中，并没有付款。当然，银行对账单上也就没有支票付款的记录了。

约翰： 是不是有可能某些经济业务被银行做了记录，但并没有记录在公司的现金账中呢？

玛丽： 有可能。公司委托银行的收款、NSF 支票及相关费用就属于这种情况。

约翰： NSF 支票？

玛丽：NSF 是"存款不足"的英文缩写。当公司把客户签发的支票存入银行账户时，银行会立刻把支票的金额记录在公司账户的贷方。但有时，支票被证明是不可收回的，因为出票人的账户中没有足够的金额。在这种情况下，银行会把支票所载金额记录在公司账户的借方，在支票上注明"NSF"并交还公司。

约翰：然后这张支票就不能再相当于现金了吗？

玛丽：不能。这张支票只能被看做是应收账款。

Section 1 Cash and Cash Equivalents

Cash is money in the form of bills or coins, which can prompt payment for goods or services in currency or by check. And cash includes cash equivalents, such as bank deposits, checks and money orders.

In the balance sheet, cash is listed first among the current assets, because it is the most liquid of all current assets and the banker, credit manager, or investor who studies a balance sheet critically is always interested in the total amount of cash as compared with other balance sheet items, such as accounts payable.

Cash and all kinds of deposits should be accounted for according to the actual amount of receipt and payment, and cash on hand, cash in bank and marketable securities shall be accounted for separately.

Section 2 Accounts Receivable

A business's **accounts receivable** are the amounts that its customers owe it and these accounts receivable are sometimes called trade creditors.

Accounts receivable are classified as current assets and appear on the balance sheet immediately after cash and cash equivalents.

Accounts receivable happen only when the term is short or when the amount to be received is not very big. However, a note receivable is used in western countries when a firm expects to collect a receivable in a longer period, or when the sum of the receivable is big. A notes receivable usually includes the maturity date and rate of interest.

If some customers will fail to pay their debts, these accounts receivable would be un-collectable. Companies recognize the fact that not all sums will be collected by reporting (on the balance sheet) accounts receivable less an allowance for bad debts.

Allowance for bad debts is the estimated amount of accounts receivable that will not be collected. Any accounts receivable, proved to be definitely un-collectable according to

regulations, should be recognized as bad debts and written off against allowance for bad debts or charged to current profit or loss, if such allowance is not set up. When an accounts receivable is written off as un-collectable, the customer still has an obligation to pay. Allowance for bad debts is a contra asset account, or you can say, a provision.

The net realizable value is the amount that a company is actually expecting to get in the future. When computing the total assets, a company uses the net realizable value.

net realizable value=accounts receivable−allowance for bad debts

Assume that a business has accounts receivable of $1,000,000, and the allowance for bad debts is $50,000. So, on the balance sheet, accounts receivable would be:

net realizable value=$1,000,000−$50,000=$950,000

Example 2.1

ABC company had the following transactions in 2007:

(1) Recognized $5,000 of sales revenue earned on account;

(2) Collected $3,000 cash from accounts receivable;

(3) Recognized $500 of bad debt expense for accounts receivable that are expected to be un-collectible in the future.

These transactions might be analyzed and recorded in the accounts as follows:

Transaction (1)

Assets (accounts receivable) and Owner's equity (sales revenue) increase by the same amount.

Assets	=	Liabilities	+	Owner's equity	Rev.	−	Exp.	=	Net Inc.	Cash Flow	
5,000	=		+	5,000		−		=			

Transaction (2)

The collection of accounts receivable acts to decrease one asset (accounts receivable) and increase another (cash).

Assets		=	Liabilities	+	Owner's equity	Rev.	−	Exp.	=	Net Inc.	Cash Flow	
3,000	(3,000)	=		+			−		=		3,000	OA

Transaction (3)

accounts receivable = $5,000 − $3,000 = $2,000

Assets	=	Liabilities	+	Owner's equity	Rev.	−	Exp.	=	Net Inc.	Cash Flow	
(500)	=		+	(500)		−	500	=	(500)		

ABC company is not able to say how much of $2,000 would be collected. But the accountants can estimate that clients could not pay $500 of accounts receivable. ABC company should recognize the anticipated future write-off of receivables in the current accounting period. So the accountants need an adjusting entry.

The transactions and the closing entry are shown as following.

	Account titles	Debit	Credit
Transaction (1)	Accounts receivable	$5,000	
	Sales revenue		$5,000
Transaction (2)	Cash	$3,000	
	Accounts receivable		$3,000
Transaction (3)	Bad debts expense	$500	
	Allowance for bad debts		$500
Closing Entry	Sales revenue	$5,000	
	Bad debts expense		$500
	Retained earnings		$4,500

Section 3 Inventory

Inventories refer to merchandise, finished goods, semi-finished goods, goods in process, and all kinds of materials, fuels, containers, low-value and perishable articles and so on that stocked for the purpose of sale, production or consumption during the production operational process. Inventories are normally accounted for at historical cost, as the cost principle requires.

The historical cost of inventory purchased includes the purchase consideration, transporttation, loading and unloading expenses, insurance, reasonable loss incurred in transit, preparatory expenses incurred before warehousing and taxes payable.

Normally, a company may account inventories under the following methods:

(1) specific identification;

(2) first-in, first-out (FIFO);

(3) last-in, first-out (LIFO);

(4) weighted average.

Specific identification is usually used when a company buys goods that are easy to identify. These items do not even need any tags to be distinguished from each other because they are big, probably unique, and generally cost a lot. This kind of items could be ships, airplanes, equipments, etc.

FIFO means that the cost of inventories purchased first must be assigned to the cost of goods sold.

Example 2.2

Suppose Simple company sells musical instruments, and at a moment it had four identical YAMAHA pianos on hand — two YAMAHA costing $80,000 each (that were purchased first) and two same type of YAMAHA costing $70,000 each (that were bought by the company after the First one). Customers don't care which one to buy since the four pianos and their prices are totally the same. If the company wants to increase its cost of goods sold, it will use $80,000 as the cost of goods sold.

LIFO is that the cost of the inventories purchased last is charged to the cost of goods sold. In the example above, the cost of goods sold would be $70,000.

Weighted Average provides that the average unit cost is included in the cost of goods sold. In order to determine the weighted average cost, you need to add all the costs of the inventories on hand and divide the result by the number of inventories. In our example, it would be:

$$(\$80,000 \times 2 + \$70,000 \times 2) / 4 = \$75,000$$

FIFO leaves the last cost in the balance sheet. On the contrary, LIFO remains the first cost in the balance sheet. And the weighted average uses the same average costs for the balance sheet.

Assume that one piano was sold by price of $100,000, look at the table below:

	FIFO	LIFO	Weighted Average
Beginning inventory	$300,000	$300,000	$300,000
Cost of goods sold	$80,000	$70,000	$75,000
Ending inventory	$220,000	$230,000	$225,000

The cost flow method a company uses in its accounting has a straight impact on the income statement, cost of goods sold, and the gross margin. So:

	FIFO	LIFO	Weighted Average
Sales	$100,000	$100,000	$100,000
Cost of goods sold	$80,000	$70,000	$75,000
Gross margin	$20,000	$30,000	$25,000

Tips: Inventory shall be accounted for by using the perpetual inventory method. The balance of the inventory account under the perpetual system should give the cost of inventory on hand at any time.

存货的核算，一般采用永续盘存制。在永续盘存制下，存货账户的余额应给出在任一时点的存货额。

Section 4 Short-term Investment

Short-term investments refer to various marketable securities, which can be realized at any time and will be held less than a year, as well as other investment with a life of no longer than a year.

Shareholders

If you own a company's stock, you would be one of the company's shareholders.

Limited Company

A limited company is an organization created by law which has at least two owners. It is the shareholders' liabilities to the amount they have paid, or agreed to pay, for their shares. There are two types of limited company: PLC and LTD.

PLC means public limited company, and **LTD** means private limited company.

A public limited company offers its shares for public subscription. A private limited company restricts its share ownership. The shares of many, but not all, PLC are traded on the Stock Exchange and these companies are known as listed companies or quoted companies.

Marketable securities include stock and debentures to be realized within one year from the balance sheet date and shall be accounted for at cost. They shall be accounted for according to historical cost as obtained and be shown in book balance in accounting statement.

When the cost includes an element of dividend declared or interest accrued, that portion relating to the dividend and interest shall be accounted for as a temporary payment and disclosed under other receivable. Dividend and interest income received or receivable from marketable securities; and profit or loss arising from disposal or liquidation of marketable securities shall be accounted for as being profit or loss on investments.

Stock Investment

Investors could buy a company's common stocks or preference stocks.

If you own a company's common stock, you would have the rights below:

(1) Vote at stockholders' meetings;

(2) Share in earnings distributions;

(3) Purchase additional stocks in proportion to the owner's present holding, if more stocks are issued by the corporation;

(4) Share in the assets if the corporation liquidates.

The owners of preferred stock usually have the right to dividends of a certain amount before owners of common stock can receive any dividends. The dividend preference is usually stated as a dollar amount per share or as a percentage of par value. For example, preferred stock might be described as "$5 par, $1 preferred stock", or "$30 par, 5% preferred stock".

Example 2.3

Assume that ABC Company is a listed company. Simple Company buys 10,000 shares of ABC Company's common stock in New York Securities Exchange on November 1, 2007, at the price of $20 per share. This transaction would be recorded below:

	Common Stock		$200,000					
	Cash			$200,000				

Assets		=	Lia.	+	Owner's equity	Rev.	−	Exp.	=	Net Inc.	Cash Flow	
200,000	(200,000)	=		+			−		=		(200,000)	IA

Dividend Distribution

Example 2.4

Assume that, on March 15, 2008, ABC company declared that they decided to give dividends at $3 per common stock. Thus, Simple Company would receive $30,000 of dividend. At this time the cash was not given but an accounting record was requested.

Common Stock Dividend Receivable $30,000
    Investment Revenue $30,000

Assets	=	Lia.	+	Owner's equity	Rev.	−	Exp.	=	Net Inc.	Cash Flow
30,000	=		+	30,000	30,000	−		=	30,000	

On April 1, Simple Company received $30,000 of cash dividend. So they need a new accounting record.

Cash $30,000
    Common Stock Dividend Receivable Cash $30,000

Assets		=	Lia.	+	Owner's equity	Rev.	−	Exp.	=	Net Inc.	Cash Flow	
30,000	(30,000)	=		+			−		=		30,000	IA

应用专栏

Useful Expressions

cash *n*.	现金
cash in bank	银行存款
cash equivalents	现金等价物
bank draft	银行汇票
credit card	信用卡
short-term investments	短期投资
stock *n*.	股票

bonds *n.*	债券
funds *n.*	基金
accounts receivable	应收账款
notes receivable	应收票据
bank acceptance	银行承兑汇票
trade acceptance	商业承兑汇票
dividend receivable	应收股利
interest receivable	应收利息
allowance for bad debts	坏账准备
prepaid *n.*	预付项目
inventory *n.*	存货
raw materials	原材料
low-value consumption goods	低值易耗品
semi-finished goods	半成品
finished goods	产成品
differences between purchasing and selling price	商品进销差价
principal *n.*	本金
interest *n.*	利息
securities exchange	证券交易所

1. In the balance sheet, cash is listed first among the current assets, because it is the most current and liquid of all assets.

现金在资产负债表中位于流动资产之首，因为它流动性最强。

2. Marketable securities shall be accounted for according to historical cost as obtained and be shown in book balance in accounting statement. Income received or receivable from marketable securities in current period and the difference between the receipt obtained from securities sold and book cost shall be all accounted for as current profit or loss.

有价证券应按取得时的实际成本记账，应当以账面余额在会计报表中列示。当期的有价证券收益，以及有价证券转让所取得的收入与账面成本的差额，计入当期损益。

3. Prepaid expenses shall be amortized according to period benefiting, and the balance shall be shown separately in accounting statement.

待摊费用应当按受益期分摊，未摊销余额在会计报表中应当单独列示。

Additional Reading Material

Every month the company will receive a statement from the bank. The bank statement will show the beginning and ending cash balance deposits, collections made by the bank for the company, checks paid, deductions from service fees and other charges. The cash balance shown on the bank statement usually does not agree with the balance of cash account shown in the accounting records. Upon receipt of the bank statement, the company prepares a bank reconciliation statement to determine the reasons for any differences in the amount of cash as shown on the bank statement and the amount of cash shown on the book of company. When the reconciliation is performed, the bank statement is adjusted for such items as outstanding checks and deposits in transit. The records of the depositor are adjusted for such items as service charges, collections of notes and drafts the bank had made for the depositor, and interest earned on the average checking account balance.

Investments of surplus cash must be in varies of government or corporation debt obligations (debt securities) or in stocks (equity securities). If the investment can be converted into cash quickly, and if management intends to hold the investments as a source of cash to satisfy the needs of current operations, the investments are called short-term investments. Investments in debt obligations usually are maintained in the accounts at cost until they are sold or mature. However, a temporary investment in equity securities must be carried at the lower of its total cost or market value at the balance sheet date. Dividends, interest, gains and losses on the investments are recorded in appropriate income statement accounts.

Prepaid expenses are payments made in advance for the use of goods and services, such as insurance, property taxes, and interest. For example, the cost of a one-year insurance policy paid in advance is a prepaid expense. Prepaid expenses are listed last among the current assets. Unlike other current assets, prepaid expenses will not be converted into cash. Nevertheless, prepaid expenses substitute for future cash payments that would be required if the expenses had not been paid. Therefore, prepaid expenses are listed as current assets until their benefit expires or they are used up.

Oral practices

Directions: *Brady is discussing his firm's financial report with Annie. Read the conversation and answer questions.*

Brady: Yes, I'd be happy to show our report to you. You'll notice that the report is divided into several sections. For example, current assets and liabilities are listed on this page.

Annie: I see that you provide a complete breakdown of all the various current accounts.

Brady: Yes, and we also include our current ratio and asset tax ratio in the footnotes. Fixed assets and long-term liabilities are noted in the next section, and the various capital, reserve and equity accounts are itemized on the next page.

Annie: You certainly do provide extremely detailed reports. Is this customary with all American firms?

Brady: Well, it's required in the case of firms whose stock is publicly held. Some European companies are reluctant to reveal too much information about their financial condition, but we have no choice.

Annie: I see you list inventory in inventory turnover figures with a note that they were computed on a LIFO basis. What does that mean?

Brady: It means last-in – first-out or a way of evaluation inventory for statement and budgetary purposes. We calculate our inventory cost in the assumption that the last inventory input is the first inventory output.

Questions:

1. What kind of company should provide detailed financial reports to the public?
2. What does LIFO mean?

Self-test Exercises

Section 2

1. Matching each of the following statements with its proper term.
   (1) accounts receivable   ( )
   (2) dishonored notes receivable   ( )
   (3) allowance method   ( )
   (4) direct write-off method   ( )

   A. The method of accounting for un-collectible accounts that provides an expense for un-collectible receivables in advance of their write-off.

   B. A receivable created by selling merchandise or services on credit.

   C. A note that maker fails to pay on the due date.

   D. The method of accounting for un-collectible accounts that recognizes the expense only when accounts are judged to be worthless.

2. At the end of the fiscal year, before the accounts are adjusted, accounts receivable has a balance of $200,000 and allowance for doubtful accounts has a credit balance of $2,500. If the estimated un-collectible accounts determined by aging the receivables is $8,500, the amount of un-collectible accounts expense is (   ).

   A. $2,500
   B. $6,000
   C. $8,500

D. $11,000

3. At the end of the fiscal year, accounts receivable has a balance of $100,000 and allowance for doubtful accounts has a balance of $7,000. The expected net realizable value of the accounts receivable is (   ).

    A. $7,000
    B. $93,000
    C. $100,000
    D. $107,000

4. What is the maturity value of a 90-day, 12% note for $10,000? (   )

    A. $8,800
    B. $10,000
    C. $10,300
    D. $11,200

5. What is the due date of $12,000, 90-day, 8% note receivable dated August 5? (   )

    A. October 31
    B. November 2
    C. November 3
    D. November 4

6. Let's assume that this company had the following transactions in 2008:

1) A customer refused to pay for the goods that was bought from this company in 2007. So the company wrote off an un-collectible accounts receivable in the amount of $200;

2) Provided $3,000 of sales on account during this year;

3) Recovered $100 of bad debt expense that was written off in 2007;

4) Recognized bad debt expense for 2008.

According to these information, discuss the accounting treatment.

Section 3

1. Assuming that net purchases cost $250,000 during the year and that the ending stock was $4,000 less than the beginning stock of $30,000, how much was cost of goods sold?

    A. $280,000
    B. $246,000
    C. $254,000
    D. $276,000

2. According to the following information, use weighted-average method and the ending inventory should be_____.

June	1	Beginning inventory	100	@	$ 1.00
	6	Purchase 1	150	@	$ 1.10
	13	Purchase 2	50	@	$ 1.20
	20	Purchase 3	100	@	$ 1.30
	25	Purchase 4	25	@	$ 1.40
	27	Sold	125	@	

3. Using the information from question 2, the LIFO method, the cost assigned to the ending inventory is _____.

4. Assuming that net purchases cost $250,000 during the year and that the ending stock was $4,000 less than the beginning stock of $30,000, the cost of goods would be _____.

5. If merchandise inventory is being valued at cost and the price level is steadily rising, the method of costing that will yield the higher net income is (   ).

   A. LIFO

   B. FIFO

   C. Average

   D. Periodic

6. Assume a company has a periodic inventory system with an opening balance of $20,000, purchases of $150,000, and sales of $250,000. The company closes its records once a year on December 31. In the accounting records, the inventory account would be expected to have a balance on December 31 prior to adjusting the closing entries that was:

   A. Equal to $20,000

   B. More than $20,000

   C. Less than $20,000

   D. Indeterminate

7. Given the following table.

Inventory	Quantity	Cost ($)	Market ($)
Item A	200	1.00	0.50
Item B	100	2.00	2.10
Item C	100	3.00	2.50
Item D	300	2.50	2.00
Item E	200	3.00	3.10

Using the item-by-item method of applying the Lower of Cost or Market Rule to valuing the inventories, the value assigned to stock Item C for inclusion in total stock on the balance sheet is:

   A. $300

B. $250

C. $50

D. None of the above

Section 4

Fill in the following blanks.

1. Short-term investments refer to various of _____.

2. Marketable securities include _____ and _____ to be realized within one year from the balance sheet date and shall be accounted for at cost.

3. If your company wants to buy another company's stock, how would you explain the importance of this investment?

参 考 译 文

第一节　现金及现金等价物

现金是钞票或硬币形式的钱，能够用通货或者支票方式迅速支付商品或劳务。现金包括现金等价物，比如银行存款、支票及汇票等。

在资产负债表中，现金处于流动资产的首位，因为在流动资产中它是最具流动性的；而且相对于资产负债表的其他项目，比如应付账款来说，银行业者、信贷经理或者审慎研究资产负债表的投资人都对现金总量很有兴趣。

现金和所有的存款都应该可以依据准确的收支量来计算，而且库存现金、银行存款和有价证券应该单独计算。

第二节　应收账款

应收账款是指公司的客户所欠的金额，有时也被称为贸易债权人。

应收账款被分类为流动资产，并且在资产负债表中位于现金及现金等价物之后。

只有在期限短或者金额不大的时候才会发生应收账款。而在西方国家，当公司应收的款项期限较长或金额较大时，则使用应付票据。应付票据通常包括到期日和利率。

如果某些客户无法支付所欠债务，则这些应付账款就属于不可收回的款项。公司(在资产负债表中)用应收账款减去坏账准备，来确认不是所有的账款都能收回这一事实。

坏账准备是指估计无法收回的应收账款金额。任何应收账款只要被证明确实无法收回，则都应确认为坏账并从坏账准备中冲销；如果没有建立坏账准备金，则应记入流动损益。当应收账款由于无法收回而被冲销时，客户仍有义务偿还账款。坏账准备属于资产的抵消账户，或者称为备抵账户。

可变现净值是指公司在未来确实能够收回的账款。计算总资产时，需要用到可变现净值。

$$可变现净值 = 应收账款 - 坏账准备$$

假设一家公司的应收账款为$1 000 000，坏账准备为$50 000。则在资产负债表中，应收账款为：

$$可变现净值 = \$1\,000\,000 - \$50\,000 = \$950\,000$$

例 2.1

ABC 公司 2007 年发生如下业务：

(1) 确认$5 000 销售收入为应收账款；
(2) 收回$3 000 应收账款；
(3) 确认$500 未来无法收回的账款为坏账费用。

这些业务经过分析记录如下：

业务(1)

资产(应收账款)和业主权益(销售收入)增加相同金额。

资产	=	负债	+	业主权益	收入	-	费用	=	净利润	现金流
5 000	=		+		5 000	-		=		

业务(2)

应收账款的收回使一项资产(应收账款)减少而另一项资产(现金)增加。

资产		=	负债	+	业主权益	收入	-	费用	=	净利润	现金流
3 000	(3 000)	=		+			-		=		3 000　OA

业务(3)

应收账款 = $5 000 - $3 000 = $2 000

资产	=	负债	+	业主权益	收入	-	费用	=	净利润	现金流
(500)	=		+	(500)		-	500	=	(500)	

ABC 公司无法准确知道$2 000 应收账款中有多少能够收回，但是会计人员估算出有$500 无法收回。ABC 公司应在当前会计期间对这笔款项的提前冲销进行确认，会计人员则应该调整账项。

业务及结转分录表示如下：

	分　　录	借　方	贷　方
业务(1)	应收账款 　　销售收入	$5 000	$5 000
业务(2)	现金 　　应收账款	$3 000	$3 000

续表

分录		借方	贷方
业务(3)	坏账费用	$500	
	坏账准备		$500
结转分录	销售收入	$5 000	
	坏账费用		$500
	留存收益		$4 500

第三节 存货

存货是在一个产品经营周期内为了销售、生产或消耗所储存起来的，包括货物、产成品、半成品、在产品，以及各种原料、燃料、包装物和低值易耗品等。根据成本原则的需要，存货一般采用历史成本来计算。

存货的历史成本包括存货的买价、运费、装卸费、保险费、途中合理损耗、入库前发生的准备费用以及应付税金等。

一般情况下，公司计算存货可采用以下方法：

(1) 个别认定法；

(2) 先进先出法(FIFO)；

(3) 后进先出法(LIFO)；

(4) 加权平均法。

个别认定法一般用于公司所购货物很容易认定之时。这类存货甚至不需要单独标签就可以彼此区别，因为它们可能是体积巨大的、独一无二的或者价值很大的。这类存货可能是诸如船只、飞机和机器设备等。

先进先出法表示，先购进的货物成本应该先结转到商品销售成本中。

例 2.2

假设 Simple 公司是一家乐器销售公司，此时库存有四台 YAMAHA 钢琴——两台 YAMAHA 钢琴，每台成本为$80 000 (先期购进的)，另两台同样型号的 YAMAHA 钢琴，每台成本为$70 000 (后期购进)。因为四台钢琴的型号和售价都是一样的，所以客户并不关心买到的是哪一台。如果公司想要增加商品销售成本，就应该以$80 000 作为销售成本。

后进先出法是指，后期购进应先结转到商品销售成本中。在上例中，商品销售成本则应为$70 000。

加权平均法是讲平均单位成本作为商品销售成本。为了确定加权平均成本，需要将全部存货成本进行累加，再除以存货的总量。在上例中，加权平均成本为：

$$(\$80\,000 \times 2 + \$70\,000 \times 2) / 4 = \$75\,000$$

先进先出法使后期进货的成本留在了资产负债表中。相反，后进先出法把先期进货的成本留在了资产负债表里。而加权平均法是使同样的平均成本留给了资产负债表。

假设本期销售了一台钢琴，售价为$100 000，请看下表：

	先进先出法	后进先出法	加权平均法
期初存货	$300 000	$300 000	$300 000
商品销售成本	$80 000	$70 000	$75 000
期末存货	$220 000	$230 000	$225 000

公司所采用的成本结转方法对于损益表、商品销售成本及毛利都有直接影响。如下表：

	先进先出法	后进先出法	加权平均法
销售收入	$100 000	$100 000	$100 000
商品销售成本	$80 000	$70 000	$75 000
毛利	$20 000	$30 000	$25 000

第四节　短期投资

短期投资是指各种有价证券，能够随时变现；并且与其他寿命短于一年的投资一样，其持有期在一年以内。

股东

如果你持有某家公司的股票，你就成为该公司的股东之一。

有限公司

有限公司是至少由两个所有人依法建立的公司组织。股东依据所拥有的股份而必须偿还或允诺偿还的，就是股东的负债。有限公司有两种形式：PLC 和 LTD。

PLC 是公共有限公司的英文缩写，而 **LTD** 是私人有限公司的英文缩写。

公共有限公司将其股份提供给社会公众进行认购。私人有限公司则限制其股份持有权。许多(但不是全部)公共有限公司的股份都在证券交易所进行交易，而且这类公司称为上市公司。

有价证券是指从资产负债表日起，一年内可变现的股票和债券，并且以成本计价。有价证券应以取得时的成本计价，以账面余额显示在会计报表中。

如果成本包括了应计股利或应计利息的因素，这部分与股利或利息相关的金额应作为暂付款记账，并显示于其他应收款中。有价证券产生的已收或应收股利和利息、存款或有价证券转让所产生的损益，都应记入投资损益。

股票投资

投资者可以购买一家公司的普通股或优先股。
如果拥有一家公司的普通股，则具有以下权利：
(1) 在股东大会上进行投票；

(2) 分享收益分配；

(3) 如果公司增发股票，能够依据当前持股比例购买增发股票；

(4) 如果公司清算，有权分得资产。

一般来说，优先股股东享有在普通股股东分红之前进行分红的权利。优先股股利也通常以××元/股或面值的一定比例来表示。例如，优先股可表示为"面值$5，股利$1 的优先股"，或"面值$30，按面值 5%分红的优先股"。

例 2.3

假设 ABC 公司为一家上市公司。2007 年 11 月 1 日，Simple 公司在纽约证券交易所以每股$20 的价格购买了 ABC 公司的股票 10 000 股。这笔业务记录如下。

普通股 $200 000
　现金 $200 000

资产	=	负债	+	业主权益	收入	−	费用	=	净利润	现金流
200 000 (200 000)	=		+			−		=		(200 000) IA

股利分配

例 2.4

假设 2008 年 3 月 15 日 ABC 公司宣告发放股利，每股普通股派$3，Simple 公司则应收入$30 000 股利。此时还没有派发现金，但需要会计记录如下：

应收普通股股利 $30 000
　投资收益 $30 000

资产	=	负债	+	业主权益	收入	−	费用	=	净利润	现金流
30 000	=		+	30 000	30 000	−		=	30 000	

4 月 1 日，Simple 公司收到了$30 000 现金股利，则需要一笔新的会计记录如下：

现金 $30 000
　应收普通股股利 $30 000

资产	=	负债	+	业主权益	收入	−	费用	=	净利润	现金流
30 000 (30 000)	=		+			−		=		30 000 IA

Unit 3　Long-term Assets

Objectives

- In Section 1, students should understand the definition, characteristics, initial and subsequent measurement of fixed assets.
- In Section 2, students ought to understand the definition, characteristics, classification and amortization of intangible assets.
- In Section 3, students should learn how to calculate depreciation expenses.

Dialogue

1. The concept of fixed assets

Alison: James. Can you tell me what fixed assets include?

James: Fixed assets, also called PPE, include property, plant and equipment.

Alison: So PPE stands for property, plant and equipment, doesn't it?

James: Yes, you are right.

Alison: Can you give me some examples of PPE?

James: Certainly. Things like land, office buildings, factories, warehouses, machinery, furniture, tools all belong to fixed assets. They are typical fixed assets.

Alison: How are fixed assets acquired?

James: They are mainly acquired by purchase and self-construction. Sometimes fixed assets can be obtained through exchange or issuance of securities.

Alison: I hear they can also be received by donation, can't they?

James: Yes.

译文：固定资产的概念

艾莉森：詹姆士，你能告诉我固定资产都包括些什么吗？

詹姆士：固定资产也称之为 PPE，它包括地产、厂房和设备。

艾莉森：PPE 代表地产、厂房和设备，是吗？

詹姆士：是的。

艾莉森：你能给我举几个固定资产的例子吗？

詹姆士：当然可以。像土地、办公楼、工厂、库房、机械、家具、工具这样的东西都属于固定资产，它们是典型的固定资产。

艾莉森：固定资产是如何取得的呢？

詹姆士： 固定资产主要通过购买和自建取得，有时也可以通过交换或发行股票取得。

艾莉森： 我听说固定资产也可以通过接受捐助的形式取得，是吗？

詹姆士： 没错。

2. Fixed assets recording

Alison: In the dialogue above we had a long discussion about fixed assets. Now can you tell me how enterprises record their fixed assets?

James: A fixed asset shall be initially measured at cost, which means the original cost or historical cost. For purchased fixed assets the cost usually includes the purchase price, related taxes and some other additional costs.

Alison: I know the purchase price and taxes, but what do you mean by additional costs?

James: Additional costs refer to the reasonable and necessary expenditures for acquiring an asset and preparing it for their intended use. For instance, if you purchase a piece of equipment, the additional costs may include delivery and handling costs, installation costs, professional fees, etc.

Alison: Oh, I see. Then how can we measure the original cost of a self-constructed fixed asset?

James: For self-constructed fixed assets, the cost comprises all the expenditures necessarily incurred for bringing the asset to working condition for its intended use. Such costs include material, labor, overhead costs, professional fees, building permit fee, etc..

Alison: When several fixed assets are acquired for a lump sum purchase price, but each asset is not priced separately, how can we determine the historical cost of each asset?

James: In such cases, the total acquisition cost should be allocated to the individual assets according to the proportion of fair value of each asset to the total fair value of all assets acquired.

Alison: How can we determine the cost of a fixed asset that is obtained through an exchange of non-monetary assets?

James: Usually the cost should be determined on the basis of the fair value of the asset given up unless it is clearly evident that the fair value of the asset received is more reliable.

Alison: How about the accounting approach of the cost of a business combination or a debt restructuring transaction?

James: Well, the cost shall be determined according to the relative items of new Accounting Standards for Business Enterprises. I'd like to remind you here that in determining the cost of a fixed asset, an enterprise should take into account any expected abandoning costs.

Alison: I see.

James: You should also remember that when fixed assets are recorded, information related to the fixed assets should be disclosed in the notes.

Alison: What do you mean by related information?

James: It includes information like recognition criteria, classification, measurement bases, depreciation methods used, useful lives, the estimated net residual values, depreciation rates and so on.

Alison: Oh, it's so complicated. Thank you for your explanation.

James: You are welcome.

译文：固定资产的入账

艾莉森：在上面的对话中，我们已经对固定资产进行了深入的讨论。那么你能告诉我，对于固定资产，企业又是如何记账呢？

詹姆士：固定资产应该按照成本进行初始计量，成本指的是原始成本或称之为历史成本。对于购置的固定资产，原始成本通常包括购买价格、相关税费和一些其他额外费用。

艾莉森：我知道什么是购买价和税费，但是你说的额外费用又是指什么？

詹姆士：额外费用指的是取得固定资产并使其达到预定可使用状态前所发生的合理的、必要的开销，比如你购买一项设备，额外费用就可能包括运输费、装卸费、安装费和专业人员服务费等。

艾莉森：我明白了。那么自建的固定资产我们又如何衡量它的原始成本呢？

詹姆士：对于自建的固定资产，它的原始成本包括该项资产达到预期可使用状态前所发生的一切必要支出。这些费用包括材料费、人工费、管理费、专业人员费和建设许可费等。

艾莉森：如果用一笔款项购入多项资产，而每项资产又没有单独标价，在这种情况下我们又如何计算每项资产的原始成本呢？

詹姆士：在这种情况下，应该按照各项固定资产公允价值比例对总成本进行分配，以此来确定各项固定资产的成本。

艾莉森：通过非货币性资产交换所取得的固定资产应该怎样确定它的成本呢？

詹姆士：一般来讲应当以换出资产的公允价值作为确定换入资产成本的基础，除非有证据表明换入资产的公允价值更加可靠。

艾莉森：对于通过合并或债务重组所取得的固定资产的成本又如何进行会计处理呢？

詹姆士：它们的成本应该按照新的《企业会计准则》的相关条款确定。在这里我还想提醒你，当确定固定资产成本的时候，应该把预计的弃置费用考虑进去。

艾莉森：我懂了。

詹姆士：你还要记住，当固定资产入账的时候，应该在附录中披露它们的相关信息。

艾莉森：你说的相关信息是指什么？
詹姆士：这些信息包括固定资产的确认条件、分类、计量基础、折旧方法、使用寿命、预计净残值和折旧率等等。
艾莉森：哦，还真复杂。多谢你的讲解。
詹姆士：不用谢。

Section 1　Fixed Assets

In contrast to current assets, long-term assets refer to those assets that will be realized or consumed within a period longer than one year of their acquisition, which are normally divided into fixed assets, intangible assets and deferred assets.

Fixed assets refer to the assets whose useful life is over one year, unit value is above the prescribed criteria and where original physical form remains during the process of utilization. According to the newly published Accounting Standards for Businesses Enterprises, fixed assets have the following two main characteristics: Firstly, they are held for use in the production or supply of goods or services, for rental to others, or for administrative purposes. Secondly, they have useful lives more than one accounting year.

Only when both of the following conditions are satisfied can fixed assets be recognized. First, it's probable that economic benefits associated with the asset will flow into the enterprise. Secondly, the cost of the asset can be measured reliably.

Section 2　Depreciation of Fixed Assets

All fixed assets are depreciable over their limited useful life except for fully depreciated fixed assets that are still in use and land that is separately valued and accounted for. Land need not to be depreciated because it never loses its functional value through use and has an indefinite life.

Depreciation is defined as the accounting process of systematically allocating the depreciable amount of a fixed asset over its useful life by a selected depreciation method. When calculating the depreciation expense of a fixed asset, an enterprise should consider its depreciable amount, estimated net residual value, estimated useful life, and the depreciation methods.

Depreciable amount refers to the original cost of a fixed asset minus its estimated net residual value. Estimated net residual value is the estimated amount which an enterprise would currently obtain from disposal of the asset, after deducting the estimated costs of disposal, if the assets were already of the age and in the condition expected at the end of its useful life. The so-called useful life refers to the period over which an asset is expected to be available for use by an enterprise or the number of units of production or service expected to be obtained from the asset by an enterprise.

The useful life and estimated net residual value of a fixed asset shall be determined reasonably and once determined they should not be changed arbitrarily. When determining the useful life and estimated net residual value an enterprise shall take the following factors into consideration: the expected production capacity or physical output; the expected physical and non-physical wear and tear; any legal or similar limits on the use of the asset.

Many methods are used to allocate the cost of a fixed asset to accounting periods through depreciation, but each of them may only be suitable for a certain circumstance. Therefore, when selecting the depreciation method, an enterprise should consider the ways to realize the expected economic benefits of a fixed asset. The four most commonly used depreciation methods are the straight-line method, the units of production method, the double declining balance method and the sum-of-the-years-digits method.

Straight-line Method

The straight-line method is the most extensively used and most conservative method to calculate depreciation charge. When we employ the straight-line method, we assume that an asset's economic revenue is the same each year, and the repair and maintenance cost is also the same for each period. Under the straight-line method, the depreciation expense is allocated equally to each period of the asset's useful life. Thus the depreciation amount is the same for each year. The formula of this method is as follows:

$$\text{Annual depreciation amount} = \frac{\text{original cost} - \text{estimated net residual value}}{\text{estimated years of useful life}}$$

The straight-line method is particularly suitable for buildings, machinery, pipelines, etc.

Example 3.1

Assume a Steyr Howo truck will be purchased for ￥200,000 by an enterprise in 2008, and the estimated net residual value is ￥20,000 with a useful life of 10 years. Under the straight-line method the annual depreciation amount will be

$$\frac{￥200,000 - ￥20,000}{10 \text{ years}} = ￥18,000/\text{year}$$

Units of Production Method

The units of production method will be employed to calculate depreciation charge when we assume that depreciation mainly results from wear and tear and that the passage of time almost has nothing to do with it. Under this method, depreciation is allocated in proportion to the degree an asset is used in the production. The formula of this method is as follows:

$$\text{Depreciation Expense per Unit} = \frac{\text{Original Cost} - \text{Estimated Net Residual Value}}{\text{Estimated Total Units of Production}}$$

Example 3.2

Assume that a duplicating machine will be purchased for ¥22,000, the net residual value is estimated at ¥100, and 300,000 copies can be made in its useful life. Then

$$\frac{¥22,000 - ¥100}{300,000 \text{copies}} = ¥0.073/\text{copy}$$

If 30,000 copies are made during the first year of its useful life, then the year's depreciation amount will be ¥0.073×30,000=¥2,190. If 40,000 copies are made during the second year of its useful life, the depreciation charge of the second year will be ¥0.073×40,000=¥2,920.

Double Declining Balance Method

The double declining balance method is also called the accelerated depreciation method. As you know, almost all assets will gradually decrease in their value with the passage of time, but the fact is that during the first few years some assets are used more often and thus can provide better service compared with later time. Therefore, the amount of depreciation charge is larger in the early years. The double declining balance method is just suitable for calculating depreciation expense for such assets.

The following should be done when calculating an asset's depreciation amount:

1. Calculate the straight-line rate. The straight-line rate can be obtained by dividing 100% by its useful life. In the example 3.1, the straight-line rate is 100%÷10=10%.

2. Calculate the double declining balance rate. The double declining balance rate can be achieved by multiplying the straight-line rate by 2. In the Example 3.1, the double declining balance rate is 10% × 2=20%.

3. Calculate the depreciation expense of each accounting period. This can be obtained through multiplying the book value of the asset in each accounting period by the double decline balance rate.

The formula of the double declining balance method is as follows: Annual depreciation amount = book value of an asset in each accounting year × double declining balance rate.

Example 3.3

Suppose that a machine is acquired for ¥10,000 with the estimated useful life of 5 years and estimated net residual value ¥1,000. If the double declining balance method is applied, the annual depreciation expense can be calculated as follows:

Unit 3 Long-term Assets

Year	Original Cost/¥	Beginning Accumulated Depreciation/¥	Beginning Book Value/¥	×	Double Straight-line Rate/%	=	Annual Depreciation Expense/¥
1	10 000	0	10 000	×	40	=	4 000
2	10 000	4 000	6 000	×	40	=	2 400
3	10 000	6 400	3 600	×	40	=	1 440
4	10 000	7 840	2 160	×	40	=	864
5	10 000	8 704	1 296			=	296
			Total Depreciation Expense				9 000

Note that the depreciation expense in the fifth year is only 1296−1000 (estimated net residual value) =296 yuan instead of 1,296× 40%= 518.40 yuan. That's because the book value of an asset ought not to be depreciated below its estimated net residual value. In this case, if the depreciation amount in the fifth year were 518.40 yuan, the book value would be 1,296−518.40=777.60 yuan, which would be less than 1,000 yuan.

Sum-of-the-Years-Digits Method

Like the double declining balance method, the sum-of-the-years-digits(SYD) method also belongs to the accelerated depreciation method, because it also assumes that the asset is used more extensively during the first few years of its purchase. The formula of this method is as follows:

Annual Depreciation Amount

$$=(\text{Original Cost} - \text{Estimated Net Residual Value}) \times \frac{\text{Remaining Useful Life}}{\text{SYD}}$$

SYD is calculated by summing up the figures from the first year when an asset is used to the last year of its useful life. For instance, if the useful life of an asset is 6 years, then SYD will be 6+5+4+3+2+1=21. Therefore, the depreciation cost for the first year will be (Original Cost − Estimated Net Residual Value)×6/21, the second year will be (Original Cost − Estimated Net Residual Value)×5/21, the third year will be (Original Cost − Estimated Net Residual Value)×4/21, and so on.

Example 3.4

Assume that a company will purchase a piece of equipment for ¥80,000 with a useful life of 5 years and an estimated net residual value ¥5,000. If the sum-of-the-years-digits method is used, the annual depreciation expense is calculated as shown in the following table.

Year	Original Cost/¥	Depreciation Base/¥	×	Depreciation Fraction	=	Annual Depreciation Expense/¥
1	80,000	80,000−5,000	×	5/15	=	25,000
2	80,000	80,000−5,000	×	4/15	=	20,000
3	80,000	80,000−5,000	×	3/15	=	15,000
4	80,000	80,000−5,000	×	2/15	=	10,000
5	80,000	80,000−5,000	×	1/15	=	5,000
SYD 15	Total Depreciation Expense					75,000

Section 3 Intangible Assets

The Definition and Characteristics of an Intangible Asset

According to the new Accounting Standard for Business Enterprises No.6, an intangible asset can be defined as any identifiable non-monetary asset without physical substance which is owned or controlled by an enterprise. From the definition we know that intangible assets have the following three characteristics: Firstly, they do not possess physical substance. Secondly, they can be recognized. Thirdly, they are non-monetary assets.

The new definition of intangible assets emphasizes the nature of recognition. It states that an intangible asset must be identifiable. An intangible asset is recognized only when both of the following conditions are met. Firstly, it is probable that the economic benefits associated with the asset will flow into the enterprise. Secondly, the cost of the asset can be measured reliably.

The intangible asset does not possess physical substance and may be represented by a document, a design, etc., but the real value is that an enterprise can gain huge benefits from the rights and privileges an intangible asset grants to the enterprises. The most commonly seen intangible assets include patents, trademarks, copyrights, franchises and licenses, Internet domain names, construction permits, land utilization right, etc.

According to the new accounting standard, internally created goodwill and internally generated brands and publishing titles are all excluded from intangible assets. Assets such as bank deposits, accounts receivable, long-term investment in bonds and stocks are not intangible assets, either.

The Initial Measurement of an Intangible Asset

When an intangible asset is recorded, it shall be measured initially at cost, which includes all costs of acquisition and expenditures incurred to make it ready for its intended use.

An intangible asset separately acquired shall be recorded at actual cost including the acquisition cost, related taxes and any reasonable and necessary expenditure to make the intangible asset ready for use. An intangible asset obtained through self-development shall be accounted at actual cost incurred in its development. If an intangible asset is received from investors, it shall be recorded at the assessed value recognized or the amount specified in the contract. When intangible assets are purchased in group, the cost should be allocated based on the fair market values or the relative sales values.

As for the intangible assets obtained through or by way of an exchange of non-monetary assets, a debt restructuring transaction, a government grant or a business combination, the cost shall be determined and recorded according to the related accounting standards.

The Amortization of an Intangible Asset

The useful lives of some intangible assets are finite while the useful lives of others are indefinite. An enterprise is supposed to analyze and assess the useful life of an intangible asset on its acquisition. Whereas an intangible asset with a finite useful life shall be amortized and amortization shall begin when the asset is available for use and cease when it is derecognized, an intangible asset with an indefinite useful life shall not be amortized but periodic impairment test shall be done. Impairment shall be accounted for in accordance with the new "Accounting Standard for Business Enterprises No. 8—Impairment of Assets."

Depreciable amount of an intangible asset is its original cost less estimated residual value and accumulated impairment losses (if a provision for impairment has been made for the intangible asset). In general, the amortization charge shall be recognized in profit and loss for the current period unless another standard requires a different treatment.

When dealing with the amortization of an intangible asset, an enterprise normally uses the straight-line method. For instance, an enterprise spent ￥120,000 purchasing a patent, whose expected useful life is 6 years. Then the annual amortization charge is ￥120,000/6 i.e., 20,000/year.

Factors Considered in Determining the Useful Life of an Intangible Asset

When an enterprise determines the useful lives of intangibles, it shall mainly consider the following factors:

   a. the provisions in the contract or legal document
   b. the provisions for renewal or extension upon expiration
   c. the historical experience and common practice
   d. the useful life of a similar asset
   e. the advice or opinions of an expert
   f. the market demand of products or service the asset provides
   g. the current situation and estimated future trend of technology, techniques, etc.
   h. the expected actions of current and potential competitors.

Tips: According to the Accounting Standards for Business Enterprises (2006), internally created goodwill and internally generated brands and publishing titles are all excluded from intangible assets.

根据《企业会计准则》(2006)，企业自创商誉以及内部产生的品牌和报刊名称等，不应确认为无形资产。

应用专栏

Useful Expressions

asset *n.*	资产
enterprise *n.*	企业
tangible assets	有形资产
economic benefit	经济利益
rental *n.*	租赁，租金额
administrative *adj.*	管理的，行政的
accounting year	会计年度
fixed assets	固定资产
property *n.*	财产，地产，资产
warehouse *n.*	库房
exchange *v.*	交换
issuance of securities	发行股票
donation *n.*	捐助
long-term asset	长期资产
economic value	经济价值
useful life	使用寿命
original cost	原始成本
historical cost	历史成本，原始成本
actual cost	实际成本，原始成本
additional cost	附加费用
expenditure *n.*	支出，花费，开销
intended use	预定可使用状态
installation cost	安装费
professional fee	专业人员服务费

overhead cost	管理费
building permit fee	建设许可费
acquisition cost	购置成本
lump sum purchase	整批购买
fair value	公允价值
non-monetary asset	非货币性资产
debt restructuring transaction	债务重组
abandoning cost	弃置费用
recognition criteria	确认条件
measurement base	计量基础
depreciation *n.*	折旧
estimated net residual value	预计净残值
net salvage value	净残值
depreciation rate	折旧率
intangible asset	无形资产
identifiable *adj.*	可以确认的
physical substance	实物形态
privilege *n.*	特权，特别待遇
finite intangibles	使用寿命有限的无形资产
indefinite intangibles	使用寿命不确定的无形资产
franchise *n.*	特许权，公民权
license *n.*	营业执照，许可证
Internet domain name	互联网域名
construction permit	建筑许可证
assessed value	评估价格
amortization	摊销
impairment test	减值测试
amortization charge	摊销费
profit and loss	损益
provision *n.*	条款，规定
common practice	惯例
depreciable amount	应计折旧额
disposal *n.*	处置，处理
deduct *v.*	扣除
straight-line method	年限平均法(直线法)
units of production method	工作量法
double declining balance method	双倍余额递减法

sum-of-the-years-digits method	年数总和法
conservative	保守的，守旧的
depreciation expense	折旧费
depreciation charge	折旧费
wear and tear	磨损，损耗
straight-line rate	直线折旧率
book value	账面价值
double straight-line rate	双倍直线折旧率
SYD	年数总和
depreciation base	折旧基数
functional value	功能价值
disposal proceeds	处置收益
accumulated amortization	累计摊销额
disposal expenses	弃置费用
organization cost	开办费
annual depreciation amount	年折旧额

1. Depreciation of a fixed asset shall be provided for monthly.
固定资产应该按月计提折旧。

2. Land never loses its functional value through use and has an indefinite useful life, so it does not need to be depreciated.
土地永远不会失去它的功能价值，且使用寿命也是无限期的，所以不需要折旧。

3. The useful life, the estimated salvage value and the depreciation method of a fixed asset should be reviewed by an enterprise at least at each financial year-end.
至少在每年年度终了时，企业应该对固定资产的使用寿命、预计净残值和折旧方法进行复核。

4. The estimated salvage value of a fixed asset ought to be adjusted if the asset is held for sale.
如果企业持有待售的固定资产，应当对其预计净残值进行调整。

5. An enterprise should disclose such information related to fixed assets in the notes as depreciation methods, useful lives, depreciation rates, etc.
企业应当在附注中披露固定资产的折旧方法、使用寿命、折旧率等。

6. The estimated net residual value of a fixed asset shall be revised if it differs enormously from its previous estimate.
如果一项固定资产的预计净残值与原先估计值有较大差异的，应当对预计净残值进行调整。

7. The intangible assets are long term in nature and subject to amortization.

无形资产属于长期资产，需要摊销。

8. Internally created goodwill, and internally generated brands and publishing titles do not belong to intangible assets.

企业自创的商誉、内部产生的品牌和报刊名不应确认为无形资产。

9. When an intangible asset is disposed, the difference between the disposal proceeds and the carrying amount should be recognized in profit or loss for the current period.

当企业处置无形资产时，应当将处置收益与该无形资产账面价值的差额计入当期损益。

10. Such things as amortization methods, accumulated amortization, useful lives, etc. shall be disclosed in the notes.

诸如摊销方法、累计摊销额、使用寿命等应该在附注中披露。

Additional Reading Material

Assets are economic resources that are possessed or controlled by an enterprise to generate revenue to the enterprise. Assets includes all property，creditor's rights and other kinds of rights. Some assets have physical substance such as land, buildings, materials, etc. while others have no physical substance such as patents, trademarks, copyrights, etc. Assets of an enterprise are usually divided into the following categories: current assets, long-term investments，fixed assets, intangible assets and other assets.

Current assets are assets that will be realized or consumed within one year or within an operating cycle that is longer than one year. Typical current assets include cash, bank deposits, short-term investments, accounts receivable, inventories and so on. Current assets are listed on the balance sheet in order of liquidity, which means the ability to be converted to cash. So cash is always listed first of all current assets because it is the most current and liquid of all. Receivables include account receivable, note receivable and other receivables. Inventories include materials, fuels, finished or unfinished goods and so on. They are kept for future sale or use.

Long-term assets, also called non-current assets, are assets that are owned by an enterprise to bring in revenue and whose useful life is more than one accounting period. Long-term assets can be divided into fixed assets and intangible assets and acquired through self-construction, purchase and trade in. No matter how a long-term asset is acquired, original cost principle must be abided by in accounting for it.

Long-term investment includes investment in stocks and bonds and investment in other projects. As you know, an enterprise can not only issue stocks or bonds but also purchase them to earn revenues. But the problem is the high risk that an enterprise may encounter when investing in such assets. An enterprise may lose money instead of yielding profits, so prompt and wise decision making is the key.

Oral Practices

Directions: *Alan is taking an accounting course and he is talking with Alina now. Read the conversation and answer the questions.*

Alina: Hi, Alan. What about your accounting lessons?

Alan: Not very well. They are a little bit difficult for me.

Alina: Really? What are you studying now? Maybe I can be of help to you.

Alan: Currently we are learning how to figure out the original cost of fixed assets. The problem is that sometimes we should take the estimated disposal expenses into account when we calculate the cost. I am not very clear under what circumstances we should put such expenses into the original cost.

Alina: Actually ordinary industrial and commercial enterprises should not consider such disposal expenses and need not put them into the original cost. But for the particular fixed assets of some special enterprises such as oil, coal or nuclear power businesses, they should put the disposal expenses into the original cost, including the cost of disposing oil wells, coal mine wells, nuclear waste, etc.

Alan: Oh, I see.

Alina: Do you have any other problems?

Alan: Yes. I don't know whether we should count such things like spare parts, repair equipment as fixed assets.

Alina: According to the definition of fixed assets, such things are normally not regarded as fixed assets. They belong to inventories. But there are exceptions. For example, some dear spare parts of airlines shall be recognized as fixed assets, because they satisfy the conditions of recognition of fixed assets.

Alan: It's so complicated. I think I need to read more. Thank you very much.

Alina: You are welcome.

Questions:

1. What enterprises should put disposal expenses into the original cost?
2. What do spare parts and repair equipment normally belong to?

Self-test Exercises

Section 1

Fill in the following blanks.

Unit 3 Long-term Assets

1. Fixed assets, also called PPE, include _____, _____ and _____.
2. Things like _____, _____, _____, _____ machinery, furniture, tools all belong to tangible fixed assets.
3. Long-term assets can be divided into two categories: _____, _____ and _____.
4. Fixed assets are mainly obtained by _____ and _____.
5. A fixed asset shall be initially measured at _____.
6. If fixed assets are purchased, the cost usually includes the _____, _____, and some other _____.
7. When a piece of equipment is acquired, the additional costs may include _____, _____, _____ and so on.
8. For self-constructed fixed assets the original cost includes material, labor, overhead costs, _____, _____, etc.
9. If a fixed asset is obtained through an exchange of non-monetary assets, the original cost is determined based on the _____.
10. In determining the cost of fixed assets, enterprises should consider any expected _____.

Section 2

Fill in the following blanks.

1. Depreciation refers to the systematic allocation of the _____ of a fixed asset over its useful life.
2. Estimated net residual value is the estimated amount which an enterprise would currently obtain from _____.
3. The four common depreciation methods are _____, _____, the double declining balance method and the sum-of-the-years-digits method.
4. _____ shall be employed when it is assumed that an asset's economic revenue is the same each year, and the repair and maintenance cost is also the same for each period.
5. When depreciation is mainly due to wear and tear, _____ are usually used.
6. Depreciable amount refers to _____ of a fixed asset less its estimated net residual value.
7. Suppose that an enterprise purchased a machine at the beginning of 2002 which cost ￥36,000. The net salvage value was estimated at ￥2,000 and the expected useful life was 5 years. Please use the straight-line method to calculate the depreciation amount of year 2002, 2003, 2004, 2005 and 2006.
8. Assume that a company bought a glass drilling machine for ￥18,000 in 2001. It was

estimated that the machine could drill 250,000 holes during its useful life. In 2001, 2002, 2003 it drilled 30,000, 40,000 and 75,000 holes respectively. Suppose the net salvage value was ￥1,000, please calculate the depreciation expense of year 2001, 2002 and 2003 under the units of production method.

9. Let us suppose a computer was bought for ￥12,000 at the beginning of the year 2001 with a useful life of 5 years and an estimated net residual value ￥1,000. Please use the double declining balance method to calculate the depreciation amount from year 2001 to 2005.

10. Assume that a machine was acquired for ￥68,000 in 2005. Its estimated useful life was 6 years and the net salvage value was ￥5,000. Please use the sum-of-the-years-digits method to calculate the depreciation charge from 2005 to 2010.

Section 3

Fill in the following blanks.

1. An intangible asset can be defined as any _____ without physical substance owned or controlled by an enterprise.

2. The new definition of intangible assets emphasizes the nature of _____.

3. The two types of intangible assets are finite and _____ intangibles.

4. The real value of intangible assets is that they can bring _____ to the enterprises.

5. Please name five most commonly seen intangibles, i.e., _____, _____, _____, _____ and _____.

6. Intangible assets do not include internally generated _____, _____ and _____.

7. Intangible assets should be measured initially at _____.

8. For intangible assets with finite useful lives enterprises shall consider their _____ while intangible assets with indefinite useful lives shall not be amortized.

9. Generally the amortization charge shall be recognized in _____ for the current period.

10. When an enterprise determines the useful life of intangible assets, it should First consider the provisions in the _____ or legal _____.

Section 4

In pairs, discuss and define the following terms.

1. long-term asset
2. fixed asset
3. tangible asset
4. intangible asset
5. useful life

Unit 3 Long-term Assets

6. depreciation

7. depreciable amount

8. estimated net residual value

9. amortization

10. goodwill

Section 5

In pairs, read and decide if the following statements are true or false. Correct the false ones.

1. Fixed assets are intangible assets.

2. Internally generated goodwill can be viewed as intangible assets.

3. Land doesn't need depreciation and is considered to have an infinite life.

4. Equipment such as machinery, furniture and tools should be amortized.

5. Fixed assets are usually purchased for business operations, not for resale.

6. Fixed assets are usually subjected to depreciation.

7. Bonds and stocks are classified as intangible assets.

8. An intangible asset, among others, is subjected to amortization over its useful life.

9. Legal and contractual provisions can determine the useful life of an intangible asset.

10. Once the expected useful life and estimated net residual value are determined, they shall not be changed under any circumstances.

Section 6

In groups, discuss the following questions.

1. What do you think of the importance of long-term assets?

2. What is the cost of a purchased fixed asset?

3. What are the most common types of fixed assets?

4. Can you name some of the intangible assets?

5. What are the four depreciation methods in the book? Which is the simplest one?

参 考 译 文

第一节 固定资产

与流动资产相比，长期资产是指那些在超过一年的时间内变现或者耗用的资产，通常分为固定资产、无形资产和递延资产。

固定资产是指使用时限在一年以上，单位价值在规定标准以上，并在使用过程中保持原来物质形态的资产。根据我国新颁布的《企业会计准则》，固定资产具有以下两个特征：

首先，固定资产是为生产产品、提供劳务、出租或经营管理而持有的；第二，固定资产的使用寿命超过一个会计年度。

只有满足下面两个条件时，固定资产才能得以确认。首先，与该资产有关的经济利益很可能流入企业。第二，该资产的成本能够可靠地计量。

第二节　固定资产的折旧

所有的固定资产在其有限的使用寿命期间都应该计提折旧。但是已提足折旧仍继续使用的固定资产和单独计价入账的土地除外。土地不需要折旧，因为在使用过程中，它永远不会失去它的功能价值，而且土地寿命也无期限。

折旧可以定义为在固定资产使用寿命内，按照确定的方法对应计折旧额进行系统分摊。当计算一项固定资产折旧费的时候，企业应当考虑它的应计折旧额、预计净残值、估计的使用寿命以及折旧方法。

应计折旧额是指应计提折旧的固定资产的原价扣除其预计净残值后的余额。预计净残值是指假定固定资产预计使用寿命已满并处于使用寿命终了时的预期状态，企业目前从该项资产处置中获得的扣除预计处置费用后的金额。所谓的使用寿命是指企业使用固定资产的预计时间，或者该固定资产所能生产产品或提供劳务的数量。

固定资产的使用寿命和预计净残值要合理确定，一经确定就不要轻易改变。当确定使用寿命和预计净残值的时候，企业要考虑以下因素：预计生产能力或实物产量；预计有形损耗和无形损耗；法律或者类似规定对资产使用寿命的限制。

许多方法都可以用来将一项固定资产的成本通过折旧的方式均摊到会计年度，但是每一种折旧方法可能只适用一种情况，所以企业应当根据与固定资产有关的经济利益的预期实现方式来选择折旧方法。最常见的折旧方法有四种：年限平均法(直线法)、工作量法、双倍余额递减法和年数总和法。

一、年限平均法(直线法)

年限平均法是一种使用最广泛也是最保守的折旧方法。当我们使用年限平均法的时候，我们是假定某项资产的年经济收入都是一样的，并且每个阶段的维修保养费也是一样的。年限平均法是将折旧费平均分摊在资产的使用寿命期内，因此每年的折旧费都是一样的。年限平均法的公式是：

$$年折旧费 = \frac{原始成本 - 预计净残值}{预计使用寿命(年数)}$$

年限平均法尤其适用于建筑、机械、管道等。

> **例 3.1**
> 假设某公司在 2008 年用 200 000 元购买了一辆斯泰尔豪沃卡车，它的预计净残值是 20 000 元，使用寿命为 10 年。如果利用直线法计算，那么每年的折旧费应该为：(￥200 000－￥20 000)/10 年＝￥18 000/年。

二、工作量法

当折旧主要来自于资产的磨损而与时间的长短并没有太大关系的时候，我们就可以使用工作量法来计算折旧费。按照工作量法折旧法，折旧费应该根据固定资产的使用程度的比例来摊配折旧费，公式如下：

$$每单位产量的折旧额 = \frac{原始成本 - 预计净残值}{预计总产量}$$

例 3.2

假设购置一台复印机，价格为 22 000 元，预计净残值为 100 元，在使用寿命内可以复印 30 万张，那么每单位产量(即每复印一张)的折旧费为：(22 000 元 − 100 元)/30 万张=0.073 元。如果第一年一共复印了 3 万张，那么第一年的折旧费就是 0.073 元×30 000=2 190 元。假如第二年一共复印了 4 万张，那么第二年的折旧费就应该是 0.073 元×40 000=2 920 元。

三、双倍余额递减法

双倍余额递减法也称为加速折旧法。正如你所知道的那样，随着时间的流逝，几乎所有的资产都会逐渐失去它的价值。但是一些资产在购置的头几年，往往比后几年使用得更为频繁，能提供更多的服务。因此这些资产头几年的折旧费就要高于后几年。双倍余额递减法正好适合计算这类资产的折旧费。

当计算一项资产的折旧费时，应该按照下面的步骤去做。

(1) 计算直线折旧率。直线折旧率的算法是拿百分数除以使用年限。在例 3.1 中，直线折旧率应为 100%÷10=10%。

(2) 计算双倍直线折旧率。双倍直线折旧率的算法是拿直线折旧率乘以 2。在例 3.1 中，双倍直线折旧率应为 10%×2=20%。

(3) 计算每个会计年度的折旧费。具体算法是用每个会计年度的资产账面价值乘以双倍直线折旧率。

双倍余额递减法的公式是：年折旧费=每个会计年度的账面价值×双倍直线折旧率。

例 3.3

假设购置一台机器，价格为 1 万元，预计使用寿命 5 年，预计净残值为 1 000 元。如果使用双倍余额递减法，每年的折旧额如下：

年份	原始成本/¥	期初累计折旧额/¥	期初账面价值/¥	×	双倍直线折旧率/%	=	年折旧费/¥
1	10 000	0	10 000	×	40	=	4 000
2	10 000	4 000	6 000	×	40	=	2 400
3	10 000	6 400	3 600	×	40	=	1 440
4	10 000	7 840	2 160	×	40	=	864
5	10 000	8 704	1 296			=	296
总计							9 000

请注意，第 5 年的折旧费只有 296 元，即 1 296 元(期初账面价值)-1 000 元(预计净残值)，而不是 518.40 元(1 296×40%)。这是因为一项资产的账面价值不能折旧到低于它的预计净残值。在这个例子中，如果第五年的折旧费按 518.40 元算的话，那么资产的账面价值就将成为 1 296-518.40=777.60 元，低于预计净残值 1 000 元。

四、年数总和法

像双倍余额递减法一样，年数总和法也属于加速折旧法，这是因为它也是假设某项资产在购置的头几年使用得更为广泛。年数总和法的公式为：

年折旧额=(原始成本-预计净残值)×(尚可使用年数÷预计使用年限的年数总和)

预计使用年限的年数总和(SYD)的算法是从使用资产的第一年起直到使用寿命结束时止的所有年数加在一起。举个例子，如果一项资产的使用寿命是 6 年，那么 SYD 应该为 6+5+4+3+2+1=21 年。那么第一年的折旧费就应该为：(原始成本-预计净残值)×6/21，第二年就应该为：(原始成本-预计净残值)×5/21，第三年就应该为：(原始成本-预计净残值)×4/21，以此类推。

例 3.4

假设某公司购买了一项设备，价格为 8 万元，使用寿命为 5 年，预计净残值为 5 000 元。如果使用年数总和法计算，每年的折旧费如下表所示。

年份	原始成本/¥	折旧基数/¥	×	折旧分数	=	年折旧费/¥
1	80 000	80 000-5 000	×	5/15	=	25 000
2	80 000	80 000-5 000	×	4/15	=	20 000
3	80 000	80 000-5 000	×	3/15	=	15 000
4	80 000	80 000-5 000	×	2/15	=	10 000
5	80 000	80 000-5 000	×	1/15	=	5 000
SYD 15	总折旧费					75 000

第三节　无形资产

无形资产的定义与特征

根据新的《企业会计准则》第 6 号，无形资产可以定义为企业拥有或控制的没有实物形态的可辨认的非货币性资产。从定义中我们可以很容易地知道无形资产具有以下三个特征：第一个特征就是它不具有实物形态，第二个特征是它的可辨认性，第三个特征就是它属于非货币性资产。

无形资产新的定义强调了它的可辨认性，说明无形资产必须是可以辨认的资产。只有当无形资产同时满足以下两个条件时，才能予以确认。第一，与该无形资产有关的经济利益很可能流入企业。第二，该无形资产的成本能够可靠的计量。

无形资产不具有实物形态，它可能只是一份文件或一个图案，但是它真正的价值在于企业可以从无形资产的权力和特权中获取巨大的利益。像专利权、商标权、版权、特许权和营业执照、互联网名称、建筑许可证和土地使用权，都是最常见的无形资产。

根据新准则，企业内部创造的商誉以及内部产生的品牌、报刊名等被排除在无形资产之外。银行存款、应收账款和长期投资的股票债券也不属于无形资产。

无形资产的初始计量

当记账的时候，无形资产应当按照实际成本进行初始计量，实际成本包括购买价格和所有使该项资产达到预定可使用状态前所发生的所有开销。

外购无形资产的成本要按照实际成本记账，其中包括购置成本、相关税费以及所有使该项资产达到预定可使用状态前所发生的合理、必要的支出。自行开发的无形资产，要按照开发过程中的实际支出记账。接受投资者投入所取得的无形资产，应按照认可的评估价格或合同规定的价格记账。对于整批购入的固定资产，各资产的入账价值应该根据各固定资产的公允价或销售价进行分配。

至于非货币性资产交换、债务重组、政府补贴和企业合并取得的无形资产，成本按照相关会计准则确定和记账。

无形资产的摊销

一些无形资产的使用寿命是有限的，而有些无形资产的使用寿命是不确定的。企业在取得无形资产时就应该分析判断其使用寿命。对于那些使用寿命有限的无形资产应进行摊销，摊销要从无形资产可供使用时起，一直到它不再作为无形资产确认时止；而对于那些使用寿命不确定的无形资产则不进行摊销，但要定期进行减值测试。减值要按照新的《企业会计准则第 8 号——资产减值》处理。

无形资产的应摊销金额为其成本扣除预计残值后的金额。已计提减值准备的无形资产，还应扣除已计提的无形资产减值准备累计金额。一般来讲，摊销费应记入当期损益，除非另有规定。

在处理无形资产摊销的时候，企业一般都采取直线法。举个例子，一个企业用 12 万元购买了一项专利，使用寿命为 6 年，那么每年的摊销费就是 2 万元(120 000/6)。

确定无形资产使用寿命时应考虑的因素

当企业确定无形资产寿命的时候，通常要考虑以下几个因素：

(a) 合同或法律所规定的条款；
(b) 到期时续约或延长情况；
(c) 历史经验和惯例；
(d) 同类资产的使用寿命；
(e) 专家的看法或建议；
(f) 该资产所能提供的产品或服务的市场需求情况；
(g) 技术、工艺等现在的情况以及未来发展趋势评估；
(h) 现有的或潜在的竞争对手可能会采取的行动。

Unit 4 Liabilities

Objectives

- In Section 1, students should understand the categories of current liabilities and their accounting treatment.
- In Section 2, students ought to learn the meaning of Long-term Liabilities and how to make the accounting treatment.

Dialogue

1. Sources of outside financing

John: What are your general views on various sources of outside financing? I understand that most American companies do not rely on bank financing to the extent the Japanese companies do.

Mary: Yes. That's probably correct. Naturally we make use of various bank sources for both long-term and short-term loans, but I would say the majority of our long-term outside financing come from the issue of bonds of debentures.

John: What about stock issues? Don't many of American firms use stock issues as a means of raising specific capital for investment projects?

Mary: Yes, that is sometimes done. Actually we often see the insurance of preferred stock designed to raise capital for specific enterprises. Of course, many firms have recently made extensive use of the Euro dollar market as a means of outside financing.

John: What about long-term obligations? Specifically for real estate and other construction ventures?

Mary: Insurance companies are very active in lending funds for these purposes. Of course, many companies, including ours, participate in the short-term call market for daily operating funds.

John: Yes. Lending and borrowing in the call money market is a rational way of utilizing idle funds.

译文：外部融资的来源

约翰：对于外部融资的来源，你有什么看法？我所理解的是，大部分的美国公司靠银行来融资，并没有达到日本公司的程度。

玛丽：情况可能的确是这样。我们很自然地都会从各种银行资源来取得长期或短期的贷款。但是我必须要说明，大部分的长期外部融资都是依靠债券的发行。

约翰：发行股票怎么样？很多美国公司不都是利用发行股票来取得资本进行投资计划的吗？

玛丽：是的，有时候确实是这样。实际上，我们经常会看到某个公司发行优先股来筹集资本。当然，许多公司最近都利用欧洲货币市场来进行外部融资。

约翰：你怎么理解长期债务，特别是房地产等建筑行业的投资？

玛丽：对于这类项目，保险公司总是很积极主动地借出资金。当然，很多公司，包括我们公司，都会利用短期资金市场来取得日常经营的周转资金。

约翰：没错。在短期资金市场中进行贷款和借款，是利用闲置资金的明智选择。

2. Accrued liabilities

(H: Helen   P: Peter)

H: What liabilities do accrued liabilities include?

P: The major liabilities are interest payable, income taxes payable, and salaries payable.

H: How did the liabilities come into being?

P: To obtain the revenue, a business has to incur a certain amount of expenses. Assume an expense benefits the current period, but the actual payment for the expense will be made in a latter accounting period. Then as the accrual basis accounting requires, the expense should be recorded in the current period. For example, the company gets a 6-month loan of $50,000 from the bank at the annual interest rate of 12%. Total of $53,000 of principal and interest won't be paid until six months later. Although $3,000 of the interest expense is to be paid in a later period, it benefits the 6 months after the loan, so it should be apportioned over the 6 months.

H: Five hundred dollars should be apportioned to each month. What's the entry for it at the end of each month?

P: Debit Interest Expense and credit Interest Payable for $500. You see, the Interest Payable account is in fact established against the Interest Expense account.

H: Then the Income Taxes Payable account is established against the Income Taxes Expense account, and the Salaries Payable account is established against the Salaries Expense account, isn't it?

P: Yes.

H: How is the unearned revenue treated in accounting?

P: First, you should understand that cash received for the unearned revenue is an asset, but the unearned revenue is a liability rather than an asset. When you receive an advance payment for goods or services from another company, you should debit Cash and credit

Unearned Revenue. According to the accrual-basis accounting, the unearned revenue should be apportioned over the following periods when goods or services are provided, and converted into sales revenue or service revenue.

H: If a company receives $3 million of advance payment for goods from a customer and will deliver $1 million of goods every month, how is the transaction to be recorded?

P: First, when $3 million of prepayment is received, the entry should consist of a debit to Cash and a credit to Unearned Revenue for $3 million. In each of the next three months when goods have been delivered, debit Unearned Revenue and credit Sales Revenue for $1 million.

H: It's understandable.

译文：应计负债

H: 应计负债有哪些？

P: 主要有应付利息、应付所得税和应付工资。

H: 这些应计负债是如何产生的？

P: 企业要获取一定的收入，就会产生一定的费用。如果一笔费用使当期受益，而这笔费用的实际支付却是在以后的某个会计期间，那么，按权责发生制的要求，这笔费用就应在本期记录。比如，公司从银行取得了 50 000 美元贷款，期限为 6 个月，年息为 12%，6 个月后偿还本息共 53 000 美元。3 000 美元的利息费用虽然在以后的会计期间支付，但该笔费用使贷款后的 6 个月受益，所以应分摊到 6 个月中。

H: 每个月应分摊 500 美元。那么每月底的会计分录应该如何做呢？

P: 以 500 美元借记利息费用账户，贷记应付利息账户。知道了吧，应付利息账户实际上是针对利息费用而设立的。

H: 那么应付所得税账户是针对所得税费用设立的，应付工资账户是针对工资费用设立的，是吗？

P: 是的。

H: 预收收入在会计上应该怎么处理？

P: 首先应该明白，虽然预收到的现金是资产，但预收收入是负债，而不是资产。当收到其他公司预付的货款或服务费时，应借记现金账户，贷记预收收入账户。按权责发生制原则，预收收入应在以后提供商品或服务的会计期间进行分摊，将其转化为销售收入或服务收入。

H: 公司如果收到客户的预付货款 300 万美元，以后每月向客户发送 100 万美元的货物，这笔交易该怎么记录？

P: 首先，在收到 300 万美元的预付款时，应以 300 万美元借记现金账户，贷记预收收入账户。在以后 3 个月每个月发货后，应以 100 万美元借记预收收入账户，贷记销售收入账户。

H: 这不难理解。

Unit 4 Liabilities

Section 1 Current Liabilities

A liability is borne by an enterprise, measurable by money value, which will be paid to a creditor using assets, or services, which are generally classified into current liabilities and long-term liabilities.

Current Liabilities are obligations that must be paid within one year or within the operating cycle, whichever is longer. This means payment for goods and services is due at a date later than the date of sale. Current liabilities can be accounts payable, short-term notes payable, the current portion of long-term debt, accrued liabilities, unearned revenue and overdraft.

1) Accounts payable

Accounts payable often are divided into the categories of trade accounts payable and other accounts payable. Trade accounts payable are short-term obligations to suppliers for purchases or merchandise. Other accounts payable include liabilities for any goods and services other than merchandise.

Example 4.1

Simple Company buys goods for $50,000 on credit. The journal entry in Simple Company's accounting records for this transaction is:

| Purchase | $50,000 | |
| Accounts payable | | $50,000 |

Assets	=	Liabilities	+	Owner's equity	Rev.	−	Exp.	=	Net Inc.	Cash Flow	
50,000	=	50,000	+			−		=		50,000	OA

2) Notes payable

Notes payable are issued whenever bank loans are obtained. Notes payable usually required the borrower to pay an interest charge. Under normal conditions, the interest rate is stated separately from the principal amount of the note.

Example 4.2

On March 1, Simple Company borrows $40,000 from its bank for a period of six months at an annual interest rate of 10 %. Six months later on September 1, Simple Company will have to pay the bank the principal amount of $40,000 plus $2,000 interest. As an evidence of this loan, the bank requires Simple Company to issue a note payable. The journal entry in Simple Company's accounting records for this March 1 borrowing is as follows:

| Cash | $40,000 | |
| Notes payable | | $40,000 |

Assets	=	Liabilities	+	Owner's equity	Rev.	−	Exp.	=	Net Inc.	Cash Flow	
40,000	=	40,000	+			−		=		40,000	FA

Borrowed $40,000 for six months at 10 % interest per year.

The liability for the interest accrues day by day over the life of the loan. On August 31, six months interest expense has been incurred, and the following adjusting entry is made:

　　　　Interest expense　　　　　　　$2,000
　　　　　　Interest payable　　　　　　　　　$2,000

Assets	=	Liabilities	+	Owner's equity	Rev.	−	Exp.	=	Net Inc.	Cash Flow	
	=	2,000	+	(2,000)		−	2,000	=	(2,000)		

The entry on September 1 to record payment of the note will be as follows:

　　Notes payable　　　　　　　$40,000
　　Interest expense　　　　　　$2,000
　　　　cash　　　　　　　　　　　　$42,000

Assets	=	Liabilities	+	Owner's equity	Rev.	−	Exp.	=	Net Inc.	Cash Flow	
(42,000)	=	(40,000)	+	(2,000)		−	2,000	=	(2,000)	(42,000)	FA

To record payment of the 10 %, six-month note on maturity date and to recognize interest expense incurred.

3) Unearned revenue

A liability for unearned revenue arises when a customer pays in advance. Upon receipt of an advance payment from a customer, the company debits Cash and credits a liability account such as unearned revenue.

Unearned revenue normally is "paid" by rendering services to the creditor, rather than by making cash payments.

Example 4.3

Simple Company signed up a contract with another company to perform services. Simple Company received an advanced cash payment in the amount of $20,000 and the term of the contract was one month. The transaction acts to increase assets (cash) and liabilities (unearned revenue). The journal entry in Simple Company's accounting records for this transaction is as follows:

　　Cash　　　　　　　　　　　$20,000
　　　　Unearned revenue　　　　　　　$20,000

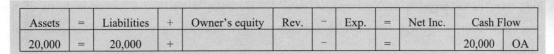

Assets	=	Liabilities	+	Owner's equity	Rev.	−	Exp.	=	Net Inc.	Cash Flow	
20,000	=	20,000	+			−		=		20,000	OA

At this time, Simple Company received cash but didn't perform the services. So the cash of $20,000 was not the real revenue. Only when Simple Company performed the services, a new journal entry would be made in the following:

    Unearned revenue $20,000

            Revenue $20,000

Assets	=	Liabilities	+	Owner's equity	Rev.	−	Exp.	=	Net Inc.	Cash Flow
	=	(20,000)	+	20,000	20,000	−		=	20,000	

4) Income Taxes Payable

The income taxes expense accrues as profits are earned. At the end of each accounting period, the amount of accrued income taxes is estimated and recorded in an adjusting entry, as shown below:

    income taxes expense $1,000

        income taxes payable $1,000

Assets	=	Liabilities	+	Owner's equity	Rev.	−	Exp.	=	Net Inc.	Cash Flow
	=	1,000	+	(1,000)		−	1,000	=	(1,000)	

The account debited in the entry, Income Tax Expense, is an expense account that usually appears as the very last deduction in the income statement. The liability account, Income Taxes Payable, ordinarily will be paid within a few months and appears as a current liability section of the balance sheet.

5) Contingent Liabilities

A contingent liabilities may be regarded as a possible liability, which may develop into a full-fledged liability or may be eliminated entirely by a future event.

For example, when a business endorses a note and turns it over to a bank for cash, the business is contingently liable to the bank. If the maker of the note pays on the maturity date, the contingent liability of the endorser is thereby ended. But if the maker defaults, the endorser must pay in his instead. In either case, the period of the contingent liability ends at the maturity date of the note.

Section 2   Long-term Liabilities

Long-term liabilities are the obligations of an enterprise that is not due within one year or an operating cycle (whichever is longer). The most common examples are bonds payable,

long-term notes payable and mortgages payable. Because bonds are a common form of a long-term debt, they will be used to explain the key accounting procedures for long-term liabilities.

Bonds payable

When a corporation needs to raise a large amount of long-term capital, it generally sells additional shares of capital stock or issues bonds payable.

The insurance of bonds payable is a technique of splitting a large loan into a great many units called bonds. As an interest-bearing (or discounted) certificate of debt issued by a government or corporation in order to raise money, each bond is a long-term interest-bearing note payable, usually in the face amount of $1,000. The bonds are sold to the investing public, thus allowing many different investors to participate in the loan.

An example of a corporate bond issue is the 8 % bond issue of the ABC Company, due March 1, 2008. With this bond issue, The ABC Company borrowed $200 million by issuing 200,000 bonds of $1,000 each.

Example 4.4   Bonds Issued at a Discount

Assume that ABC Company plans to issue $1,000,000 face value of 10 %, 10-year bonds. At the issuance date of May 1, the going market rate of interest is slightly above 10 % and the bonds sell at a market price of only $950. The issuance of the bonds will be recorded by the following entry:

Cash   950,000
Discount on bonds payable   50,000
    Bonds payable   1,000,000

Assets		=	Liabilities	+	Owner's equity	Rev.	−	Exp.	=	Net Inc.	Cash Flow	
950,000	50,000	=	1,000,000	+			−		=		950,000	FA

The amount of the discount is deducted from the face value of the bonds payable to show the carrying value or book value of the liability. At the date of issuance, the carrying value of bonds payable is equal to the amount for which the bonds were sold. Over the life of the bonds, we will see that this carrying value gradually increases until it reaches the face value of the bonds at the maturity date.

Example 4.5   Amortization of Bond Discount

In this example, the discount on bonds payable has a beginning debit balance of $50,000. Each year $5,000 will be amortized into Bond Interest Expense.

Assuming that the interest payment dates are October 31 and April 30, the entries to be made each six months to record bond interest expense are as follows:

(1) Paid semi-annual interest on $1,000,000 of 10 %, 10-year bonds.
Bond interest expense   50,000
    Cash   50,000

Assets	=	Lia.	+	Owner's equity	Rev.	−	Exp.	=	Net Inc.	Cash Flow	
(50,000)	=		+	(50,000)		−	50,000	=	(50,000)	(50,000)	FA

(2) Amortized discount for six months on 10-year bond issue ($50,000 ÷ 20 = $2,500).
Bond interest expense   2,500
        Discount on Bonds Payable   2,500

Assets	=	Liabilities	+	Owner's equity	Rev.	−	Exp.	=	Net Inc.	Cash Flow
	=	2,500	+	(2,500)		−	2,500	=	(2,500)	

应用专栏

Useful Expressions

current liability	短期负债
overdraft *n.*	透支
notes payable	应付票据
account payable	应付账款
unearned revenue	预收账款
accrued wages	应付工资
dividends payable	应付股利
tax payable	应交税金
value added tax payable	应交增值税
consumption tax payable	应交消费税
income tax payable	应交所得税
personal income tax payable	应交个人所得税
other payables	其他应付款
drawing expense in advance	预提费用
long-term liabilities	长期负债
long-term loans	长期借款
long-term loans due within one year	一年内到期的长期借款
long-term loans due over one year	一年后到期的长期借款

debentures, bonds	债券
bonds payable	应付债券
face value, par value	债券面值
the maturity date	到期日
premium on bonds	债券溢价
discount on bonds	债券折价
accrued interest	应计利息
contingent liability	或有负债
default *n. & vi.*	未履行责任

1. There are different types of bonds. Bonds secured by pledge of specific assets are called mortgage bonds.

债券的种类有很多，以某种资产做保的债券称为抵押债券。

2. A contingent liability may be regarded as a possible liability, which may develop into a full-fledged liability or may be eliminated entirely by a future event.

或有负债被看做是一种可能发生的债务，它可能成为一种必须支付的债务，也可能由于未来经济业务的发生而完全消除。

Additional Reading Material

Long-term liabilities are obligations of business that are due to be paid after one year or beyond the operating cycle, whichever is longer. Decisions related to long-term debt are critical because how a company finances its operations is the most important factor in the company's long-term liability. The amount and type of debt a company incurs depends on many factors, including the nature of the business, its competitive environment, the state of the financial markets, and the predictability of its earnings. Growing businesses frequently need long-term financing to invest in R&D activities and long-term assets. Two key sources of long-term funds are as follows:

1) Issuance of capital stock;
2) Issuance of long-term debt such as bonds, notes, mortgages, and leases.

Failure to make timely payments could force a company into bankruptcy.

The interest coverage ratio (ICR) is a measure of how much risk a company is undertaking with its debt. The ICR measures the degree of protection a company has from default on interest payments.

$$ICR = (Operating\ Profit - Interest\ Payable) / Interest\ Payable$$

Oral Practices

Directions: *Read the following conversation and then answer the questions.*

John: Good morning, Sir. Would you tell me what I should do to have money transferred from abroad?

Sir: Yes, I'm glad to. Where is it from?

John: It's from my company in New York. They will send me a check. But I don't know how soon I can receive the money.

Sir: If you ask your company to apply for a check drawn on our bank in Beijing, we can cash it right away.

John: Thank you. But how would they do that?

Sir: Through your company's bank in New York, you should ask them to issue a check drawn on our bank. That would be the easiest way, because we maintain a correspondent relationship with your bank in New York. I will call you when the check arrives.

John: Thank you so much.

Sir: Not at all. Goodbye.

Question:

How could you receive the money transferred from abroad?

Self-test Exercises

Section 1

Fill in the following blanks.

1. The account of _____ should be decreased when the service paid for in advance has been provided.

2. The account of _____ should be recorded when the business purchased supplies on credit.

3. The account of _____ used to show what the business owes the bank.

4. Liabilities are what the business owes everyone except _____.

5. Contingent liabilities do not become liabilities unless _____.

6. Recording a utility bill payment for this accounting period will not increase _____ liabilities. (long-term or current)

7. On June 1, Simple Company borrows $60,000 from its bank for a period of six months

at an annual interest rate of 8 %. As an evidence of this loan, Simple Company issues a note payable. According to this information, please finish the relevant entries.

Section 2

1. Given the following information, which of the following accounting transactions is true?

Gross payroll　　　　　　　　　　　　$20,000
Federal income tax withheld　　　　　　$4,000
Social security tax withheld　　　　　　$1,600

　　A. $1,600 is recorded as salary expense.
　　B. $14,400 is recorded as salary payable.
　　C. The $1,600 deducted for employee social security tax belongs to the company.
　　D. Payroll is an example of an estimated liability.

2. Assume that ABC Company plans to issue $2,000,000 face value of 9 %, 10-year bonds. At the issuance date of January 1, the going market rate of interest is slightly above 10 % and the bonds sell at a market price of only $980. The interest payment dates are June 30 and December 31. According to this information, please finish the accounting treatment below:

(1) Bonds Issued at a Discount.
(2) Paid semi-annual interest.
(3) Amortized discount for six months.

参考译文

第一节　流动负债

负债由企业产生，可以用货币价值衡量，用资产或劳务偿还给债权人，一般被分为流动负债和长期负债。

流动负债是必须在一年或一个经营周期内进行偿还的债务。也就是说，商品和劳务的支付是在销售日期之后的某段时间内。流动负债包括应付账款、短期应付票据、长期债务的流动部分、应计负债、预收账款及透支等。

1) 应付账款

应付账款通常分为应付货款和其他应付款。应付货款是由于商品采购而应向供货方偿还的短期债务。其他应付款则包括除商品采购以外的所有货物或劳务所发生的负债。

例 4.1

Simple 公司赊购$50 000 的货物。对于这笔交易，Simple 公司的会计记录如下。

借：采购　　　　　　　　　　　$50 000
　　贷：应付账款　　　　　　　　　　　$50 000

资产	=	负债	+	业主权益	收入	-	费用	=	净利润	现金流
50 000	=	50 000	+			-		=		50 000　OA

2) 应付票据

取得银行借款时发生应付票据。应付票据通常需要借款人支付利息费用。在一般情况下，票据的利率和本金会分别列示。

例 4.2

3月1日，Simple 公司从银行借款$40 000，期限为6个月，年利率为10％。六个月后即9月1日，Simple 公司必须向银行支付$40 000 的本金再加上$2 000 的利息。作为此笔贷款的凭证，银行需要 Simple 公司签发一张应付票据。Simple 公司在3月1日发生借款所做会计记录如下。

借：现金　　　　　　　　　　　$40 000
　　贷：应付票据　　　　　　　　　　　$40 000

资产	=	负债	+	业主权益	收入	-	费用	=	净利润	现金流
40 000	=	40 000	+			-		=		40 000　FA

此笔借款本金为$40 000，期限6个月，年利率10%。

利息的负债是在借款的期限中一天天累加的。到8月31日，已经发生了六个月的应计利息，调整分录如下。

借：利息费用　　　　　　　　　$2 000
　　贷：应付利息　　　　　　　　　　　$2 000

资产	=	负债	+	业主权益	收入	-	费用	=	净利润	现金流
	=	2 000	+	(2 000)		-	2 000	=	(2 000)	

9月1日记录票据支付如下。

借：应付票据　　　　　　　　　$40 000
　　利息费用　　　　　　　　　　$2 000
　　贷：现金　　　　　　　　　　　　　$42 000

资产	=	负债	+	业主权益	收入	-	费用	=	净利润	现金流
(42 000)	=	(40 000)	+	(2 000)		-	2 000	=	(2 000)	(42 000)　FA

记录了到期日偿还票据本金，并确认了应计利息费用。

3) 预收账款

当客户提前支付款项时，发生预收账款。收到客户提前支付的款项时，公司应借记现金,贷记负债账户,即预收账款。

预收账款通常是靠提供劳务来"偿还",而不是支付现金。

例 4.3

Simple 公司与另一家公司签署劳务合同。Simple 公司提前收到对方支付的现金 $20 000,合同期限为 1 个月。此业务增加了资产(现金)和负债(预收账款)。Simple 公司此笔业务的会计记录如下。

借:现金　　　　　　　　　　　$20 000

　贷:预收账款　　　　　　　　　　　　$20 000

资产	=	负债	+	业主权益	收入	−	费用	=	净利润	现金流
20 000	=	20 000	+			−		=		20 000 OA

此时,Simple 公司只收到了现金而没有提供劳务。因此,$20 000 现金并不是真实的收入。只有在 Simple 公司向对方提供劳务后,才会做如下会计记录:

借:预收账款　　　　　　　　$20 000

　贷:收入　　　　　　　　　　　　$20 000

资产	=	负债	+	业主权益	收入	−	费用	=	净利润	现金流
	=	(20 000)	+		20 000	−		=	20 000	

4) 应付所得税

公司取得利润时发生所得税。在每一个会计期末,要估算出应计所得税的金额并做调整分录,如下所示。

借:所得税费用　　　　　　　　$1 000

　贷:应付所得税　　　　　　　　　$1 000

资产	=	负债	+	业主权益	收入	−	费用	=	净利润	现金流
	=	1 000	+	(1 000)		−	1 000	=	(1 000)	

此分录中借方账户为"所得税费用",属于费用类账户,在损益表中通常处于最后一个抵减项目。负债账户"应付所得税"一般会在几个月内支付,并显示在资产负债表的流动负债中。

5) 或有负债

或有负债可以看做是一项可能发生的负债,随着未来事项的发生,可能转变为真实的负债,也可能完全消除。

例如,公司对一张票据进行背书,再转给银行并从银行取得现金,则该业务使背书人对银行产生了或有责任。如果发票人在到期日支付了款项,背书人的这项或有完全消除。但是如果发票人未履行责任,那么背书人必须替发票人偿还款项。也就是说,这项或有负债的期限是在票据到期日终止的。

第二节　长期负债

长期负债是指公司在一年或一个经营周期以上需要偿还的债务。常见的长期负债有应付债券、长期应付票据及应付抵押贷款。债券是最常见的长期债务，所以可以用债券来说明长期负债的会计处理程序。

应付债券

当一家公司需要获得大量的长期资本时，一般都会采取增发股本或发行应付债券。

应付债券的发行就是把一笔大额贷款分为很多份额，这些份额就是债券。当政府或一家公司为了筹集资金而发行带息债券或折扣债券时，每一份债券都是带息的长期应付票据，通常面额都为$1 000。债券可以销售给社会公众，这样就使得许多不同的投资人都能够参与到这项融资中。

举例说明公司债券的发行：ABC 公司发行债券，年利率为 8%，到期日为 2008 年 3 月 1 日。在这项业务中，ABC 公司发行了 200 000 份债券，每份面额为$1 000，共筹集资金 2 亿元。

例 4.4　折扣发行债券

假设 ABC 公司计划发行总价值$1 000 000 的债券，年利率为 10%，期限为 10 年。在发行日即 5 月 1 日，当时市场利率略微高于 10%，每份债券仅以$950 的市场价格销售。发行该笔债券的会计分录如下。

借：现金　　　　　　　　$950 000
　　应付债券折扣　　　　$50 000
　　贷：应付债券　　　　　　　　$1 000 000

资产		=	负债	+	业主权益	收入	-	费用	=	净利润	现金流	
950 000	50 000	=	1 000 000	+			-		=		950 000	FA

为了表示这笔债务的账面价值，应付债券的折扣额要从面值中减除。在发行日，应付债券的账面价值等于销售债券取得的金额(每份$950)。在债券的整个期限中，账面价值是逐渐增加的，直到到期日时账面价值与面值相等。

例 4.5　债券折扣的分摊

在本例中，应付债券折扣的期初借方余额为$50 000。每年都将有$5 000 的金额被分摊到债券利息费用中。

假设该债券的付息日为每年的 10 月 31 日和 4 月 30 日，则每六个月的债券利息费用将做会计分录如下：

(1) 支付半年的利息(债券面值$1 000 000，年利率10% 期限10年)
借：债券利息费用　　　　　　$50 000
　　贷：现金　　　　　　　　　　　　$50 000

资产	=	负债	+	业主权益	收入	-	费用	=	净利润	现金流	
(50 000)	=		+	(50 000)		-	50 000	=	(50 000)	(50 000)	FA

(2) 分摊6个月的折扣 ($50 000 ÷ 20 = $2 500)
借：债券利息费用　　　　　　　$2 500
　　贷：应付债券折扣　　　　　　　$2 500

资产	=	负债	+	业主权益	收入	-	费用	=	净利润	现金流
	=	2 500	+	(2 500)		-	2 500	=	(2 500)	

Unit 5   Owner's Equity

Objectives

- In Section 1, students should know the difference between partnership and corporation, and identify a corporation and its major characteristics.
- In Section 2, students ought to know partnership accounting.
- In Section 3, the focus is to learn to differentiate between common stock and preferred stock.
- In Section 4, students ought to make clear the difference between paid-in capital and capital surplus.
- In Section 5, students should know stockholders' equity section of a corporation balance sheet.
- In Section 6, students must learn to explain cash dividends and stock dividends.

Dialogue: The accounting of Owner's Equity

(H: Hellen   P: Peter)

H: I think there are more partnerships than corporations, aren't there?

P: Yes. The reason is that partnerships are easy to form. But nowadays more and more enterprises adopt the form of corporation.

H: I think that the income of the partnership is also owned by all the partners.

P: The income of the partnership is distributed according to the partnership agreement. Some partnerships distribute the income in proportion to the partners' investment, and some distribute the income equally to the partners.

H: Does the accounting for partnerships have anything special?

P: The partnership maintains a separate capital account and a separate drawing account for each partner.

H: What are the characteristics of the incorporated business?

P: First, the incorporated business, namely the corporation, is a legal entity. Stockholders are not personally liable for the debts of a corporation. Thus, the most that a stockholder may lose by investing in a corporation is the amount of his investment. To many investors, this is the most important advantage of the corporation.

H: How is the cost to form a company treated in accounting?

P: It's charged to an account entitled Organization Cost which belongs to Other Assets. Many corporations amortize this asset to expense over a period of around 5 years. The entry for the amortization is to debit Organization Expense and Credit Organization Costs.

H: Dose the corporation maintain withdrawing accounts for stockholders?

P: The capital paid in by stockholders is permanent, so it is not subject to withdrawal, so the corporation doesn't maintain any withdrawing accounts.

H: The section of owner's equity in some balance sheets consists of only two items-capital stock and retained earnings, but some balance sheets carry detailed items of owner's equity.

P: That's true. Detailed items of various preferred and common stocks can be included in the capital stock, and detailed items of various dividends and other distributions can be included in retained earnings. In China there are four sections in the owner's equity, i.e., paid-in capital, capital surplus, revenue surplus and undistributed profit.

译文：业主权益的核算

H: 我想合伙企业的数量比公司多吧？

P: 是的。这是因为合伙企业的组建非常容易。但是，现在越来越多的企业选择公司这一组织形式。

H: 我想合伙企业的收益也是所有合伙人共同分享的。

P: 合伙企业的收益是按合伙协议分配的。有的按合伙人的投资比例分配，而有的是平均分配。

H: 合伙企业的会计有什么特别指出的吗？

P: 合伙企业的每个合伙人开设有独立的资本账户和资本提取账户。

H: 公司制企业有哪些特点？

P: 首先，公司制企业即公司，是一个法律实体。另外，股东个人不对公司的负债负责，因此股东的损失最大不超过其对公司的投资额。对于大多数投资者而言，这是公司的最大优点。

H: 创办公司的成本在会计上是怎么处理的呢？

P: 记入一个叫组织成本的资产账户，属于其他资产。在5年左右把这项资产分摊到费用账户中。分摊时，借记组织费用账户，贷记组织成本账户。

H: 公司为股东设立资本提取账户吗？

P: 不设立。股东缴入的资本是公司的永久性资本，一般不能提取，因此公司也就不设立资本提取账户。

H: 有些资产负债表上的所有者权益只有股本和留存收益两个项目，而有些却分得较细。

P: 是的。股本部分可以详细地列出各种优先股和普通股的金额，留存收益部分可以详细地列出各种股利以及其他的分配。在中国，所有者权益分为四个部分：实收资本、资本公积、盈余公积和未分配利润。

Section 1　Ownerships of Business Entities

In general, businesses take out of the following three alternative legal forms: sole proprietorship, partnerships and corporations.

1. Proprietorships and Partnerships

A proprietorship is a business that is owned by one person and is not organized as a corporation. A partnership is an unincorporated association of two or more persons to carry on a business for profit as co-owners. Proprietorships and partnerships are not separate entities; they do not exist apart from the owners. And the owners are personally responsible for the liabilities of the entities. This means that the personal assets of the owner(s) are available to satisfy the claims of the business creditors. Proprietorships and partnerships are not subject to income taxes. Instead, the income is taxed as personal income of the owner(s), whether the owner(s) withdraw(s) cash from the business or not.

In case of a proprietorship, the owner's equity is reported by means of a single capital account. In a partnership, capital accounts are established for each partner. Investments by owners' are credited to Capital account. Withdrawals and distributions are debited to Capital account, or to separate contra-equity accounts, closing to Capital account at the end of the accounting period.

2. Corporations

A corporation is a separate legal entity chartered (or incorporated) under laws in different jurisdiction. The ownership (or equity) of a corporation is divided into units called shares of stock, and the individuals or organizations that own these shares are called shareholders or stockholders. The advantages of corporations are as follows:

a. Corporations are separate legal entities. This characteristic means that a corporation is responsible for its own acts and its own debts as a person. However, because a corporation is not a person, it can only go through its agents, who are managers.

b. Corporations have continuity of life. A corporation's life may continue indefinitely because it is not tied to the physical lives of its owners.

c. Shareholders are not liable for the corporation's debts. This limited liability feature is a major reason why corporations are able to obtain resources from investors who are not active participants in managing the affairs of the business.

d. Stockholders are not agents of the corporation. Instead, they participate in the affairs of the corporation only by voting in the stockholders' meeting.

e. Ownership rights can be easily transferred. Also, the transfer of shares from one stockholder to another usually has no effect on the corporation or its operations.

There are also disadvantages to incorporating a business. The income of a corporation is taxed twice, First as income of the corporation and again as personal income to the stockholders when cash is distributed to them as dividends. Another disadvantage is that corporations are generally subject to more regulations than other businesses, such as Securities Law and Company Law, reporting requirements for listed corporations.

Section 2   Sole Proprietorship and Partnerships Accounting

In most respects, partnership accounting is similar to that in a sole proprietorship except there are more owners. As a result, a separate capital account and drawing account is maintained for each partner. Partnerships recognize no salaries expense for services provided to the organization by the partners. Accounts paid to partners are recorded by debiting partner's drawing account.

1. Opening the accounts of a new partnership

Example 5.1

On January 1, Joan Adams and Richard Brown decide to form a partnership by consolidating their two retail stores. A capital account will be opened for each partner and credited, with the agreed valuation of the net assets that the partner contributes. The journal entries to open the accounts of the partnership of Adams and Brown are as follows:

(1) To record the investment by Joan Adams in the partnership of Adams and Brown.

Dr. Cash	40,000	
Accounts Receivable	60,000	
Inventory	90,000	
Accounts Payable		30,000
Cr. Joan Adams, Capital		160,000

(2) To record the investment by Richard Brown in the partnership of Adams and Brown.

Dr. Cash	10,000	
Inventory	60,000	
Land	60,000	
Building	100,000	
Accounts Payable		70,000
Cr. Richard Brown, Capital		160,000

2. Additional investments

Example 5.2

After six months of operation the firm is in need of more cash, and the partners make additional investments of $10,000 each on July 1. These additional investments are credited to the capital accounts as shown below:

To record additional investments

Dr. Cash   20,000
    Cr. Joan Adams, Capital   10,000
        Richard Brown, Capital   10,000

3. Closing the accounts of a partnership at year-end

At the end of the accounting period, the balance in the Income Summary account is closed into the partners' capital accounts. The profits or losses of a partnership may be divided among the partners in any manner agreed upon by the partners.

Example 5.3

Adams and Brown have agreed to share profits equally. Assuming that the partnership earns net income of $60,000 in the First year of operations, the entry to close the Income Summary account is as follows:

(1) To divide net income for the year in accordance with partnership agreement to share profits equally.

The next step in closing the accounts is to transfer the balance of each partner's drawing account to his capital account. Assuming that withdrawals during the year amounted to $24,000 for Adams and $16,000 for Brown, the entry at December 31 to close the drawing accounts is as follows:

Dr. Income Summary   60,000
    Cr. Joan Adams, Capital   30,000
        Richard Brown, Capital   30,000

(2) To transfer debit balances in partners' drawing accounts to their respective capital accounts.

Dr. Joan Adams, Capital   24,000
    Cr. Richard Brown, Capital   16,000
Dr. Joan Adams, Drawing   24,000
    Cr. Richard Brown, Drawing   16,000

4. Income statement for a partnership

The income statement of a partnership for Adams and Brown is shown as follows below:

ADAMS AND BROWN

Income Statement

For the year ended December 31, 2003 $

Sales		600,000
goods		400,000
Gross profit on sales		200,000
Operating expenses		
Selling expense	100,000	
General & administrative expenses	40,000	140,000
Net income		60,000
Division of net income		
To Joan Adams (50%)	30,000	
To Richard Brown (50%)	30,000	60,000

5. Statement of partners' equity

The statement of partners' equity for Adams and Brown appears below:

ADAMS AND BROWN

Statement or partners' Equity

for the Year Ended December 31, 2003 $

	Adams	Brown	Total
Balances, Jan. 1, 2003	160,000	160,000	320,000
Add: Additional investments	10,000	10,000	20,000
Net income for the year	30,000	30,000	60,000
Subtotals	200,000	200,000	400,000
Less: Drawings	24,000	16,000	40,000
Balances, Dec. 31, 2003	176,000	184,000	360,000

Section 3 Rights and Privilege of Shareholders

1. Rights and Privilege of Common Shareholders

As we know, stockholders are the owners of a company. The ownership of a corporation can be divided into shares of capital stock. Capital stock is the number of shares authorized for issuance by a company's charter, including both common stock and preferred stock. The interest of stockholder is determined by the number of shares that he or she owns.

Individual investors can purchase and own shares of capital stock. We then call these individual investors stockholders or shareholders.

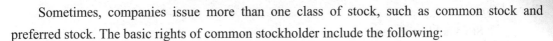

Sometimes, companies issue more than one class of stock, such as common stock and preferred stock. The basic rights of common stockholder include the following:

(1) Voting right

A stockholder has one vote for each share owned. They can vote for directors and on certain other key issues. Stockholders have no managerial authority unless they have been appointed by the board to a management role. Stockholder(or group of stockholders) who owns more than 50% of the capital stock has the power to elect the board of directors and to set basic corporate policies. Therefore, these stockholders control the corporation.

(2) Dividends & Liquidation participation right

A stockholder has the right to get dividends declared by the board of directors. The directors may elect to distribute some or all of the earnings of a profitable corporation to its stockholders in the form of cash dividends. Dividends can be distributed only after they have been formally declared (authorized) by the board of directors and paid in proportion to the number of shares owned. Stockholders in a corporation could make withdrawals of company assets when the corporation liquidates. After paying creditors, any remaining assets are divided among the shareholders again, in proportion to the number of shares owned.

(3) Preemptive right

A stockholder has the right to maintain his or her percentage ownership if the corporation increases the number of shares outstanding.

2. Rights and Privilege of Preferred Shareholders

Preferred shareholders are owners who have certain rights superior to those of common shareholders. These rights will pertain to either the earnings or the assets of the corporation. Preferences as to earnings exist when the preferred shareholders have a stipulated dividend rate. Preferences as to assets exist when the preferred shareholders have a stipulated liquidation value. Preferred shares may also have the following features: participation in earnings beyond the stipulated dividend rate; a cumulative feature, affording the preferred shareholders the protection that their dividends in arrear, if any, will be fully satisfied before the common shareholders participate in any earnings distribution; and convertibility or call ability by the corporation.

In exchange for the preferences, the preferred shareholders' rights are limited. The right to vote, and the right to participate without limitation in the earnings of the corporation, may be restricted to common shareholders.

Section 4 Capital vs. Retained Earnings

Owner's equity in a corporation is defined as stockholders' equity, shareholders' equity, or corporate capital. An example of a stockholders' equity section of a corporation balance sheet is shown below:

> Stockholders' equity
> Paid-in capital
>   Common stock.   330,000
>   Retained earnings   80,000
>   Total stockholders' equity   410,000

Stockholders' equity normally includes the following three categories:

Capital stock

Additional paid-in capital (In China, it is called capital surplus.)

Retained earnings (In China, it is called undistributed profit.)

Capitals stock and additional paid-in capital constitute contributed (paid-in) capital while retained earnings represent the earned capital of the enterprise.

It is quite essential for us to distinguish between paid-in capital and retained earnings in the chart of accounts for corporations. Only earnings of the corporation can be distributed as dividends by law. Corporations cannot legally distribute dividends exceeding the cumulative balance in retained earnings so as to protect their creditors. We will First explain the accounts used to record paid-in capital transactions and then discuss retained earnings.

Section 5 Issuance of Shares

1. Par value stock

As we have learned, par value of a bond represents the amount that an issuer agrees to repay at the date of maturity. But the par value of a share is an arbitrarily assigned dollar amount. There is no necessary relationship between the price at which a corporation issues stock, and the price at which the stocks trades in the marketplace, and the par value of the stock.

If the stock has "par value", stockholder's permanent investment is equal to the number of shares outstanding times the par value of each share.

Sometimes a corporation may issue par value stock at a price in excess of par, then the stock is said to be issued at a premium.

Issuance of par value stock

When shares are issued, net assets and equity increase by fair value of assets given to the corporation. The capital stock account is credited for the par value of the stock issued. The excess over par is credited to a descriptively named paid-in capital in excess of par account to record source in detail.

In China, we use capital surplus account instead of paid-in capital in excess of par account.

Example 5.4

The issuance of 100,000 shares of common stock, par $1, for cash of $1.2 per share would be recorded as follows:

Dr. Cash	120,000	
Cr. Common Stock, par $1 (100,000 shares)		100,000
Paid-in Capital in Excess of Par, common stock		20,000

2. No-par value stock

If the stock is "No-par value" stock, investment of stockholder is an arbitrary amount that the board assigns to the stated capital account.

Corporations may issue no-par value stock for the following reasons:

To avoid the stocks were issued at a discount;

To avoid confusion over the relationship between the par value and fair market value.

Issuance of no-par value stock

Please notice that treatment of par value stock is quite different from no-par value stock. No-par stock with a stated (or assigned) value is accounted for in the same manner as discussed for par value stock because the stated value places the no-par stock on essentially the same basis as par value stock.

True no-par stock, when sold, is recorded as a credit to the capital stock account. Thus the capital stock account should be credited for the full amount received. In this case, no paid-in capital "in excess" is recorded.

Example 5.5

Assume that a corporation issues 10,000 shares of no-par common stock at $40 a share and at a later date issues 1,000 additional shares at $36. The entries to record the no-par stock are as follows:

Dr. Cash	400,000	
Cr. Common stock		400,000

Issued 10,000 shares of no-par common stock at $40.

Dr. Cash	36,000	
Cr. Common stock		36,000

Issued 1,000 shares of no-par common stock at $36.

Section 6   Retained Earnings

The amount of retained earnings represents the cumulative net income of the firm since its beginning, less the total dividends that have been distributed to shareholders. It is important to note that retained earnings are not the assets, but the existence of retained earnings means that net assets generated by profitable operations have been kept in the company to help it grow or to meet other business needs. However, a credit balance in Retained Earnings does not mean that cash or any designated set of assets is directly associated with retained earnings. The fact that earnings have been retained means that net assets as a whole have been increased.

Retained Earnings may carry a debit balance. Generally, this happens when a company's losses and distributions to stockholders are greater than its profits from operations. In such a case, the firm is said to have a deficit (debit balance) in retained earnings. This is shown in the stockholders' equity section of the balance sheet as a deduction from paid-in capital.

1. Appropriated retained earnings

A corporation may voluntarily designate or bound by law or by contract an amount of retained earnings for some special purpose as a means of explaining to stockholders why dividends are not being declared. For example, the board of directors may appropriate part of retained earnings for expansion. A debit to retained earnings and a credit to a separate account-- retained earnings appropriated for expansion (in China, the account title is reserve fund). Reserve fund appears directly in the owner's equity on the balance sheet.

In China, companies must provide "legal reserves." Each year a certain percentage of income is appropriated if the corporation has net profit until the reserve amount equals 50% percentage of legal capital stockholders' equity. Thus, the main purpose of legal reserves is to protect creditors from overpayment of dividends and it is good for expansion.

Today in USA, appropriations of retained earnings are seldom seen on balance sheets. Instead, management's reasons for not declaring dividends usually are conveyed in a letter to stockholders that is published with the financial statements.

2. Dividends and stock split

If you had your own business and wanted to withdraw money for personal use, you would simply withdraw it from the company's checking account or cash register. In a corporation, a formal action by the board of directors is required before money can be distributed to the owners. In addition, such payments must be made on a pro rata basis of ownership percentage. These pro rata distributions to owners are called dividends. Dividends usually have two forms, i.e., cash and stock dividends. Cash dividends and stock dividends are declared with some frequency in practice, and will be the focus of discussion in this lesson.

1) Cash dividends

Cash dividend is a pro rata distribution of cash to stockholders. For cash dividend to be paid, a corporation must have sufficient cash.

There is no necessary relationship between the balance in the retained earnings account and the balance in the cash account. The fact that the company reports large earnings does not mean

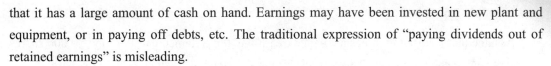

that it has a large amount of cash on hand. Earnings may have been invested in new plant and equipment, or in paying off debts, etc. The traditional expression of "paying dividends out of retained earnings" is misleading.

The amount of distributed dividend is subject to retained earnings limit. Since dividends represent a distribution of earnings to stockholders, the theoretical maximum for dividends is the total undistributed net income of the company, represented by the credit balance of the Retained Earnings account. In practice, many corporations limit dividends, in the belief that a major portion of the net income must be retained in the business if the company is to grow and to keep pace with its competitors.

2) Stock dividends

Dividends may also be paid in the form of additional shares of stock rather than cash. This type of dividend is called stock dividend. A company may want to retain funds in the business to finance expansion, pay off debts, and this precludes paying a cash dividend; but the company still wants its shareholders to receive a dividend of some kind. Such a company may declare a stock dividend, which increases every shareholder's number of shares by the same percentage.

Stock dividend is quite different from cash dividend. If dividends paid are in the form of cash, those dividends are taxable. When a company issues a stock dividend, rather than cash, there usually are not tax consequences until the shares are sold.

Sometimes corporation's objective to distribution of a stock dividend is to reduce the market price of its stock and thus more attractive to a wider range of investors. The declaration of a stock dividend does not create a liability because the corporation is not obligated to pay assets.

A stock dividend does not change the balance of income, assets, or shareholders' proportionate equity, but it increases the number of outstanding shares. Accordingly, it will reduce the per share market price of the stock. However, in practice stock dividends are so small — usually less 20 percent of the number of issued shares — that the market price of the shares occasionally remains unchanged. A large stock dividend significantly increases the number of shares available in the market and usually lowers the stock price.

The entry to record a stock dividend in USA depends on its size.

Large stock dividend (25% or more of issued stock) significantly increases the number of shares available in the market and usually lowers the stock price. A common practice is to transfer the par value of the dividend shares from retained earnings to common stock, as shown in next example.

Small stock dividend (less than 20 — 25% of issued stock) is less likely to affect the price of the company's stock significantly. Hence, to record a stock dividend, retained earnings are debited with the fair value of the additional shares issued, with the credit being to the paid-in capital in excess of par account.

To illustrate the accounting for stock dividends, let us look at the following example.

Example 5.6

Assume that a corporation has a balance of $300,000 in retained earnings and 50,000 shares of $10 par value common stock. The current fair market value of its stock is $15 per share.

If the corporation declares a 10% stock dividend, the entry to record this transaction at the declaration and payment date is as follows:

The date of declaration

Dr. Retained Earnings	75,000	
Cr. Common Stock to Be Distributed		50,000
Paid-in Capital in Excess of Par		25,000

The date of payment

Dr. Common Stock to Be Distributed	50,000	
Cr. Common Stock		50,000

If the corporation declares a 40% stock dividend, the entry to record this transaction at the declaration and payment date is as follows:

Declaration date

Dr. Retained Earnings	200,000	
Cr. Common Stock to Be Distributed		200,000

The date of payment

Dr. Common Stock to Be Distributed	200,000	
Cr. Common Stock		200,000

In Chinese practice, accounting record of all stock dividends are the same as large stock dividends. The entry of stock dividends is recorded at the date of payment that combined the entries of the date of declaration and the date of payment together. Stock dividends should be disclosed in financial statement.

3) Dividend declaration

Things we must remember are that, dividends are not paid automatically and the board of directors is necessary to declare a dividend.

The following three dates are important in connection with dividends: (1) the declaration date (2) the record date, and (3) the payment date. Normally, there is a time span of two to four weeks between dates. As explained below, accounting entries are required on two of the dates – the declaration date and the payment date.

On the declaration date, the board of directors announces the intention to pay the dividend. The declaration creates a liability for the corporation. Thus, an entry is required to recognize the decrease in retained earnings and the increase in the liability, dividends payable, that have occurred.

Example 5.7

Assume that on December 1, 2005, the directors of A corporation declare a 40 cents per share cash dividend on 100,000 shares of $10 par value common stock. The dividend is $40,000 (100,000 × 0.4), and the entry to record the declaration is as follows:

Dr. Dividends   40,000
   Cr.   Dividends Payable   40,000

At the end of the year, the dividends account is closed to retained earnings by the following entry:

Dr. Retained earnings   40,000
   Cr. Dividends   40,000

From this entry, you can see that a declaration of dividends reduces retained earnings and, eventually, the amount of cash on hand. Thus, though not considered to be an expense, dividends do reduce the amount a company could otherwise invest in productive assets.

Those stockholders who own the stock on the date of record will receive the dividend when it is paid. The corporation makes no journal entry on the date of record because no transaction occurs and the corporation's liability recognized on the declaration date is unchanged.

On payment date, payment of the dividend is recorded by debiting dividends payable, crediting cash. Note that payment of the dividend reduces both current assets and current liabilities but has no effect on stockholders' equity. The entry to record the payment is as follows:

Dr. Dividends payable   40,000
   Cr. Cash   40,000

The cumulative effect of the declaration and payment of a cash dividend on a company's financial statements is to decrease both stockholders' equity and total assets.

4) Stock split

Stock split is an increase in the number of outstanding shares of a company's stock, such that proportionate equity of each shareholder remains the same. That means a stock split doesn't change the total par or stated value of the stock and contributed capital. Hence, no transfer is made from retained earnings to common stock when a stock split is affected.

To illustrate a stock split, look at the following example:

Example 5.8

Assume that Hongxin Corporation has 10,000 shares of $100 par common stock outstanding with a current market price of $150 per share. The board of directors declares a 5-for-1 stock split, reduces the par to $20, and increases the number of shares to 50,000. The amount of common stock outstanding is $1,000,000 both before and after the stock split. Only the number of shares and the par per share are changed. Each shareholder owns the same total par amount of stock before and after the stock split. For example, a stockholder who owned 4 shares of $100 par stock before the split (total par of $400) would own 20 shares of $20 par stock after the split (total par of $400).

Some companies decide to split their stock if the price of the stock rises significantly and is perceived to be too expensive for small investors to afford. The price per share immediately adjusts to reflect the stock split, since buyers and sellers of the stock all know about the stock split (in the case of two-for-one split, the share price would be cut in half). However, sometimes the price reduction is not quite proportional to the split because stock with a low price tends to be more attractive than stock with a high market price per share.

The difference between a stock dividend and a stock split is a matter of intent. The intent of a stock dividend is to give shareholders "ostensibly separate evidence" of their interests in the firm without having to distribute cash. The intent of a stock split is to reduce the market price of the shares so as to improve their marketability.

Table 5-1 lists the comparison of stock dividends and stock split.

Table 5-1 The comparison of stock dividends and stock split.

Stock Dividends	Stock Split
Par value of a share does not change	Par value of a share decreases
Total number of shares increases	Total number of shares increases
Total stockholders' equity does not change	Total stockholders' equity does not change
The composition of equity changes (less of retained earnings; more of stock)	The composition of equity does not change (same mounts of stock and retained earnings)
Stock dividends require journal entries	Stock splits do not require journal entries

应用专栏

Useful Expressions

partnership	*n.*	合伙
partner	*n.*	合伙人
corporation	*n.*	公司
own	*v.*	拥有
amortize	*v.*	分期清偿
distribution	*n.*	分配

Unit 5 Owner's Equity

convenient *adj.*	方便的
combine *v.*	联合
recognize *v.*	承认，认可
consolidate *v.*	巩固，加固
divide *v.*	划分
share *v.*	分配，分享
evidence *n./v.*	证实，证明
subtotal *n.*	小计
ordinarily *adv.*	普通地
issuance *n.*	发行
common stock	普通股
preferred stock	优先股
shareholder(stockholder) *n.*	股东
dividend	股利，股息
preemptive right	优先权
owner's equity	所有者权益
par value stock	有面值股票
no-par value stock	无面值股票
paid-in capital	实收资本
additional paid-in capital	多收资本，增收资本
capital surplus	资本公积
issuing corporation	发行公司
retained earnings	留存收益
cash dividend	现金股利
stock dividend	股票股利
declaration of dividend	股利宣布，股利公告
dividend distribution	股利分配
reserve *vt./n.*	计提准备金, 准备金
stockholders' equity	股东权益
appropriation of retained earnings	留存收益的分配
at the option of	有选择权
appropriated retained earnings	核定的留存收益
reserve found	盈余公积
stock split	股票分割
charter *n.*	宪章，章程
bylaw *n.*	附则、细则、公司章程
generate *vt.*	产生

1. The incorporated business, namely the corporation, is a legal entity. Stockholders are not personally liable for the debts of a corporation. Thus, the most that a stockholder may lose by investing in a corporation is the amount of his investment.

公司制企业即公司，是一个法律实体。另外，股东个人不对公司的负债负责。因此股东的损失最大不超过其对公司的投资额。

2. Detailed items of various preferred and common stocks can be included in the capital stock, and detailed items of various dividends and other distributions can be included in retained earnings. In China there are four sections in the owner's equity, i.e., paid-in capital, capital surplus, revenue surplus and undistributed profit.

股本部分可以详细地列出各种优先股和普通股的金额，留存收益部分可以详细地列出各种股利以及其他的分配。在我国，所有者权益分为四个部分：实收资本、资本公积、盈余公积和未分配利润。

3. In general, businesses take out of the following three alternative legal forms: sole proprietorship, partnerships and corporations.

一般地说，企业可以采用三种法律组织形式：独资企业、合伙企业和公司。

4. As we know, stockholders are the owners of a company. The ownership of a corporation can be divided into shares of capital stock. Capital stock is the number of shares authorized for issuance by a company's charter, including both common stock and preferred stock.

我们知道，股东是公司的所有者。公司的所有权可以分割成股本，股本代表公司所有者权益的分割。股本是公司章程核准的发行股数，包括普通股和优先股。

5. When shares are issued, net assets and equity increase by fair value of assets given to the corporation. The capital stock account is credited for the par value of the stock issued. The excess over par is credited to a descriptively named paid-in capital in excess of par account to record source in detail.

发行股票时，按照公司获得资产的公允价值增加净资产和权益，"股本"科目贷记发行股票面值的金额。超过面值部分，贷记"附加投入资本"，以详细反映其来源。

6. True no-par stock, when sold, is recorded as a credit to the capital stock account. Thus the capital stock account should be credited for the full amount received. In this case, no paid-in capital "in excess" is recorded.

无票面价值股票发行时，贷记股本账户。这样股本账户按应收到的金额全额贷记。在这种情况下，不用记录超过设定价值的资本公积。

7. The amount of retained earnings represents the cumulative net income of the firm since its beginning, less the total dividends that have been distributed to shareholders.

留存收益的数额等于企业开办以来累计的净利润减去已分配给股东的股利。

8. A corporation may voluntarily designate or bound by law or by contract an amount of retained earnings for some special purpose as a means of explaining to stockholders why

dividends are not being declared. This is a separate account — retained earnings appropriated for expansion (in China, the account title is reserve fund).

公司可能会出于自愿，或由于受到法律及合同的约束，为某些特定用途拨定一定数量的留存收益，并以此向股东解释为什么没有宣告股利的原因，这就是为扩大经营而拨定的留存收益(在中国，这个账户是盈余公积)。

9. Cash dividend is a pro rata distribution of cash to stockholders. For cash dividend to be paid, a corporation must have sufficient cash.

现金股利是按比例分配给股东的现金。要支付现金股利，公司必须有足够的现金。

10. Dividends may also be paid in the form of additional shares of stock rather than cash.

股利也可以不通过现金，而以额外的股利形式来发放，这种形式的股利就叫股票股利。

Tips：Derivative A derivative is a financial instrument whose value depends on the price of an underlying instrument, such as currencies, commodities or securities. Common examples of derivatives include swaps, options, futures and FRAs. These particular types of derivatives are called over-the-counter (OTC) derivatives and futures in particular are traded on an exchange. In terms of options, the most common are called put (sell) and call (buy) options. Swaps on the other hand, come in many different forms. The most common forms include interest-rate swaps, currency swaps and credit swaps.

衍生工具：衍生工具就是一种金融工具，其价值取决于基础工具的价格，比如货币、商品或有价证券。衍生工具的常见例子包括互换(掉期)、选择权(期权)、期货和远期。这些特殊类型的衍生工具被称为非上市证券市场(OTC)衍生工具，尤其是期货，是在外汇基础上交易的。关于选择权，最常见的称为抛出(出售)和买进(购买)选择权。另一方面，互换是以多种形式出现的。最常见的形式包括利率互换、通货互换和信用互换。

Additional Reading Material

Owner's Equity

The owner's equity in a business represents the resources invested by the owners. It is called stockholders' equity in a corporation. "Owner's equity" is a broader term because the concepts being presented are equally applicable to the ownership equity in corporations, partnerships, and single proprietorships.

Owner's equity in corporations and single proprietorships.

The owner's equity of the following a corporation consists of the following two elements: capital stock and retained earnings, as shown in the following illustration: Owner's equity

Stockholders' equity:

Capital stock	1,000,000
⋮	
Retained earnings	278,000
Total Stockholders' equity	1 278,000

The $1,000,000 shown under the caption capital stock represents the amount invested in the business by its owners. The $ 278,000 of retained earnings represents the portion of owner's equity which has been accumulated through profitable operation of the business. The corporation has chosen to retain this $ 278,000 in the business rather than to distribute these earnings to stockholders as dividends. The total earnings of the corporation may have been considerably more than $ 278,000, because any earnings which were paid to stockholders as dividends would not appear on the balance sheet. The term retained earnings describes only the earnings which were not paid out in the form of dividends. The amount of the retained earnings account at any balance sheet date represents the accumulated earnings of the company since the date of incorporation, minus any losses and minus all dividends distributed to stockholders.

A single proprietorship is not required to maintain a distinction between invested capital and earned capital. Consequently, the balance sheet of a single proprietorship will have only one item in the owner's equity section, as illustrated below:

Owner's equity:	
Bill White Capital	$ 30,000

Changes of owner's equity

The equity of the owners is a residual claim because the claim of the creditors legally come first. If you are the owner of a business, you are entitled to whatever remains after the claims of the creditors are fully satisfied. Thus, owner's equity is equal to the total asset minus the liabilities. For example, a company has total assets of $ 350,000, and its total liabilities amounting to $ 80 000, therefore, the owner's equity must be equal to $ 270,000($ 350,000 − $ 80,000).

Suppose that the company borrows $ 20,000 from a bank. After recording the additional asset of $ 20,000 in cash and recording the new liability of $ 20,000 owed to the bank, now the company has total assets of $370,000 and the total liabilities of $ 100,000 and therefore the owner's equity still is equal to $ 270,000.

It is apparent that the total assets of the business were increased by the act of borrowing money from a bank, but the increase in total assets was exactly offset by an increase in liabilities, and the owner's equity remained unchanged. The owner's equity in a business is not increased by the incurring of liabilities of any kind.

Increases in owner's equity

The owner's equity comes from two sources: (1) investment by the owners; (2) earnings from profitable operation of the business.

For a proprietorship, the owner's equity is represented by the term capital. The total capital comes from the owner's initial investment and net income. The net income is the excess of revenue over expenses for the accounting period and it is the increase in capital resulting from profitable operation of a business.

For a corporation, the caption capital stock in the balance sheet represents the amount invested by the owners of the business, as previously mentioned. When the owners of a corporation invest cash or other assets in the business, the corporation issues in exchange shares of capital stock as evidence of the investor's ownership equity. Thus, the owners of a corporation are termed stockholders.

The basic unit of capital stock is called share, but a corporation may issue capital stock certificates in denominations of 1 share, 100 shares, or any other number. The total number of shares of capital stock outstanding at any given time represents 100% ownership of the corporation. Outstanding shares are those in the hands of stockholders. The number of shares owned by an individual investor determines the extent of his or her ownership of the corporation. Capital provided to a corporation by stockholders in exchange for shares of either preferred or common stock is called paid-in capital, or contributed capital.

The earning of net income, or profits, is a major goal for almost every business enterprise, large or small. Profits increase the owner's equity in the business and the increase is usually accompanied by an increase in total assets. The resources generated by profitable operations may be retained in the business to finance expansion, or they may be distributed as dividends to the stockholders. Some of the largest corporations have become large by retaining their profits in the business and using these profits for growth. Retained profits may be used, for example, to acquire new plant and equipment, to carry on research leading to new territories. But remember, retained earnings is not an asset; it is an element of stockholders' equity.

Decreases in owner's equity

Decreases in owner's equity also are caused in two ways, (1) distribution of cash or other assets by the business to its owners; (2) losses from unprofitable operation of the business.

The distribution of cash for a single proprietorship takes the form of personal withdrawals, and a drawing account is used to show the decrease in capital. A dividend is a distribution of assets (usually cash) by a corporation to its stockholders. In some respects, dividends are similar to expenses in that they reduce both the assets and the owners' equity in the business. However, dividends are not an expense, and they are not deducted from revenue in the income statement. The reason that dividends are not viewed as an expense is that these payments do not serve to generate revenue. Rather, they are a distribution of profits to the owners of the business. Since the declaration and payment of a dividend reduce the stockholders' equity, the dividend could be recorded by debiting the Retained Earnings account. However, a clearer record is created if a separate Dividends account is debited for all amounts distributed as dividends to stockholders. At the end of a period the Dividends account is credited and the Retained Earnings account is debited to close the Dividends account.

An expense always causes a decrease in owner's equity. Expenses are the cost of the goods and services used up in the process of earning revenue. When the expenses exceed the revenue generated, the business is said to be operating at a loss.

Oral Practices

Directions: *Steven meets Tony after he has taken the Owner's equity course. Read the conversation and answer the questions.*

Tony: Hi, Steven. How are you getting on with your lessons?

Steven: I am still struggling with my Owner's equity course.

Tony: Oh, don't get discouraged. Not everyone can do as well as you.

Steven: Thanks. Tony, can you give me an example of a stockholders' equity section of a corporation balance sheet?

Tony: An example of a stockholders' equity section of a corporation balance sheet is shown below:

Stockholders' equity
Paid-in capital
 Common stock   330,000
 Retained earnings   80,000
Total stockholders' equity   410,000

Steven: What is the Retained earnings?

Tony: The retained earnings represents the cumulative net income of the firm since its beginning, less the total dividends that have been distributed to stockholders.

Steven: What is the difference between the capital stock and capital surplus?

Tony: When shares are issued, net assets and equity increase by fair value of assets given to the corporation. The capital stock account is credited for the par value of the stock issued. The excess over par is credited to a descriptively named paid-in capital in excess of par account to record source in detail. In China, we use capital surplus account instead of paid-in capital in excess of par account.

Steven: Can you make it more specific?

Tony: For example, the issuance of 100,000 shares of common stock, par $1, for cash of $1.2 per share would be recorded as follows:

Dr. Cash   120,000
 Cr. Common Stock, par $1 (100,000 shares)   100,000

Paid-in Capital in Excess of Par, common stock   20,000

Steven: I begin to understand. I think I need to do a lot of study today.

Tony: Keep up. Steven, you will make it.

Questions:

1. What is owner's equity?

2. What examples can you tell Steven to help him understand the section of owner's equity?

3. What is the difference between paid-in capital and capital surplus?

Self-Test Exercises

Sections 1 & 2

Complete the following sentences.

1. A corporation's balance sheet contains assets, liabilities, and _____.

2. _____ and _____ are the two common capital stocks issued by a corporation.

3. _____ is the legal value of a share of stock.

4. The stocks that have been issued to shareholders and have not been bought back by the corporation is called_____stocks.

5. _____ and _____ are the usual forms of distribution to shareholders.

6. A_____ is a proportional distribution to shareholders of additional shares of the corporation's common or preferred stocks.

7. _____involves a constraint on a specific portion of retained earnings for a specific purpose.

8. _____represents the corporation's accumulated net income, less accumulated dividends and other amounts transferred to paid-in capital accounts.

9. A_____shows the charges in the retained earnings of a corporation during an accounting period.

Sections 3 & 4

Mark the correct items by "T" and the wong items by "F".

1. After the shares of capital stocks have been sold to the investors, they are referred to as issued shares. (T   F)

2. When a corporation issues one type of capital stocks, common stocks are always issued. (T   F)

3. Par value is strictly a legal matter, and it establishes the legal capital of a corporation. (T   F)

4. A stock is issued at a premium when the par exceeds the selling price. (T   F)

5. The balance of the additional paid-in capital account represents a gain on the sale of stocks and increases net income. (T   F)

6. Treasury stocks are presented at the bottom of the shareholders' equity section as a deduction on the balance sheet. (T   F)

7. Income Tax levied on a corporation's income should be accounted as an operating expense. (T   F)

8. A corporation must, by law, pay a dividend once a year. (T   F)

9. Dividends are an expense of a corporation and should be charged to the periodic income. (T   F)

10. The appropriation of retained earnings is to establish a cash fund for a specific purpose. (T   F)

11. On the date of dividends declaration, the corporation become liable to shareholders for the amount of a cash dividend. (T   F)

12. Appropriation of retained earnings has no effect on total shareholders' equity. (T   F)

Sections 5 & 6

Choose the correct answers to the following questions.

1. If a corporation has outstanding 1,000 shares of $9 cumulative preferred stock of $100 par and dividends have been passed for the preceding three years, what is the amount of preferred dividends that must be declared in the current year before a dividend can be declared on common stock?

  A. $9,000 B. $27,000 C. $36,000 D. $45,000

2. All of the following are reasons for purchasing treasury stock except to_____.

  A. make a market for the stock

  B. increase the number of shareholders

  C. increase the earnings per share and return on equity

  D. give employees as compensation

3. Paid-in capital for a corporation may arise from which of the following sources?

  A. Issuing cumulative preferred stock.

  B. Receiving donations of real estate.

  C. Selling the corporation's treasury stock.

  D. All of the above.

4. Under the equity method, the investment account is decreased by all of the following

except the investor's proportionate share of _____.

  A. dividends paid by the investee

  B. declines in the fair value of the investment

  C. the losses of the investee

  D. all of the options

 5. Cash dividends are paid on the basis of the number of shares _____.

  A. authorized

  B. issued

  C. outstanding

  D. outstanding less the number of treasury shares

 6. The stockholders' equity section of the balance sheet may include _____.

  A. common stock   B. preferred stock

  C. donated capital   D. all of the above.

 7. Declaration and issuance of a dividend in stock _____.

  A. increases the current ratio

  B. decreases the amount of working capital

  C. decreases total stockholders' equity

  D. has no effect on total assets, liabilities, or stockholders' equity

 8. If a corporation reacquires its own stock, the stock is listed on the balance sheet in the _____.

  A. current assets section

  B. long term liability section

  C. stockholders' equity section

  D. investments section

 9. A corporation has issued 25,000 shares of $100 par common stock and holds 3,000 of these shares as treasury stock. If the corporation declares a $2 per share cash dividend, what amount will be recorded as cash dividend?

  A. $22,000   B. $25,000   C. $44,000   D. $50,000

 10. A company declared a cash dividend on its common stock on December 15, 2004, payable on January 12, 2005. How would this dividend affect shareholders' equity on the following dates?

December 15, 2004	January 12, 2005
A. Decrease.	Decrease.
B. No effect.	No effect.
C. No effect.	No effect.
D. Decrease.	Decrease.

参考译文

第一节 企业实体的所有权形式

一般来说,企业可以选择三种法律组织形式:独资企业、合伙企业和公司。

1. 独资企业和合伙企业

独资企业,是指仅有一个业主拥有的非合作形式的企业。而合伙企业是由两个或多个合伙人共同经营,共享利润的合作企业。独资企业和合伙企业的资产并非是独立的,并不独立于业主的资产而单独存在,且业主对企业的债务负完全责任,这就意味着业主个人资产也要对企业债权人的债务承担偿还责任。

独资企业和合伙企业的所得不交企业所得税,而是以业主的名义申报个人所得税,不论业主是否在企业提款。

在独资企业下,所有者权益仅反映一个单独的资本账户。在合伙企业,资本账户要合伙人分别设立,合伙人的投资计入资本账户的贷方,提款和利润分配计入资本账户的借方,或当一个会计期结束时,从资本账户结转计入一个独立的资本对立账户。

2. 公司

公司是在不同法律条例下允许独立经营的独立法律实体。公司的所有权被分割成等额股份,拥有这些股份的个人或组织被称为股东。公司的优点有以下几点。

(1) 公司是独立的法律实体。这个特征意味着公司作为一个独立的"人",对他的行为和债务承担责任,然而,由于公司并非一个真正的人,实际上仅是通过他的代理,即管理者来承担责任的。

(2) 公司有持续的寿命周期。一个公司的寿命可以永久持续下去,因为他并不受所有权人生理生命的局限。

(3) 股东对公司债务承担有限责任。正是这种有限责任的特征,可以使公司能够从投资者那里获取资源,而这些投资者并不参与公司事务的管理。

(4) 股东并非是公司的代理人。他们仅是在股东会议上通过表决权参与公司事务。

(5) 所有权很容易被转移,而且股份从一个股东转移到另一个股东,对公司的运作不会产生任何影响。

公司制企业也有一些缺点。公司的所得被征税两次。首次是公司所得交税,再一次是股东作为现金股利的分配的所得,还要交税。另一个缺点是,公司和其他企业相比,要遵守更多的规则,如证券法、公司法和报告规则等。

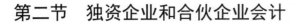

第二节 独资企业和合伙企业会计

除合伙企业拥有多个业主之外，在许多方面，合伙企业会计与独资企业相似。因此，应为每个合伙人拥有一个单独的资本账户和提用账户。与独资企业一样，合伙企业不把合伙人为企业提供的服务作为工资费用。支付给合伙人的款项借记合伙人提用账户。合伙人权益表取代业主权益表，单独反映每个合伙人资本账户的变化。

1. 新合伙企业开立账户

例 5.1

1月1日艾德姆斯和布朗决定把他们的两家零售商店合并，共同组建一个新的合伙企业。为每个合伙人开立一个资本账户，并把合伙人投入的净资产的协议价格贷记到相应的资本账户。艾德姆斯和布朗合伙企业开立账户的日记账分录如下：

① 记录艾德姆斯对合伙企业的投入。

借：现金　　　　　　　　40 000
　　应收账款　　　　　　60 000
　　存货　　　　　　　　90 000
　　应付账款　　　　　　30 000
　　贷：艾德姆斯，资本　　160 000

② 记录布朗对合伙企业的投入。

借：现金　　　　　　　　10 000
　　存货　　　　　　　　60 000
　　土地　　　　　　　　60 000
　　建筑物　　　　　　　100 000
　　应付账款　　　　　　70 000
　　贷：布朗，资本　　　160 000

2. 增加投资

例 5.2

假设企业经营6个月之后需要更多的现金，合伙人同意在7月1日每人增资10 000美元。这些增加的投资贷记如下的资本账户：

借：现金　　　　　　　　20 000
　　贷：艾德姆斯，资本　　10 000
　　　　布朗，资本　　　　10 000

3. 合伙企业年末结账

在会计期末，收益汇总账户的余额结转到合伙人资本账户。合伙企业的损益在合伙人之间按他们约定的方式进行分配。

例 5.3

艾德姆斯和布朗约定平均分配利润。假设该合伙企业在经营的第一年获得净收益 60 000 美元，收益汇总账户的结账分录如下：

① 根据合伙协议平均分配本年度净收益。下一步是把每个合伙人的提用账户结转到其资本账户。假设本年度艾德姆斯提用 24 000 美元，布朗提用 16 000 美元，12 月 31 日提用账户的结账分录如下：

借：收益汇总　　　　　　　　　60 000
　　贷：艾德姆斯，资本　　　　　　　　30 000
　　　　布朗，资本　　　　　　　　　　30 000

② 把合伙人提用账户的借方余额转入他们各自的资本账户。

借：艾德姆斯，资本　　　　　　24 000
　　贷：布朗，资本　　　　　　　　　　16 000
借：艾德姆斯，提用　　　　　　24 000
　　贷：布朗，提用　　　　　　　　　　16 000

4. 合伙企业的收益表

艾德姆斯和布朗合伙企业的收益表如下所示：

艾德姆斯和布朗合伙企业

收益表

2003 年度　　　　　　　　　　　　　　　　　　　　　　　　　　美元

销售收入		600 000
销货成本		400 000
销售毛利		200 000
营业费用		
推销费用	100 000	
管理费用	40 000	140 000
净收益		60 000
净收益分配		
艾德姆斯(50%)	30 000	
布朗(50%)	30 000	60 000

5. 合伙人权益表

艾德姆斯和布朗合伙企业的合伙人权益表如下所示：

艾德姆斯和布朗合伙企业

合伙人权益表

2003 年度 美元

	艾德姆斯	布 朗	合 计
期初余额	160 000	160 000	320 000
加：增加的投资额	10 000	10 000	20 000
本年度净收益分配	30 000	30 000	60 000
小计	200 000	200 000	400 000
减：提用	24 000	16 000	40 000
期末余额	176 000	184 000	360 000

第三节 股东的权利

1．普通股股东的权利

我们知道，股东是公司的所有者。公司的所有权可以分割成股本，股本代表公司所有者权益的分割。股本是公司章程核准的发行数，包括普通股和优先股。股东的权益由其持有的数量决定。

私人投资者可以购买和拥有股本。我们把私人投资者称为股票持有者或股东。公司有时不只发行一种股票，如普通股和优先股。

普通股股东通常拥有以下权利：

(1) 选举权。股东每拥有一份额股票便有一份选举权，选举董事并决定其他重要事务。除非董事会授权，股东没有管理权限。任何一个股东或股东团体，只要拥有股本的 50%及其以上的份额，就拥有选举董事会和制定公司基本方针的权力，所以这些股东实质上控制着公司。

(2) 股利和清算参与权。公司股东有权获得董事会宣告的股利。董事会可以将公司盈利的一部分或全部以现金股利的形式发给股东。股利只有在董事会宣布(核定)后才可发放。股利是根据股东持有股票数量按比例分配给所有股东的。

股东可以在公司清算时从公司撤资。只有清偿债务后，才可以将剩余的资产在股东之间按比例分配。

(3) 优先购股权。若公司增发配股，股东有权利维持其所有权比例。

2．优先股股东的权利

优先股股东相对于普通股股东有特定的优先权，这些权利体现在收益分配和对公司资产的权利上。在收益分配上的优先权体现在优先股股东具有约定的股利分配率，在公司资产上的优先权体现在优先股股东具有约定的清算价值。优先股也许还有以下特征：在约定股利分配率的基础上参与额外收益的分配；在公司拖欠股利时，在以后年度可以累积。总之，在收益分配上，优先股股东比普通股股东有完全的满足，且具有灵活性。

相对于他们的优先权，优先股股东的权力也受限制，选举权和参与公司收益分配的权利会受到普通股股东的限制。

第四节　公司资本和留存收益

公司所有者权益被定义为股东权益、股票持有者权益或公司资本。公司资产负债表中所有者权益的部分示例如下：

股东权益
实收资本　　　　　　　　　　330 000
留存收益　　　　　　　　　　 80 000
　总股东权益　　　　　　　　410 000

股东权益通常被分为以下三部分：

- 股本
- 附加投入资本(在中国被称为资本公积)
- 留存收益(在中国，被称为未分配利润)

股本和附加投入资本构成认缴资本，留存收益代表公司挣得的资本。

公司账目表必须区分实收资本和留存收益。这种区别是相当关键的，因为根据法律，只有公司实际挣得的盈余才可以作为股利发放。为保护债权人，公司依法发放的股利不可以超过留存收益的累计账面余额。我们首先解释用来记录实收资本交易处理的账户，然后讨论留存收益。

第五节　股票发行

1. 票面价值

我们已经学过，债券的票面价值表示发行者同意到期日归还的金额。但是股票的票面价值是对每股任意设定的价值。公司股票的发行价、股票交易的市场价，和股票面值之间并没有必然联系。

如果股票有票面价值，股东的长期投资就等于股东持有股数乘以每股票面价值。

如果公司以高于票面价值的价格发行股票，该股票就被称为溢价发行。

有面值股票的发行

发行股票时，按照公司获得的资产的公允价值增加资产和权益。"股本"科目贷记发行股票面值的金额。超过面值部分贷记"附加投入资本"，以详细反映其来源。

在中国，我们用资本公积代替附加投入资本。

例 5.4

发行 100 000 股普通股，面值 1 美元，以每股 1.2 美元发行，记录如下：

借：现金　　　　　　　　　　　　　　　　120 000
　　贷：普通股(面值 1 美元，100 000 股)　　100 000
　　　　附加投入资本—普通股　　　　　　　 20 000

2. 无票面价值

若股票无票面价值，股东的投资就等于董事会分配记入设定资本账户的任意值。公司可能会因为以下原因而发行无面值的股票：

(1) 为了避免股票可能折价发行；
(2) 为了避免票面价值和公允市价的混淆。

无票面价值股票的发行

无票面价值股票发行的财务处理和有票面价值股票发行的账务处理不同。具有设定价格的无票面价值股票和有面值股票记账方法一样，因为设定价值实际上赋予了无票面价值与有票面价值股票同样的计价基础。

无票面价值股票卖出时贷记股本账户。这样，股本账户应按收到的金额全额贷记。在这种情况下，不用记录超过设定价值的资本公积。

例 5.5

假设公司以每股 40 美元发行 10 000 股无票面价值股票，后来又以每股 36 美元发行 1 000 股。记录无票面价值股票的分录如下：

以每股 40 美元发行 10 000 股无票面价值股票。

借：现金　　　　　　　400 000
　　贷：普通股　　　　　　　400 000

以每股 36 美元发行 1 000 股无票面价值股票。

借：现金　　　　　　　360 000
　　贷：普通股　　　　　　　360 000

第六节　留存收益

留存收益的数额等于企业从开办以来累计的净利润减去已分配给股东的股利。需要注意的是，留存收益本身并不是资产，但留存收益的存在，意味着由盈利经营行为产生的净资产已经在公司中累积，帮助公司壮大并满足其他经营需求。但留存收益的贷方余额并不意味着留存收益直接与现金或某种特定形式的资产相关联，而是意味着净资产总体上增加了。

留存收益也可能是借方余额，这通常发生在公司的损失和对股东的分配大于经营利润之时。在这种情况下，企业产生了留存收益(借方余额)，这在资产负债表的所有者权益部分作为实收资本的减项。

1. 法定留存收益

公司可能会出自自愿，或由于受到法律及合同的约束，为某些特定用途拨定一定数量的留存收益，并以此作为向股东解释为什么没有宣告股利的原因。例如，董事会可以拨定一部分留存收益来扩大经营。借记留存收益，贷记一项专门账户——为扩大经营拨定的留存收益(在中国，这个账户是盈余公积)。盈余公积直接出现在资产负债表的所有者权益中。

在中国，公司必须有法定公积金。如果公司有净利润，每年需按利润的一定百分比提取法定公积金，直到公积金金额达到法定资本的50%。因此，法定公积金的主要目的是通过防止过度发放股利来保护债权人，并且这也有利于扩大经营。

如今在美国，留存收益的拨定很少出现在资产负债表上。作为替代，管理层不宣告股利的理由通常会在给股东的信里说明，这封信和资产负债表一起公布。

2. 股利和股票分割

如果你有自己的公司，并且想从中撤回一些出资供自己使用，你只需要从公司的支票账户或收银机中提取即可。而在公司中，必须通过董事会的正式举措把钱分给所有者，并且，这种支付必须以所有者权益的比例为基础。这种按比例对所有者的支付就叫做股利。股利通常有两种方式：现金股利和股票股利。现金股利和股票股利在实际中应用很多，是本节讨论的重点。

1) 现金股利

现金股利是按比例分配给股东的现金。要支付现金股利，公司必须有充足的现金。

留存收益的余额和现金账户的余额之间并不存在必然的联系。公司报告的利润额很大，并不代表其手头的现金多。利润可能被用于投资购买新厂房和设备，或是偿还贷款等。那种"用留存收益支付股利"的传统观点是错误的。

股利分配的金额受制于留存收益的限制。既然股利代表分配给股东的收益，理论上的可发放股利的最大值是未分配净利润的总额，即留存收益的贷方余额。实际上，很多公司限制股利的发放，因为他们认为，如果公司要壮大并且与其对手并驾齐驱，大部分净利润必须留存在企业中。

2) 股票股利

股利也可以不通过现金而是通过额外的股份来发放，这种形式的股利就是股票股利。有时公司想要留存资金来扩大运营，偿还负债，这种情况下就不适合支付现金股利；但公司仍然希望股东可以得到某种形式的股利。这样的公司会宣告股票股利，以相同的比例增加每个股东持有的股票数量。

股票股利不同于现金股利。如果股利以现金形式发放，这些股利需要纳税。当公司发放股票股利而不是现金股利时，除非股票出售，否则不需要纳税。

有时公司分配股票股利的目的是降低股票的市价，以吸引更广泛的投资者。股票股利的宣告不会产生负债，因为公司没有付出资产的义务。

尽管股票股利并不改变公司的收益、资产或每个股东的所有者权益比例，但它确实增加了发行在外的股票的数目。所以从理论上讲，这种股利会减少股票的每股市价。但在实务中，股票股利的比例很小——通常占不到已发行股票总数的20%——因此股票的市价时常保持不变。大量的股票股利会使市场上可购买的股票数量有明显的增加，从而降低股价。

在美国，记录股票股利的分录取决于股利的规模。

大量股票股利(等于或多于已发行股票的25%)：显著地增加了市场上可购买的股票数量，通常会使股价降低。实务中，通常的做法是把股利的面值由留存收益转到普通股，如下例所示。

少量股票股利(少于已发行股票的20%到25%)：不会明显影响公司股价。因此，记录股票股利的方法是，以额外发行的股票的公允价值借记留存收益，贷记超过面值的投入资本。

为了说明股票股利的会计处理，我们来看下面的例子。

例5.6

假设某公司留存收益余额为300 000美元，50 000股面值为10美元的普通股。股票当前的市价是每股15美元。

如果公司宣告10%的股票股利，在宣告日和支付日这笔交易的分录如下：

宣告日：

借：留存收益　　　　　　　　75 000
　　贷：待分配的普通股　　　　　　50 000
　　　　超过面值的投入资本　　　　25 000

支付日：

借：待分配的普通股　　　　　50 000
　　贷：普通股　　　　　　　　　　50 000

如果公司宣告了40%的股票股利，在宣告日和支付日这笔交易的分录如下：

宣告日：

借：留存收益　　　　　　　　200 000
　　贷：待分配的普通股　　　　　200 000

支付日：

借：待分配的普通股　　　　　200 000
　　贷：普通股　　　　　　　　　200 000

在中国会计实务中，所有股票股利的会计处理都和大量股票股利相同。股票股利的分录是在支付日记录，将宣告日和支付日的分录合并起来。股票股利应当在财务报表中有所披露。

3. 股利宣告

应该记住的是，股利不会自动被支付。董事会必须通过正式行动来宣告股利。

和股利有关的重要日期有三个：(1)宣告日；(2)登记日；(3)支付日。通常，每两个日期之间都会有 2 到 4 周的间隔。正如下面解释的那样，在宣告日和支付日都要求做会计分录。

在宣告日，董事会宣告了要支付股利的意图。这项宣告使公司产生了负债。因此，要求做一笔确认留存收益减少和负债(应付股利)增加的分录。

例 5.7

假设在 2005 年 12 月 1 日，A 公司董事会宣告 100 000 股面值为 10 美元的普通股每股可得 40 美分现金股利。股利是 40 000 美元(100 000×0.4)，记录这项宣告的分录是：

借：股利　　　　　　　　　40 000
　　贷：应付股利　　　　　　　　40 000

在年底时，股利账户由以下分录结转到留存收益：

借：留存收益　　　　　　　40 000
　　贷：股利　　　　　　　　　　40 000

由这笔分录，可以看到宣告股利减少了留存收益，并最终减少了现金。因此，尽管股利不被认为是费用，但它确实减少了公司可以投资在其他生产性资产上的资金。

那些在登记日持有股票的股东在股利支付的时候将收到股利。因为没有任何交易发生，公司在登记日不做日记账，并且公司在宣告日当天确认的负债金额也不变。

在支付日，股利支付借记应付股利，贷记现金。注意股利的支付同时减少流动资产和流动负债，但对所有者权益无影响。记录支付的分录是：

借：应付股利　　　　　　　40 000
　　贷：现金　　　　　　　　　　40 000

宣告和支付现金股利对公司财务报表的累积影响减少了所有者权益和总资产。

4. 股票分割

股票分割仅仅会增加发行在外的股票数量，每位股东所持股票的比例没有改变，股票的总面值或总设定价格，以及已投资本也不会发生改变。所以当分割股票时，不需要把留存收益转到普通股。

为了说明股票分割，请看下面的例子。

例 5.8

假设红新公司有 10 000 股面值为 100 美元的发行在外普通股，市价为每股 150 美元。董事会宣告 5 对 1 股票分割，将面值降到 20 美元，将股数增加到 50 000 股。发行在外普通股的总金额在股票分割前后都为 1 000 000 美元，只有股数和每股面值改变了，每个股东在股票分割前后拥有股票面值的总金额仍是相同的。例如，一个股东在分割前持有 4 股面值为 100 美元的股票(总面值为 400 美元)，拆股后将持有 20 股面值为 20 美元的股票(总面值仍为 400 美元)。

一些公司在其股票价格大幅上升时会进行股票分割，防止股价过高阻碍小股东投资。

股票分割会自动减少股票的市价,因为买卖双方都明白股票分割的机理(在 2 对 1 的情况下,股价会下降一半)。然而,在某些情况下,价格的下降与股票分割并不成比例,因为每股市价低的股票比每股市价高的股票要更有吸引力。

股票股利和股票分割之间的区别仅仅在于其目的。发放股票股利是为了不以现金的形式给股东以其在公司的利益上的"表面上分散的凭证",股票分割的目的是降低股票市价来提高其可销售性。

表 5-1 列示了股票股利和股票分割的比较。

表 5-1　股票股利和股票分割的比较

股票股利	股票分割
股票面值不改变	股票面值减少
股票总数量增加	股票总数量增加
总所有者权益不变	总所有者权益不变
所有者权益的组成改变(留存收益减少;股票增加)	所有者权益的组成不变(留存收益和股票都和分割前相同)
股票股利要求做日记账	股票分割不要求做日记账

Unit 6 Revenue & Expense

Objectives

- In Section 1, students should be able to describe what revenue is and identify different types of revenue.
- In Section 2, students should be able to understand the accounting expenses and identify the different types of expenses.

Dialogue

1. sales revenue

Mary: We know that enterprises should recognize revenue rationally and account for the revenue on time. But what are the rules specifying when revenue should be recognized in different situations?

John: That's a good question. Let's talk about the sales revenue first. It can't retain effective control over the goods sold. The economic benefits associated with the transaction will flow to the enterprise and the relevant amount of revenue and costs can be measured reliably. Mary, there is a question for you: Do you know how sales revenue is determined?

Mary: That's easy. I guess sales revenue should be determined in accordance with the amount stipulated in the contract or agreement signed by the enterprise and the buyer or with an amount agreed between them. Is it right?

John: Yeah. And there is another question: what about the cash discounts?

Mary: I think the cash discounts should be recognized as an expense in the period in which they are actually incurred.

John: That's right. Otherwise, sales allowances should be recorded as a reduction of revenue in the period when the allowances are actually made.

译文：销售收入

玛丽：我们知道，企业应该合理地确认收入，并及时将已经实现的收入入账。但是，收入是如何确认和计量的呢？

约翰：问得好。先来说销售收入吧。企业不能对已售出的商品实施控制，与交易相关的经济利益必须能够流入企业，相关的收入和成本能够可靠地计量。问你个问题，你知道销售收入是怎样确定的吗？

玛丽： 这个简单。销售商品的收入应该按照企业和买方签定的合同或协议的金额，或者双方同意的金额来确定，对吧？

约翰： 嗯，对。再问你个问题，现金折扣应该怎么处理呢？

玛丽： 我觉得现金折扣应该在实际发生的时候确认为当期费用。

约翰： 是这样的。否则，销售折让在实际发生时就应当冲减当期收入。

2. service revenue

Mary: We know that revenue can also arise from the rendering of services. Then, what is the appropriate method to determine the stage of completion of the services?

John: What do you think should be the first step?

Mary: Survey the work performed?

John: Exactly. Then you should check the proportion of services performed to the total services to be performed, or the proportion of costs incurred to the estimated total costs.

Mary: Is that all?

John: No. Finally you should determine total revenue arising from the rendering of services in accordance with the amount stipulated in the contract or agreement.

译文：劳务收入

玛丽： 除了销售收入，提供劳务也会产生收入。那么，确定劳务完成程度有什么合适的方法呢？

约翰： 你觉得首先应该做什么？

玛丽： 计量已经完成的工作？

约翰： 完全正确。然后就要计量已经提供的劳务占应提供劳务总量的比例，或已发生的成本占估算的总成本之比。

玛丽： 就这样吗？

约翰： 不是。最后还得确认提供劳务的总收入与合同或协议中规定的金额是否相符。

3. other operating revenues

Mary: Sales revenue and service revenue are prime operating revenues, or main revenues, and I think revenue can also arise from the use of enterprise assets by others.

John: Yes. These revenues can result from wrappage lease and remised right of assets.

Mary: Then what condition should these revenues be measured by?

John: The economic benefits associated with the transaction will flow to the enterprise, and the amount of the revenue can be measured reliably.

Mary: What about the cash of the enterprise used by others? I mean, the interest.

John: Interest should be measured based on the application interest rate and the length of time for which the enterprise's cash is used by others.

译文： 其他业务收入

玛丽： 销售收入和劳务收入都是主营业务收入。我想，收入还可以通过他人使用本企业资产而发生。

约翰： 是的。这些收入可以通过出租包装物和出让资产使用权而产生。

玛丽： 那么，在确定这些收入时，必须满足什么条件呢？

约翰： 能使交易相关的经济利益流入企业并能够可靠地计量收入的金额。

玛丽： 那企业被他人使用的现金呢？我是指，这部分现金产生的利息。

约翰： 利息收入则应该按照他人使用本企业现金的时间和适用利率来计算和确定。

4. period expense

Mary: Period expenses are composed of operating expense, administrative expense, finance expense and so on. Am I right?

John: Yes. Operating expenses are expenses incurred during the sales process, including freight charges, insurance, advertising expense, etc.

Mary: Then administrative expenses are expenses incurred in organizing and managing the operating activities of an enterprise.

John: Finance expenses are expenses incurred by an enterprise in raising funds required for operations. Finance expenses include interest expenses that should be included as period costs, exchange losses, and other relevant handling charges.

译文： 期间费用

玛丽： 期间费用包括营业费用、行政管理费用和财务费用等，对吗？

约翰： 是的。营业费用是指企业在销售商品过程中发生的费用，包括运输费、保险费和广告费等。

玛丽： 行政管理费用就是企业为组织和管理企业生产经营所发生的管理费用了。

约翰： 财务费用就是指企业为了筹集生产经营所需资金等而发生的费用，包括利息支出、汇兑损失和相关的手续费等。

Section 1　Revenue

Revenue is the gross inflow of economic benefits arising in the course of the ordinary activities of an enterprise from such events as the sale of goods, the rendering of service and the use of enterprise by others. Revenue growth is an important indicator of the market reception of a company's products and services.

When a business renders services to its customers or delivers merchandise to them, it either receives immediate payment in cash or acquires an account receivable which will be collected

Unit 6 Revenue & Expense

and thereby become cash within a short time. The revenue for any given period is equal to the inflow of cash and receivables from sales made in that period. For any single transaction, the amount of revenue is a measurement of the asset values received from customers.

Revenues causes an increase in owner's equity. The inflow of cash and receivable from customers increases the total assets of the company; on the other side of the accounting equation, the liabilities do not change, but owner's equity is increased to match the increase in total assets. Thus revenue is the gross increase in owner's equity resulting from business activities.

When is revenue recorded in the accounting records? The realization principle states that a business should record revenue at the time services are rendered to customers or goods sold are delivered to customers. In short, revenue is recorded when it is earned, without regard as to when the cash is received.

Sales revenue arises from the sale of goods. When an accountant confirms sales revenue, several conditions must be noticed. First, the enterprise has transferred the significant risks to the buyer. Secondly, the enterprise can't retain continuing managerial involvement to the degree usually associated with ownership.

Service revenue arises from the rendering of services. When services provided are started and completed within the same accounting year, revenue should be recognized at the time of completion of the services. To calculate the revenue, the conditions of transactions and computing methods are very important. An accountant needs to make sure that the total amount of service revenue and costs of completion of the services provided can be measured reliably. Besides, the economic benefits associated with the transaction will flow to the enterprise.

Sales for cash—While some businesses sell for cash or on credit, others sell for cash only. Examples include snack shops, food stores, and some gas stations. Various procedures are used to handle cash sales and cash registers are usually employed. The cash register is a means of internal control since the total cash sales for the day should be reconciled to the cash in the register drawer. Sales tickets are normally prepared in duplicate form. One copy is given to the customer as receipt, and the second copy is retained in the register and later removed by a person in the accounting department who will analyze and record the sales.

Installment sales—Property such as appliances, stereo equipment, furniture, clothes, automobiles, real estate, and many other types of merchandise may be sold on an installment basis. Such a method refers to a plan whereby the seller agrees to give the buyer physical possession of the goods in exchange for a promise to make payments periodically over a specified time interval. The agreement between the buyer and seller is reflected in legal terms as a conditional sales contract. Quite often a down payment is required. The sales contract will contain wording to the effect that the seller will retain title to the property until payment is made in full. A high price is usually charged for goods sold on installment to offset the added risk imposed on the seller for waiting to collect payments and the additional record-keeping expenses involved.

Trade and Cash Discounts—Manufacturers and wholesalers publish catalogs in order to describe their products and list their retail prices. Usually, they offer deductions from these list prices to dealers who buy in large quantities. These deductions are known as trade discounts. By offering these discounts, a business can adjust a price at which it is willing to bill its goods without changing the list price in the catalog. For example, XYZ company wants to advertise its stereo radio at a list price of $150.00. However, the radio is offered to dealers at a trade discount of 30 percent, which amounts to $45.00. Therefore, the dealer pays only $105.00 for the set.

While trade discounts are used to make price differentials among different classes of customers and as a means of avoiding catalog revisions, cash discounts are used primarily to induce prompt payment by customers. In other words, the seller may allow the buyer to deduct a certain percent of the bill if he or she makes the payment before the amount is due. The payment terms should be clearly stated on the face of the invoice. In the following are examples of some commonly used terms.

2/10, n/30. This is read as "two ten, net thirty" and means that a 2 percent discount of the invoice price is allowed if payment is made within 10 days following the invoice date, and the gross invoice price is due 30 days from the invoice date.

2/EOM, n/60. This is read as "two EOM, net sixty" and means two percent discount may be deducted if the invoice is paid by the end of the month. The discount may not be taken after the end of the month, and payment is due 60 days from the invoice date.

Tips: Revenue is recognized in the case that goods are sold or services are rendered, no matter whether cash or other assets are received or not. If we still have control over the goods or the services, revenues cannot be recognized.

确认收入的条件是已经售出了产品或提供了劳务, 而不论现金或其他资产是否已经到账。如果对产品或者劳务仍有管理权, 则不应确认为收入。

Section 2　Expenses

Expenses refer to the outlays incurred by an enterprise in the course of production and operation. It means the outflows or other using up of assets or incurrence of liabilities during a period. According to the relationship with products, we can divide expenses into two categories: product costs and period expense.

Product costs are directly related to the products, which are composed of direct material costs, direct labor costs and the indirect costs. Direct material costs are raw material costs. Direct labor costs mean the wages and salaries of the personnel connected with the manufacturing

Unit 6 Revenue & Expense

process.

Indirect costs mainly refer to manufacturing overhead, such as water and electricity expenses, leasing charges, maintenance and so on.

Period expenses are not directly associated with products, but they are indispensable for generating the current revenue. Period expenses are composed of operating expense, administrative expense, finance expense and so on.

应用专栏

Useful Expressions

sales revenue	销售收入
service revenue	劳务收入
prime operating revenue	主营业务收入
render *vt.*	提供(服务等)
period expense	期间费用
direct material cost	直接材料成本
direct labor cost	直接人工成本
manufacturing overhead	制造费用
leasing charge	租赁费
maintenance *n.*	维修费
allocate *vt.*	分摊
freight charges	运输费
advertising expenses	广告费

1. For any single transaction, the amount of revenue is a measurement of the asset values received from customers.

就某一项经济业务来说，收入的金额相当于从客户那里收到的资产的价值。

2. When is revenue recorded in the accounting records? The realization principle states that a business should record revenue at the time services are rendered to customers or goods sold are delivered to customers.

收入应在什么时候登记入账呢？收入实现的原则主张企业在其劳务已提供给客户或所销售的产品已经发送于客户的时候确认收入。

3. While trade discounts are used to make price differentials among different classes of customers and as a means of avoiding catalog revisions, cash discounts are used primarily to induce prompt payment by customers.商业折扣的目的是在不同的客户中使用不同的产品价格，同时又不需要更改价格目录。现金折扣则主要是为了吸引顾客及早付款而提供的折扣。

Additional Reading Material

The procedure of accounting for costs

Accounting for a department's costs is a five-step procedure. First, the flow of production in physical output units is determined. Secondly, equivalent units of production are computed for units completed and transferred out and for ending work in process inventory. Thirdly, the total cost to account for is determined by adding the beginning balance of work in process to costs incurred during the current period. Fourth, unit costs are computed for each input category. And fifth, physical units are cost by multiplying equivalent units of production from step 2 by equivalent –unit costs from step 4.

Use cost of goods manufactured to compute cost of goods sold. Cost of goods manufactured is the cost of finished goods that a business completes during a period. A manufacturer's cost of goods manufactured replaces a merchandiser's purchases. For a manufacturer, the beginning balance of Finished Goods Inventory plus the cost of goods manufactured minus the ending balance of Finished Goods Inventory gives the company's cost of goods sold.

Oral Practices

Directions: *Steven and Tony are talking about the financial accounting course they had just now. Read the conversation and answer the questions.*

Tony: Revenue and expenses are both important for a company to obtain profit, and I think there must be a point at which total revenue equal total expenses.

Steven: Yeah. I know that is called break-even point.

Tony: Then sales below the break-even point result in a loss, and sales above break-even point provide a profit.

Steven: Right.

Tony: So I guess the managers will pay much attention to this point.

Steven: I'm afraid not. Maybe the break-even point is only incidental to the managers of ongoing operations because they focus on the sales level needed to earn a target

Unit 6 Revenue & Expense

profit. But when managers are evaluating a new product or market opportunity, or when demand for an established product is declining, the break-even point will be more significant, I think.

Tony: Sounds right. I have another question about the expenses, and I want to hear your ideas.

Steven: I am glad if I could help.

Tony: We know that expenses are all the costs incurred to gain revenues, but there is also terms of " revenue expenses" and "capital expenses". How to explain this?

Steven: Revenue expenses only influence the benefits of the current accounting year, such as property insurance, subscription of newspapers and magazines. Some long-term assets, such as buildings and equipments, will be transferred gradually during ten or even more years. So the expenses used to acquire these are called capital expenses.

Tony: Thank you so much. You are really somebody!

Questions:

1. What is break-even point?
2. How to distinct the revenue expenses and the capital expenses?

Self-test exercises

1. Select the best answer for each of the following questions.

(1) Which of the following can be recognized as revenue? (   )

    A. interest income

    B. freight charges

    C. sales returns

    D. cash discount

(2) Product costs are composed of direct material cost, direct labor cost and (   ).

    A. advertising expense

    B. administrative expense

    C. insurance

    D. manufacturing overhead

2. Mark the correct items by "T" and the wrong items by "F".

(1) A present reduction in cash required to generate revenues is called an expense. (   )

(2) Revenue increases owner's equity. (   )

(3) The revenue expenses are paid to influence the current operating result. (   )

(4) Revenue is recognized when we receive cash from the buyers. (   )

(5) Advertising expense is usually collected as period expense. (   )

(6) Interest revenue should be measured based on the length of time. (   )

(7) Sales returns should be recorded as a reduction of revenue. (   )

(8) If revenues exceed expenses for the same accounting period, the entity is deemed to suffer a loss. (   )

参考译文

第一节　收入

　　收入是在企业销售产品、提供劳务和让渡资产使用权等日常活动中产生的经济利益的总流入。收入增长是市场接纳企业产品或服务的一个重要指示器。

　　当企业向其顾客提供劳务或发送产品时，企业立即获得现金收入，或者是一项应收账款，在未来某时收回这项账款，转为现金收入。那么一定时期内的收入总额就等于该期间由于销售业务而产生的现金收入和应收账款的总和。就某一项经济业务来说，收入的金额即相当于从客户那里收到的资产的价值。

　　收入引起所有者权益的增加。现金的流入和应收账款的发生增加了企业的资产总值，在会计等式左方，负债没有变化，而所有者权益增加了，与总资产增加相适应。可见，收入就是由于企业经济活动引起的所有者权益增加的总数。

　　收入应在什么时候登记入账呢？收入实现的原则主张企业在其劳务已提供给客户或所销售的产品已经发送给客户时确认收入。简言之，即当收入赚得的时候入账，不论那时是否收到现金。

　　销售收入来自销售的商品。会计师确认销售收入时，必须要注意几个条件。首先，企业已将主要风险转移给了买方。第二，企业不能保留通常与所有权相关的继续管理权。

　　劳务收入来自于所提供的劳务。当提供的劳务在同一会计期间开始并结束，收入应该在劳务完结时确认。为了计算收入，交易条件和计算方法非常重要。会计人员需要确信劳务收入的总金额和所提供劳务的完工成本能可靠计量。除此之外，与交易相关的经济利益将会流入企业。

　　现金销售　有些企业既有现金销售业务，也有信用销售业务，而有的企业只有现金销售业务，如快餐店、食品店和一些汽车加油站。在处理现销业务时，将使用与赊销业务不同的程序，并常常使用现金出纳机。因为每日要将现金销售总额与收款机里的实有现金核对相符，所以现金出纳机实际上是进行内部控制的一种手段。发生现销业务时，要编制一式两份的销货票，一份交于顾客作为依据，另一份留在出纳机中，然后由会计人员集中起来进行分析并入账。

分期付款销售 诸如仪器、立体声设备、家具、服装、汽车、房地产和许多其他种类的商品都可以按分期付款的方式销售。按这种方式，卖方要将商品交于买主，买方同意定期按一定的间隔期付款。卖方与买方之间的这一协议，从法律的角度就是一种有条件的合同，往往需要先支付一笔定金。销售合同中必定包括这样的措辞，即在买主付清货款之前，货物的所有权仍在卖主。分期付款销售商品价格往往较高，以便抵消卖主等待付款所带来的风险以及有关的记账费用。

商业折扣和现金折扣 制造商和批发商印制价格目录以介绍其产品的零售价格，他们往往对大量购买的客户提供价格折扣，这种折扣被称为商业折扣。通过提供商业折扣，企业可以在不改变价格目录的条件下，按其所愿意接受的价格出售商品。如，某某公司需按每件 150 美元的价格为其立体声收录机打广告，但是公司将为代理商提供 30%的商业折扣，每件折扣金额为 45 美元，这样一来，代理商每件商品只需支付 105 美元。

商业折扣的目的是在不同的客户中使用不同的产品价格，同时又不需要更改价格目录。现金折扣则主要是为了吸引顾客及早付款而提供的折扣。换句话说，如果买方能在货款到期前付款，卖方将允许买方享受一定的折扣。付款条件在销售发票上要明确写明，下面列示的是一些常见的付款条件：

2/10，n/30，意思是如果买方在发票开出日起 10 日内付款，可以按发票价格打 2%的折扣，全部货款将在发票开出之日起 30 日到期。

2/EOM，n/60，意思是如果在月末之前付款，买方可以享受 2%的折扣，月末以后付款不享受折扣，货款将在自发票开出日起 60 天到期。

第二节 费用

费用是指企业在生产和经营过程中产生的支出。它意味着某一会计期间资产的流出或使用，或是发生了负债。根据与产品的关系，费用可分为两类：产品成本和期间费用。

产品成本直接与产品相关，它包括直接材料成本，直接人工成本和间接成本。直接材料成本是原材料成本。直接人工成本指与生产过程相关人员的工资。

间接成本主要指制造费用，如水费、电费、租赁费、维修和保养费等。

期间费用并不直接与产品相关，但对产生当期收入不可缺少。期间费用包括营业费用、管理费用和财务费用等。

Unit 7 Financial Statements

Objectives

- In Section 1, students should understand the balance sheet and know how to finish a balance sheet.
- In Section 2, students ought to learn the meaning of the Income Statement and the two common forms of income statements: the multiple-step income statement and the single-step income statement.
- In Section 3, students ought to learn the meaning of the Statement of cash flow.

Dialogue: What is Balance Sheet

Mary is applying for a bank loan to start her new business. She describes her concept to John, a loan officer at the bank.

John: How much money will you need to get started?

Mary: I estimate $100,000 for the beginning inventory, plus $40,000 for counters and cash registers, plus $20,000 working capital to cover operating expenses for about three months. That's a total of $160,000 for the start-up.

John: How are you planning to finance the investment of the $160,000?

Mary: I can put in $100,000 from my savings, and I'd like to borrow the remaining $600,000 from the bank.

John: Suppose the bank lend you $60,000 on a one-year note, at 10% interest, secured by a lien on the inventory. Let's put together projected financial statements from the figures you gave me. Your beginning balance sheet would look like what you see on my computer screen. (It is shown in Table 7-1)

Table 7-1 The Balance Sheet of Mary's Store $

Asset		Liabilities and Equity	
Cash	20,000	Bank loan	60,000
Inventory	100,000	Current liabilities	60,000
Current assets	120,000	Owner capital	100,000
Equipment	40,000	Equity	100,000
Fixed assets	40,000	Liabilities and Equity	160,000
Total assets	160,000		

Mary: The left side shows your company's investment in assets. It classifies the assets into "current "(which means turning into cash in a year or less) and "non-current"(no turning into cash in a year). The right side shows how the assets are to be financed: partly by the bank loan and partly by your equity as the owner.

John: Now I see why it's called a "balance sheet". The money invested in assets must equal the financing available — it's like the two sides of a coin. Also, I see why the assets and liabilities are classified as "current" and "non-current" — the bank wants to see if the assets turning into cash in a year or less will provide enough cash to repay the one-year bank loan. Well, in a year there should be cash of $120,000. That's enough cash to pay off more than double amount of the $60,000 loan. I guess that guarantees approval of my loan!

Mary: We're not quite there yet. We need some more information. First, tell me, how much do you expect your operating expenses will be?

John: For the First year, I estimate as follows:

Store rent	$36,000
Phone and utilities	$14,400
Assistants' salaries	$40,000
Interest on the loan	$6,000(10% on $60,000)
Total	$96,400

Mary: we also have to consider depreciation on the store equipment. It probably has a useful life of 10 years. So each year it depreciates by 10% of its cost of $40,000. That's $4,000 a year for depreciation. So operating expenses must be increased by $4,000 a year, from $96,400 to $100,400.

译文：什么是资产负债表

玛丽正在为开新公司而申请银行贷款。她在对银行负责贷款的职员约翰描述她的想法。

约翰： 你开这家新公司需要多少钱？

玛丽： 我估计期初存货需要$100 000，加上柜台和收银机等$40 000，再加$20 000 大约三月之久的营运资金。大概启动资金需要$160 000。

约翰： 你如何计划这$160 000 的融资？

玛丽： 我可以从个人积蓄中拿出$100 000，剩余的$60 000 我想从银行借。

约翰： 假设银行以一年期10%的票面利率，借你$60 000，用存货作为抵押担保，根据你给我的数据来编一张预期的财务报表。你的期初资产负债表正如我的电脑屏幕所示。(如表7-1 所示)

表 7-1　Mary's Store 资产负债表　　　　　　　　　　　　　　　　　　　　$

资　产		负债和所有者权益	
现金	20 000	银行贷款	60 000
存货	100 000	流动负债	60 000
流动资产	120 000	实收资本	100 000
设备	40 000	所有者权益	100 000
固定资产	40 000	负债和所有者权益	160 000
总资产	160 000		

　　左边表示你公司投资的资产，把资产分类为"流动"(在一年或者短于一年变现的)和"非流动"(不准备在一年或者短于一年变现的)；右边表示资产是如何通过融资得来的：一部分是从银行贷款，另一部分是你的所有者权益。

玛丽：现在我明白为什么叫"资产负债表"了。投资在资产上的钱一定等于可利用资金，就像硬币的两面一样。同时，我明白了资产和负债为什么被归类为"流动"和"非流动"，银行想要搞清楚公司的资产是否能变成足够的现金来偿还一年内到期的银行贷款。在一年内到期的流动资产有$120 000，那已有足够清偿$60 000 贷款的两倍了。我想我的贷款能成功！

约翰：现在还不行，我们需要再多一些数据。首先，告诉我，你希望有多少经营费用？

玛丽：第一年，我估计如下：

店租	$36 000
电话等公用费用	$14 400
店员薪水	$40 000
贷款的利息	$6 000 (利率 10%，面值$60 000)
总计	$96 400

约翰：我们还必须考虑店内设备的折旧。使用寿命大概是 10 年。因此每年$40 000 的成本，10%的折旧率，就是一年$4 000 的折旧费用。因此每年必须要增加$4 000 经营费用，即从$96 400 增加到$100 400。

Section 1　Balance Sheet

A **balance sheet** is a summary of a company's balances. Assets, liabilities and owner's equity are listed as of a specific date, such as the end of its financial year. A balance sheet is often described as a snapshot of a company's financial condition.

A company's balance sheet has three parts: assets, liabilities and owner's equity. The main categories of assets are usually listed First and are followed by the liabilities. The difference between the assets and the liabilities is known as equity or the net assets of the company.

According to the accounting equation, net assets must equal assets minus liabilities.

Another way to look at the same equation is that assets equals liabilities plus owner's equity. This is how a balance sheet is presented, with assets in one section and liabilities and owner's equity in the other section. The sum of these two sections must be equal; they must "balance".

A balance sheet summarizes a company's asset, equity and liabilities at a specific point in time. Small businesses tend to have simple balance sheets. Larger businesses tend to have more complex balance sheets, and these are presented in the organization's annual report. Large businesses also may prepare balance sheets for segments of their businesses. A balance sheet is often presented alongside one for a different point in time (typically the previous year) for comparison.

Example 7.1

The following balance sheet structure is just an example. It does not show all possible kinds of assets, equity and liabilities, but it shows the most usual ones.

以下是资产负债表的结构举例。表中并没有包括所有资产、负债和所有者权益的项目，但显示了最常用的一些项目。

A Sample Balance Sheet

$

Assets		Liabilities and Owner's Equity	
Cash	6,600	Liabilities	
Accounts receivable	6,200	Notes payable	30,000
		Accounts payable	
		Total liabilities	30,000
Equipment	25,000	Owner's equity	
		Capital stock	7,000
		Retained earnings	800
		Total owner's equity	7,800
Assets Total	37,800	Liabilities and Owner's Equity Total	37,800

Section 2 the Income Statement

The income statement is a financial statement that summarizes the results of a company's operation by matching revenue and related expenses for a particular accounting period. It shows the net income or net loss. It is also called earnings statement, statement of operations, and profit and loss statement.

There are two common forms of income statements: the multiple-step income statement and

the single-step income statement. The multiple-step income statement contains the series of steps in which costs and expenses are deducted from revenues. As a First step, the cost of goods sold is deducted from sales to produce an amount for gross profit. As a second step, operating expenses are subtracted from the gross profit to obtain operating income (or operating profit). As a final step, income tax expenses are subtracted to determine net income. The multiple-step income statement is shown in Table 7-2.

Table 7-2 Income Statement of ABC Inc.

December 31, 2008 $

ITEM	
Sales	1,180,000
Cost of goods sold	790,000
Gross profit	390,000
Operating expenses:	
Depreciation expense	7,000
Other operating expenses	196,000
Total operating expenses	203,000
Income from operations	187,000
Other income:	
Gain on sale of land	12,000
Other expense:	
Interest expense	8,000
Income before income tax	191,000
Income tax expense	83,000
Net income	108,000

The single-step statement is another format of income statement which groups all revenues together and then lists and deducts all expenses together without drawing any intermediate subtotals. The single-step statement is shown in Table 7-3.

Table 7-3 Income Statement of ABC Inc.

December 31, 2008 $

ITEM	
Sales	1,180,000
Gain on sale of land	12,000
Total revenues	1,192,000
Expenses:	
Cost of merchandise sold	790,000

续表

Depreciation expense	7,000
Other operating expenses	196,000
Interest expense	8,000
Income tax expense	83,000
Total expenses	1,084,000
Net income	108,000

Tips: The purpose of the income statement is to show managers and investors whether the company made or lost money during the period being reported.

The important thing to remember about an income statement is that it represents a period of time. This contrasts the balance sheet, which represents a single moment in time.

损益表的目的是向管理者和投资人表明公司在报告期内是否有赢利或损失。

记住一个要点，损益表表示的是某一时期内的损益状况。相反，资产负债表是表明某一时间点上的财务状况。

Section 3 Cash Flow Statement

The cash flow statement is a financial statement that reports the cash receipts and cash payments of an entity during a particular period. The term cash refers not only to the bills and coins we normally think of as cash, but also to cash equivalents. Cash equivalents are highly liquid short-term investment that can easily and quickly be converted into cash, usually with maturity of three months or less at the date of purchase.

The cash flows of an entity usually come from cash flows from operating activities, cash flows from investing activities, and cash flows from financing activities. Operating activities include the sale and the purchase or production of goods and services, including collecting accounts receivable from customers, paying suppliers or employees, and paying for items such as rent, taxes, and interest. Investing activities include acquiring and selling long-term assets and securities held for long-term investment purposes. Financing activities include obtaining resources from owners and creditors and repaying amounts borrowed.

The creation of the statement of cash flows is simple. Firstly, Listthose activities that increased cash (that is, cash inflows) and those that decreased cash (cash outflows). Secondly, place each cash inflow and outflow into one of the three categories according to the type of activities, which are introduced above. There are two main methods to make a cash flow statement.

Direct method

The **direct method** for creating a cash flow statement reports major classes of gross cash receipts and payments. Here's a sample cash flow statement using direct method.

Example 7.2

A Sample Cash Flow Statement $

Cash flows from operating activities		
Cash receipts from customers	27,500	
Cash paid to suppliers and employees	(20,000)	
Cash generated from operations (sum)	7,500	
Interest paid	(2,000)	
Income taxes paid	(2,000)	
Net cash flows from operating activities		3,500
Cash flows from investing activities		
Proceeds from the sale of equipment	7,500	
Dividends received	3,000	
Net cash flows from investing activities		10,500
Cash flows from financing activities		
Dividends paid	(12,000)	
Net cash flows used in financing activities		(12,000)
Net increase in cash and cash equivalents		2,000
Cash and cash equivalents, beginning of year		1,000
Cash and cash equivalents, end of year		3,000

Indirect method

The **Indirect Method** uses net income as a starting point, makes adjustments for all transactions for non-cash items, then adjusts for all cash-based transactions. An increase in an asset account is subtracted from net income, and an increase in a liability account is added back to net income. This method converts accrual-basis net income (loss) into cash flow by using a series of additions and deduction.

The following shows the cash flow statement of ABC Inc. with indirect method.

Example 7.3

The Cash Flow Statement of ABC Inc.

December 31, 2008 $

ITEM			
Cash flows from operating activities:			
Net income		108,000	
Add: Depreciation	7,000		
Decrease in inventories	8,000		

续表

Increase in accrued expenses	2,200	17,200	125,200
Deduct: Increase in account receivable	9,000		
Decrease in accounts payable	3,200		
Decrease in income tax payable	500		
Gain on sale of land	12,000	24,700	
Net cash flow from operating activities			100,500
Cash flow from investing activities:			
Cash from sale of land		72,000	
Less: Cash paid to purchase land	15,000		
Cash paid for purchase of building	60,000	75,000	
Net cash flow from investing activities			(3000)
Cash flow from financing activities:			
Cash received from sale of common stock		48,000	
Less: Cash paid to retire bonds payable	50,000		
Cash paid to dividends	24,000	74,000	
Net cash flow from financing activities			(26,000)
Increase in cash			71,500
Cash at the beginning of the year			26,000
Cash at the end of the year			97,500

Tips: People and groups interested in cash flow statements include:

- Accounting personnel, who need to know whether the organization will be able to cover payroll and other immediate expenses;
- Potential lenders or creditors, who want a clear picture of a company's ability to repay;
- Potential investors, who need to judge whether the company is financially sound;
- Potential employees or contractors, who need to know whether the company will be able to afford compensation.

对现金流量表有兴趣的人包括：
- 公司的会计人员，他们想要知道公司能否及时支付员工工资及其他随时发生的费用；
- 潜在的贷款人，他们想要搞清楚公司的偿还能力；
- 潜在的投资人，他们要判断公司的财务状况是否稳定；
- 潜在的员工或生意伙伴，他们想了解公司是否有能力支付赔偿金。

应用专栏

Useful Expressions

inventory *n.*	存货
markup *n.*	成本加成
projected *adj.*	预期的
drawings *n.*	提款
particular *adj.*	特定的
alternatively *adv.*	替代地
summarize *v.*	汇总
multiple-step *n.*	多步式
single-step *n.*	单步式
deduct *v.*	扣减
subtract *n.*	减去，扣除
subtotals *n.*	小计
liquid *adj.*	流动的
maturity *n.*	到期
rent *n.*	租金
interest *n.*	利息
securities *n.*	证券
creditor *n.*	债权人
financial position	财务状况
operating results	经营成果
the balance sheet	资产负债表
the income statement	利润表，损益表
the statement of cash flows	现金流量表
net income	净收益
net loss	净损失
multiple-step income statement	多步式利润表
single-step income statement	单步式利润表
the cost of goods sold	商品销售成本
gross profit	毛利
income tax expenses	所得税费用

cash receipts	现金收入
cash payments	现金支出
cash equivalents	现金等价物
operating activities	经营活动
financing activities	筹资活动(融资行为)
accounts payable	应付账款
long-term assets	长期资产

Additional Reading Material

Computerized Accounting Systems

Computerized accounting systems have become more widely used as the cost of computer hardware and software has declined. Given this wide usage, why did we study manual accounting systems? The reason is that the concepts we described for a manual system also apply to computerized systems.

Computerized accounting systems have three main advantages. First, in a computerized accounting system, transactions are simultaneously recorded in journal and posted electronically to general and subsidiary ledger accounts. The posting process is done without manual effort, since the original transactions include the required information for posting to the ledger. Thus, computerized accounting systems simplify the record-keeping process. Secondly, computerized accounting systems are generally more accurate than manual systems. Computer systems will not make common mistakes, such as math errors, posting errors, and journal recording errors. Thus, computerized systems avoid the time lost in correcting common errors. Thirdly, computerized systems provide management current account balance information, since account balances are posted as the transactions occur. Thus, computerized accounting system provides management more current information to support decision-making.

How do computerize accounting systems work? Computerized accounting systems consist of various subsystems. Examples include the accounts receivable and the accounts payable subsystems.

Assume that ABC company renders services to four customers on May 5. These four customers need to be billed (invoiced) for the services. A computer operator sits at console and enters billing data for each customer into the computer. The data include the date, customer's account number, and the amount billed. An electronic listing of this information in the computer is termed an invoice file. This process is much like recording information in a revenue journal in a manual system. The computer uses the invoice file information to print bills for mailing to the customers. In addition, the computer electronically posts each of the four amounts in the invoice file as debits to the appropriate customer accounts in the subsidiary ledger and to Accounts Receivable in the general ledger. At the same time, a credit is electronically posted to the fees earned account in the general ledger. The posting is automatic. The accounting software is programmed to take the information in the invoice file and automatically create the appropriate debits and credits in the electronic ledger.

Assume that ABC company also received five checks from customers on May 5 in payment for services rendered in April. The computer operator inputs the check information into the computer before depositing the checks at the bank. The data include the date of receipt, customer's account number, and amount of the check.

An electronic listing of this information in the computer is termed a cash receipts file. This process is much like recording information in a cash receipts journal in a manual system. The computer uses this information to electronically post each of the five checks as credits to the appropriate customer accounts in the subsidiary ledger and to Accounts Receivable in the general ledger. At the same time, a debit is electronically posted to Cash in the general ledger.

Periodically, management may need report to use in making decisions. Three common reports from the accounts receivable system are the customer invoice summary report, cash receipts summary report, and customer account balance report.

Oral Practices

Directions: *Roger meets Ruth after he has taken the financial accounting course. Read the conversation and answer the questions.*

Ruth: Hi, Roger. How are you getting on with your lessons?

Roger: I am still struggling with my financial statement course.

Ruth: Oh, don't get discouraged. Not everyone can do as well as you.

Roger: Thanks. Tony, can you tell me the difference between gross margin and net income?

Ruth: Gross margin on sales is a subtotal to measure the profit before selling, administrative, interest, and tax expense.

Roger: What is net income?

Ruth: Net income (or loss) is the residual of revenues less all expense for a given accounting period, such as a year, a three-month quarter, or a month. Net income increases shareholders' equity and a net loss decreases shareholders' equity. Such changes in shareholders' equity are shown in the retained earnings account on the balance sheet. Net income is transferred to retained earnings once each year soon after the fiscal year has ended.

Roger: I begin to understand. I think I need to do a lot of study today.

Ruth: Keep up. Steven, you will make it.

Questions:

1. What is the difference between gross margin and net income?
2. Please explain how the following amounts are arrived at.

   (1) gross profit   (2) net income   (3) pre-tax profit

Self-test Exercises

Section 1

According to the following information

(1) make entries for each transaction;

(2) finish the balance sheet.

Emily started her business — Emily's Bakery. The transactions in the year of 2008 are as follows:

(1) Emily contributed $10,000 in cash.

(2) The company borrowed $3,000 from a bank.

(3) The company purchased equipment for $5,000 cash.

(4) The company performed service for $12,000. The costumer paid $8,000 in cash and promised to pay the rest amount at a later date.

(5) The company paid $9,000 for expenses (wages, interest and maintenance).

(6) The company paid dividend of $1,000.

The Balance Sheet of Emily's Bakery
December 31, 2008

Current Assets	Current Liabilities
Long-term Assets	Long-term Liabilities
	Owner's Equity
Total Assets	Total Liabilities and Owner's Equity

Section 2

1. ABC company began business in January, 2005. Complete the following table.

$

Totals as of	December 31,2005	2006	2007
Assets	46,000	100,000	?
Liabilities	8,000	32,000	20,000
Shareholders' equity	?	?	?
Net income (loss)	20,000	?	32,000
Dividends	?	16,000	12,000
Shareholders' investment	24,000	10,000	20,000

2. Please explain how the following amounts are arrived at.

(1) current asset (2) current liability (3) pre-tax profit

(4) net profit (5) total assets (6) total shareholders' equity

Section 3

Choose the best answers to the following questions.

1. An example of a cash flow from an operating activity is _____.

　　A. the receipt of cash from issuing stock

　　B. the receipt of cash from issuing bonds

　　C. the payment of cash for dividends

　　D. the receipt of cash from customers on account

2. An example of a cash flow from an investing activity is _____.

　　A. the receipt of cash from the sale of equipment

　　B. the receipt of cash from issuing bonds

　　C. the payment of cash for dividends

　　D. the payment of cash to acquire treasury stock

3. An example of a cash flow from a financing activity is _____.

　　A. the receipt of cash from customers on account

　　B. the receipt of cash from the sale of equipment

　　C. the payment of cash for dividends

　　D. the payment of cash to acquire marketable securities

参考译文

第一节 资产负债表

资产负债表是公司账目余额的汇总。资产、负债和所有者权益将被列示在特定日期的资产负债表中,如年末资产负债表。资产负债表经常被描述为公司财务状况的"快照"。

公司的资产负债表包括三部分:资产、负债和所有者权益。各主要类型的资产列示在表的首位,其后是负债。公司的资产与负债的差额称为所有者权益或净资产。根据会计等式,净资产 = 资产-负债。

观察会计等式的另一种方法是,资产=负债+所有者权益。这也是提供资产负债表所用的方式:资产是一部分,而负债和所有者权益是另一部分。这两部分的金额必须相等,也就是必须"平衡"。

资产负债表汇总了某一特定时间点上公司的资产、负债及所有者权益的状况。小型公司多使用简单的资产负债表。大型公司多使用更为复杂的资产负债表,并且在公司的年度报告中也要提供资产负债表。大公司也可能会为了某一部分业务而提供资产负债表。公司经常提供不同时间的(尤其是上一年度的)资产负债表,以便于对比分析。

例 7.1

资产负债表			$
资 产		负债和所有者权益	
现金	6 600	负债	
应收账款	6 200	应付票据	30 000
		应付账款	
		总负债	30 000
机器设备	25 000	所有者权益	
		股本	7 000
		留存收益	800
		总权益	7 800
资产合计	37 800	负债和所有者权益合计	37 800

第二节 损益表

损益表是用来汇总公司在某一会计期间发生的经营收入和相关费用状况的财务报表。损益表表明了净利润或净损失,也被称为收入表、经营报表或盈亏表。

损益表有两种常见格式:多步式损益表和单步式损益表。多步式损益表是罗列一系列步骤，在各步骤中，成本费用逐渐从收入中减除。第一步，从销售收入中减去产品销售成本，得出毛利。第二步，从毛利中减去经营费用，得出经营收入(或经营利润)。最后一步，再减去所得税费用，则确定出了净利润。多步式损益表如表7-2所示。

表7-2　ABC 公司损益表

2008年12月31日　　　　　　　　　　　　　　　　　　　　　　　　　　　　$

项　目	金　额
销售收入：	1 180 000
产品销售成本	790 000
毛利	390 000
经营费用：	
折旧费用	7 000
其他经营费用	196 000
经营费用合计	203 000
经营利润	187 000
其他收入：	
土地变卖收益	12 000
其他费用：	
利息费用	8 000
税前所得	191 000
所得税费用	83 000
净利润	108 000

另一种形式的损益表是单步式损益表，是将所有的收入汇总到一起进行排列，并减去所有的费用，不需要进行中间步骤的"小计"。单步式损益表如表7-3所示。

表7-3　ABC 公司损益表

2008年12月31日　　　　　　　　　　　　　　　　　　　　　　　　　　　　$

项　目	金　额
销售收入	1 180 000
土地变卖收益	12 000
总收入	1 192 000
费用：	
商品销售成本	790 000
折旧费用	7 000
其他经营费用	196 000
利息费用	8 000
所得税费用	83 000

续表

项 目	金 额
费用合计	1 084 000
净利润	108 000

第三节 现金流量表

现金流量表是记录公司在特定期间现金收入和支出状况的财务报表。现金不仅是指我们常认为的钞票和硬币，也包括现金等价物。现金等价物是具有高流动性的短期投资，能够很容易地迅速变现，一般从持有之日起，期限都不超过3个月。

公司的现金流一般包括经营行为现金流、投资行为现金流及融资行为现金流。经营行为包括商品和劳务的销售和采购，包括应收账款的收回、向供货商或员工付款，也包括支付租金、税金及利息等。投资行为包括长期资产和长期有价证券的取得和销售。融资行为包括从所有者和债权人处取得资金和偿还资金。

编制现金流量表并不复杂。首先，列出各种增加现金的行为(现金流入)和减少现金的行为(现金流出)。第二步，根据以上三种行为的类型，把所有行为适当归类。编制现金流量表有两种主要方法。

1. 直接法

采用直接法编制现金流量表，是按照现金收入和现金支付的主要类型来编制。用直接法编制一张简单的现金流量表，如下例所示。

例 7.2

现金流量表		$
经营行为现金流		
来自于客户的现金收入	27 500	
向供货商及员工支付现金	(20 000)	
小计	7 500	
利息支付	(2 000)	
所得税支付	(2 000)	
经营行为净现金流		3 500
投资行为现金流		
销售机器设备的现金流入	7 500	
股利收入	3 000	
投资行为净现金流		10 500

续表

融资行为现金流		
股利支付	(12 000)	
融资行为净现金流		(12 000)
现金及现金等价物的净流量		2 000
现金及现金等价物的期初余额		1 000
现金及现金等价物的期末余额		3 000

2. 间接法

间接法是以净利润作为出发点，将所有非现金事项进行调整，得出所有现金交易的结果。资产账户的增加，将从净利润中减除；而负债账户的增加，将累加到净利润中。这种方法是利用一系列的加减，把权责发生制下的净利润(或净损失)转变为现金流。

利用间接法编制 ABC 公司的现金流量表，如下例所示。

例 7.3

ABC 公司现金流量表

2008 年 12 月 31 日 $

项 目			
经营行为现金流：			
净利润		108 000	
加：折旧	7 000		
存货减少额	8 000		
应计费用增加额	2 200	17 200	125 200
减：应收账款增加额	9 000		
应付账款减少额	3 200		
应付所得税减少额	500		
土地变卖收益	12 000	24 700	
经营行为净现金流			100 500
投资行为现金流			
销售土地的现金流		72 000	
减：购买土地的现金支出	15 000		
购买建筑物的现金支出	60 000	75 000	
投资行为净现金流			(3 000)
融资行为净现金流			
销售普通股的现金收入		48 000	

续表

项 目			
减：应付债券现金支出	50 000		
支付股利的现金支出	24 000	74 000	
融资行为净现金流			(26 000)
现金增加额			71 500
年初现金余额			26 000
年末现金余额			97 500

Unit 8   Interpretations of financial statements

Objectives

- In Section 1, students should be able to display an ability to think critically and to communicate effectively by analyzing, interpreting and comparing company (including group) financial information, considering performance and prospects and evaluating company securities in the light of such analysis.
- In Section 2, students should know the major limitations of financial ratio analysis.

Dialogue

1. profitability

(A: Annie   B: Brady)

A: The profitability of a company depends largely on its ability to obtain the net income, doesn't it?

B: Yes. The dividends and capital gains by investors come from a corporation's net income.

A: What are the ratios that can be used to evaluate the profitability of a company?

B: The principal ratios are return on stockholders' equity, return on assets, assets turnover, return on investment, earnings per share, price/earning ratio, dividends yield, book value per share, equity ratio, and …

A: OK. Please explain to me some of the principal ones.

B: The return on stockholders' equity can be said the most important ratio in evaluating the company's profitability. This ratio shows how much is earned for each dollar invested by owners.

A: How is it computed?

B: First, deduct preferred dividends from the net income, and then divide the difference by the average common stockholders' equity. In this way, you can work out the return on stockholders' equity. The average common stockholders' equity is the mean of the beginning common stock balance and the ending common stock balance of the period.

A: In these ratios, the term "average" always seems to refer to the mean of the beginning balance and the ending balance.

Unit 8 Interpretations of financial statements

B: Right. Return on net sales is equal to the net income divided by sales revenue, and it is also an important indicator. It shows how much net income is produced by each revenue dollar. Also important are return on assets and assets turnover.

A: Is the return on assets the ratio of net income to assets?

B: Right. Assets turnovers is the ratio of net sales to total assets. This ratio reflects how many times the total assets turn over during the period, and it can show the ability of the company generating sales through the use of total assets. Oh, I'd like to tell you something about the famous Dupont return on assets.

A: Was it developed by Dupont Company?

B: Yes. The return on assets is equal to the net income divided by the total assets. I'll write it down for you… If the equation includes the sales revenue, it can be expressed like this… Look, what is the term for the ratio of net income to sales revenue?

A: Return on net sales.

B: What's the term for the ratio for sales revenue to average total assets?

A: Assets turnover.

B: Therefore, the return on assets is equal to the product of the return on net sales and the assets turnover. This indicator is important, for it reveals a theory like this: if a company is to increase the return on assets, it should increase the return on net sales, or increase the assets turnover.

A: A simple math equation can have such material meaning. Return on investment is the ratio of income to stockholders' investment, isn't it?

B: The investors the ratio involves include the long-term creditors as well as stockholders.

A: Do you have a book which carries the formula for these ratios?

B: Yes. Just a moment, I'll find it for you… Here it is. Look, on the right side of the return on investment equation, the denominator is average long-term funds. Under the formula is an explanation saying that long funds include long-term liabilities and stockholders' equity.

A: Very detailed. Let me have a close study of these ratios.

译文：获利能力

(A：安妮　　　B：布瑞迪)

A: 公司的获利能力在很大程度上取决于公司获取净收益的能力，是吗？

B: 是的。投资者得到的股利和资本收益来自公司实现的净收益。

A: 分析公司获利能力的比率有哪些？

B: 主要有股东权益收益率、资产收益率、资产周转率、投资收益率、每股收益、市盈率、股利收益率、每股账面价值、权益比率，还有……

A: 好了。请给我讲几种主要的吧。

B: 股东权益收益率可以说是评价公司获利能力最主要的比率,它表示投资者投资的每一美元所能得到的回报。

A: 这项比率怎么计算?

B: 首先用净收益减去优先股股利,再除以平均普通股收益,就可求出股东权益收益率了。平均普通股是普通股期初余额和期末余额的平均值。

A: 这些比率中,"平均"这个词的意思似乎都是期初余额和期末余额的平均值。

B: 对。销售利润率等于净收益除以销售收入,也是一项重要指标,它反映的是单位销售收入能够产生的净收益。还有,资产收益率和资产周转率也是非常重要的评估指标。

A: 资产收益率是不是净收益与资产的比率?

B: 对。资产周转率是销售收入与资产总额的比率。它表示某一期间总资产周转了多少次,能反映公司利用资产产生销售收入的能力。哦,我想给你说一下著名的杜邦资产收益率。

A: 是不是由杜邦公司开发的?

B: 是的。资产收益率是净收益除以平均总资产,我写下来让你看看……这个式子如果把销售收入考虑进去,可以这样表示……你看,净收益与销售收入的比率是什么比率?

A: 销售利润率。

B: 销售收入与平均总资产比率是什么比率?

A: 资产周转率。

B: 所以,资产收益率就等于销售利润率与资产周转率的乘积,这就是著名的杜邦资产收益率。该指标非常重要,因为它揭示了这么一个道理:如果一个公司想提高资产收益率,就得提高其销售利润率或资产周转率。

A: 简单的数学等式竟然有这么大的意义。投资收益率是收益与股东投资的比率吧?

B: 投资收益率所涉及的投资者除股东外,还包括公司长期债务的债权人。

A: 你有没有哪本书上有这些比率的公式?

B: 有,你等一下,我找找……找到了。你看,投资收益率等式右端的分母是平均长期资金,下面解释说长期资金包括长期负债和股东权益。

A: 这么详细。让我把这些比率好好看一看。

2. solvency

(M: Mike   T: Tom)

M: We often speak of the company's solvency. Can you explain it to me?

T: Solvency refers to the company's ability to pay the debts to the creditors. The degree of solvency directly affects the survival and development of the company. Therefore, accountants should pay close attention to relative indicators.

M: Relative indicators are a series of ratios, aren't they?

Unit 8 Interpretations of financial statements

T: Yes. The major indicators for evaluating the company's short-term solvency include current ratio, quick ratio, receivable turnover, inventory turnover, operating cycle, and operating cash flows to current debt ratio. The major indicators for evaluating the company's long-term solvency include debt ratio and times interest earned.

M: Is current ratio relevant to current assets or current liabilities?

T: Yes. The computation of current ratio is to divide current assets by current liabilities. It's the most common ratio used to evaluate a company's liquidity and short-term debt paying ability. However, if you want to know the immediate paying ability of a company, you may use quick ratio. Quick ratio is an improvement to the current ratio and the computation is to divide quick assets by current liabilities.

M: What are quick assets?

T: They mean cash, marketable securities, and accounts receivable. Even cash ratio is used in evaluating the short-term solvency.

M: I guess the ratio is cash to current liabilities, isn't it?

T: Absolutely right. To evaluate the debt-paying ability of a business, some turnover ratios are used as the indicator, like the receivable turnover and inventory turnover. The receivable turnover expresses the firm's ability and speed of collecting cash from customers.

M: What's the computation of the receivable turnover?

T: Sales revenue divided by average accounts receivable.

M: What do you mean by "average" here?

T: I mean the mean of the beginning accounts receivable balance and the ending balance of the year.

M: Does the average inventory refer to the mean of the beginning inventory balance and the ending inventory balance of the year?

T: You are right. This ratio expresses the speed of goods selling.

M: Can the inventory turnover be expressed in days?

T: Yes. Now, people pay more and more attention to cash flow, so you can also use the cash flow as an indicator to evaluate the solvency of a business. A ratio named operating cash flows to current debt ratio is very frequently used.

M: Just now you said a ratio named debt ratio is used to evaluate the long-term solvency of a business, isn't it?

T: Yes, it is. The debt ratio is computed by dividing total liabilities by total assets.

M: The lower the ratio is, the better. Right?

T: Yes. The higher the ratio is, the higher the strain of paying principal and interest is, and the higher the risk of solvency is. Besides the debt ratio, another ratio named times interest earned can also be used to evaluate the long-term solvency of the company. The computation of times interest earned is the income before taxes and interest divided by the interest expense.

M: That means dividing the income including interest and taxes by the interest expense, doesn't it?

T: Yes. I want to point out that when these ratios are used to make financial analysis, the ratios should be compared with those of the industry and those of the past years.

M: Yes, they should.

译文：偿付能力

(M：迈克　T：汤姆)

M: 我们经常提起公司的偿付能力，你能给我解释一下吗？

T: 偿付能力就是指公司向债权人清偿债务的能力。偿付能力的大小，直接影响到公司的生存和发展，所以会计师应密切关注相应的指标。

M: 相应的指标也就是一系列的比率吧？

T: 是的。评价公司短期偿付能力的主要指标有流动比率、速动比率、应收账款周转率、存货周转率、营业周期、营业现金流量与流动负债比率，评价公司长期偿付能力的主要指标有负债比率和利息所得倍数。

M: 流动比率与流动资产或流动负债有关吗？

T: 有关。流动比率计算方法是流动资产除以流动负债。它是评价公司的流动性和短期偿付能力最常用的指标。但如果要知道公司当即偿付债务的能力，可以采用速动比率。速动比率是对流动比率的一种改进，计算公式是速动资产除以流动负债。

M: 什么叫速动资产？

T: 速动资产是指现金、有价证券和应收账款。在评价短期偿付能力时，有时还使用现金比率。

M: 我猜想，现金比率是现金与流动负债的比率，是吗？

T: 完全正确。在评价企业的债务清偿能力时，还经常使用一些周转率作为指标，如应收账款周转率和存货周转率。应收账款周转率表示企业能够从客户手中收回现金的能力和速度。

M: 该怎么计算呢？

T: 销售收入除以平均应收账款。

M: 你这里所说的"平均"是什么意思？

T: 就是指年初余额和年末余额的平均数。

M: 平均存货就是年初存货余额与年终存货余额的平均值吗？

T: 说得对。这项比率表示存货的销售速度。

M: 也可以用天数来表示存货周转的速度吗？

T: 是的。现在，人们越来越重视现金流量，所以也可以用现金流量指标来衡量企业的偿付能力。有一个比率叫营业现金流量与流动负债比率，就很常用。

Unit 8 Interpretations of financial statements

M: 你刚才说衡量企业长期偿付能力的一个指标叫负债比率,是吗?

T: 是的。负债比率的计算公式是用负债总额除以资产总额。

M: 这项比率是越低越好吧?

T: 是的。负债比率越高,偿还债务本息的压力就越大,偿付能力方面的风险也就越大。除负债比率外,还有一个叫利息所得倍数的比率也可以用来衡量公司的长期偿付能力。利息所得倍数的计算方法是用息税前收益除以利息费用。

M: 也就是扣除利息和税款前的收益除以利息费用,是吗?

T: 是的。需要说明的是,在使用这些比率进行财务分析时,应与行业比率或公司过去的比率进行比较。

M: 是应该比较。

Tips: The major objective of financial analysis is to evaluate the past performance, analyze the current financial position, and forecast opportunities and challenges of the future.

财务分析的主要目的是评价过去的绩效,分析目前的财务状况,预测未来的挑战和机遇。

Section 1 Introduction to Financial Analysis

Ratio analysis

Once you understand how a set of accounts is constructed, you need to be able to analyze them to find out what they really disclose. Interpreting and analyzing financial statements will enable you, as a manager, to compare the performance of your company this year with last year, to compare your company with its competitors, and to detect weaknesses which you can improve.

Absolute figures in financial statements do not tell you much. For example, to be told that Retail Stores Plc made $196 million profits before tax is not a useful piece of information unless it is related to, say, the turnover which produced the profit or to the capital employed in the group.

Ratio analysis is a useful tool with which to interpret financial accounts. But for ratios to be meaningful, they must be compared with equivalent ratios calculated for previous years and with those of the industry in which the company is positioned. Industrial ratios are produced by a variety of clearing houses for industrial statistics.

Ratios reduce the amount of data contained in the financial statements to workable form. This aim is defeated if too many are calculated. You must learn which combination of ratios will be appropriate to your needs.

Liquidity

Your first concern as a manager is to ensure the short-run survival of the company. Is the company able to meet its short-term obligations?

Current ratio=Current Assets/Current Liabilities, it is a comparison of current assets to current liabilities, is a commonly used measure of short-run solvency, i.e., the immediate ability of a firm to pay its current debts as they come due. Current ratio is particularly important to a company thinking of borrowing money or getting credit from their suppliers. Potential creditors use this ratio to measure a company's liquidity or ability to pay off short-term debts. Comparatively speaking, small companies should have higher current ratios to meet unexpected cash requirements. The rule of thumb current ratio for small companies is 2:1. Current ratio is best compared to the industry.

Quick ratio(or Acid Test Ratio) = (Current Assets−Inventory)/Current Liabilities, it is a more rigorous test than the current ratio of short-run solvency. This ratio considers only cash, marketable securities (cash equivalents) and accounts receivable because they are considered to be the most liquid forms of current assets. A quick ratio less than 1.0 implies "dependency" on inventory and other current assets to liquidate short-term debt.

Capital structure

The net assets of a company can be financed by a mixture of owner's equity and long-term debt. Gearing ratios analyze this mixture by measuring the contributions of shareholders against the funds provided by the lenders of loan capital. Retail Stores Plc has no long-term debt; but the significant ratio is:

= (Long-term debt) / Net assets ×100%

The profit and loss account provides another useful angle on the capital structure. Is there a healthy margin of safety in the profits to meet the fixed interest payments on long-term debt? An overgeared company may show signs of running out of profit to pay this fixed burden.

Times Interest Earned (TIE) = Profit before tax / Interest charges

The TIE ratio is used by bankers to assess a firm's ability to pay their liabilities. Normally, a banker will be looking for a TIE ratio to be 2.0 or greater, showing that a business is earning the interest charges two or more times each year. A value of 1.0 or less suggests that the firm is not earning sufficient amounts to cover interest charges.

To be sure that their dividend is safe, shareholders will want profits compared with the dividend payable.

Dividend cover = profit for the financial year / Dividend payable

Activity and efficiency

The ratios showing inventory turnover and average collection period help managers and outsiders to judge how effectively a company manages its assets. The figure of sales is compared with the investment in various assets. Manufacturing companies tend to show a much slower turnover.

Average Collection Period = Debtors/Sales per day.

This ratio measures the length of time it takes to convert your average sales into cash. This measurement defines the relationship between accounts receivable and cash flow. A longer average collection period requires a higher investment in accounts receivable. A higher investment in accounts receivable means less cash is available to cover cash outflows.

Inventory Turnover = Sales/Inventory.

It measures the average efficiency of the firm in managing and selling inventories during the last period, i.e., how many inventory turns the company has per period and whether that is getting better or worse. The faster the inventory turns, the more efficiently the company manages their assets. However, if the company is in financial trouble, on the verge of bankruptcy, a sudden increase in inventory turns might indicate they are not able to get product from their suppliers.

Profitability

Profitability is the ability of an entity to earn profits. This ability to earn profits depends upon the effectiveness and efficiency of operations as well as resources available to the enterprise.

Return on Capital Employed (ROCE) is a measure of how effectively the company is using its capital. The formula to measure the return on all the assets the company is using: Profit before interest and tax (PBIT) / (total assets − current liabilities)

It shows the percentage return on the capital invested in the business. It indicates how efficiently management is using the business resources to earn profits.

There are several alternative methods of calculating this ratio, depending upon the definition of "capital employed" and upon whether the user prefers to use profit before taxation or profit after taxation.

Net profit ratio

Net profit ratio = Net profit /Sales ×100%

The net profit ratio is net profit as a percentage of sales. It shows how much net profit is earned for every $1 of sale revenue.

Gross profit margin(GPM)

Gross profit margin = Gross profit/Sales×100%

GPM shows the relationship between sales and the direct cost of products/services sold. The gross profit margin should be stable over time. A persistent gradual decrease is likely to indicate that productivity needs to be increased to return profitability back to previous levels.

The difference between gross profit margin and net profit margin would indicate the efficiency of expenses control.

Earnings Per Share (EPS)

The ordinary shareholder gains from investment in a limited company in two ways.

(1) Dividends: these represent the amount of income actually distributed to the shareholders. Dividend Policy is dependent on various factors in addition to the profits earned in a particular year.

(2) Retained profits: these increase the reserves of the company and increase the capital value of the shares.

Earnings per share helps to assess the overall performance of the ordinary shareholder's investment in a company.

Earnings per share relates the profits earned by the ordinary shares(irrespective of the size of the dividend) to the number of issued ordinary shares.

Price Earnings Ratio (P/E)

The price /earnings ratio relates the market value of a share to the earnings per share. This facilitates the comparison of the performance of the shares of different companies.

	2008	2009
Market value		
Earnings per share		
(P/E)		

A high (P/E) ratio indicates a high demand for the shares in relation to their performance. When demand for the shares is stimulated by the rumor of a take-over bid, the (P/E) ratio will rise sharply.

Tips: Since shares represent ownership of a company's dividend, profit, revenue, as-set and cash flow, the ways to value shares will be based on these five categories of figures. Financial ratio analysis is based on these five categories of data in a company's balance sheet and income statement, and turns them into ratios for comparison.

既然股票代表了公司的股息、盈利、营业额、资产及现金流量的拥有权，评定股票价值的方法就从上述五方面着手。比率分析就是将一间公司资产负债表与损益表中的这五项数字，转化为可供比较的财务比率。

Section 2　Limitations of financial ratio analysis

Major limitations of financial ratio analysis are:

1) Ratio selection

It is difficult to choose ratios for analysis. For example, there are different definitions of gearing ratio. The second example is to assess asset turnover.

Unit 8 Interpretations of financial statements

2) Historical Cost Accounting

The financial statements of most organizations are drawn up using the historical cost concept. Little or no account is taken of inflation, which invariably leads to undervalued assets on the balance sheet. Also many companies do not include a value for intangible assets such as goodwill on their balance sheets.

3) Seasonal Fluctuations

The level of activity of many organizations varies on a seasonal basis, e.g. the Christmas card trade. Balance sheet lists the assets and liabilities that may not be representative of the year as a whole.

4) Time Lag

Most users of financial statements must rely on the audited published accounts of an organization. Many months may elapse before these accounts are published, by which time the information is out of date.

5) Different Patterns of Asset Ownership

Most organizations use fixed assets in carrying out their activities. Some organizations choose to purchase the fixed assets they use, while others choose to use fixed assets belonging to somebody else and to pay a hire charge or rent for their use.

应用专栏

Useful Expressions

profitability *n.*	获利能力
solvency *n.*	偿付能力
financial analysis	财务分析
current ratio	流动比率
quick ratio	速动比率
return on stockholders' equity	股东权益收益率
return on owner's equity	所有者权益收益率
return on assets	资产收益率
assets turnover	资产周转率
return on investment	投资收益率
earnings per share (EPS)	每股收益
price/earning ratio	市盈率

dividends yield	股利收益率
book value per share	每股账面价值
equity ratio	权益比率
times interest earned	已获利息倍数
receivable turnover	应收账款周转率
inventory turnover	存货周转率
operating cycle	营业周期
operating cash flows/current debts ratio	营业现金流量与流动负债比率
debt ratio	负债比率
average collection period	平均收款期
dividend cover	股利报酬率
profit margin	销售利润率
preferred dividend	优先股股利

1. Ratio analysis is a useful tool with which to interpret financial accounts. But for ratios to be meaningful, they must be compared with equivalent ratios calculated for previous years and with those of the industry in which the company is positioned.

比率分析是用于分析财务报表的一种有用工具。但是要使得比率有意义的话，它们必须与以前年度计算的相应比率进行比较，与公司所在行业比率进行比较。

2. There are several ratios to evaluate a corporation's liquidity and short term debt paying ability.

有几个基本比率可以评价公司的流动性和短期偿债能力。

3. The current ratio means how many times the current assets are compared to the current liabilities.

流动比率表示流动资产与流动负债相比是流动负债的多少倍。

4. The ratios showing inventory turnover and average collection period help managers and outsiders to judge how effectively a company manages its assets.

这些反映存货周转率和平均收款期的比率有助于管理者和外部人士判断一个公司管理资产的效率。

5. We can use different approaches to analyze the profitability and solvency of a company.

我们可以使用不同的方法分析公司的盈利能力和偿付能力。

6. The ratio analysis may be the most popular and important approach.

比率分析法可能是最常用、最重要的方法。

Unit 8 Interpretations of financial statements

Additional Reading Material

Financial Statement Analysis for Decision Making

Perform a horizontal analysis of comparative financial statements. Acenoting provides information for decision making. Banks loan money, investors buy stocks, and managers run businesses on the basis of the analysis of accounting information. Horizontal analysis shows the dollar amount and the percentage change in each financial statement item from one period to the next. Perform a vertical analysis of financial statements. Vertical analysis shows the relationship of each item in a financial statement to its total: total assets on the balance sheet and net sales on the income statement.

Prepare common-size financial statements. Common-size statements — a form of vertical analysis — show the component percentages of the items in a statement. Investment advisory services report common-size statements for various industries, and analysis use them to compare a company with its competitors and with the industry averages.

Use the statements of cash flows in decision making. The statement of cash flows shows the net cash inflow or outflow caused by a company's operating, investing, and financing activities. By analyzing the inflows and outflows cash listed to this statement, an analyst can see where a business's cash comes from and how it is being spent.

Compute the standard financial ratios used for decision making. Ratios play an important part in business decision making because they show relationships between financial statement items.

Use ratios in decision making. Analysis of ratios over a period of time is an important way to track a company's progress.

Oral Practices

Directions: *Read the following conversation and answer questions.*

Mike: What are the methods of financial analysis?

Johnson: There are numerous methods for financial analysis, and new methods keep emerging.

Mike: Then tell me some basic methods.

Johnson: Basic methods may roughly fall into three categories — that is, horizontal analysis, vertical analysis, and ratio analysis. Under horizontal analysis, financial statement amounts are placed together, and change amounts and percentages between one year and others are computed.

Mike: Can you illustrate it for me with an example?

Johnson: Here I happen to have a comparative balance sheet of Times Corporation for 2000 and 2001, which takes the horizontal analysis approach. This exhibit lists the amounts of each item at the end of 2000 and 2001. First, deduct the amounts of 2000 from those of 2001, and the result is the increase or decrease amount in this column. Then divide the increase or decrease amount by the relative amount of 2000. In this way we can get change percentage of 2001 over 2000.

Mike: Let me have a look... This company's total assets rise by $ 90,000 from $ 860,000 of 2000 to $ 950,000 of 2001. That is an increase of 10.5% over the basic year 2000.

Johnson: Yes. Look, this income statement takes a vertical analysis approach. First, the sales revenue is assumed to be 100%, and then calculate the percentages of the cost of goods sold, net income and other items to the sales revenue.

Mike: Why is it net sales here?

Johnson: It actually means the sales revenue; the term "net sales" emphasizes that it doesn't include returns or discounts. So sales revenue and net sales mean the same.

Mike: Why does the net income of 2001 only account for 8.3% of sales revenue?

Johnson: Not bad already. Many successful corporations have a net income of between 5% and 15% of sales revenue. For many famous corporations, this figure is only around 2%.

Mike: Then what is the ratio analysis approach?

Johnson: It's based on a series of financial ratio indicators, which show the relationship of one item to another.

Mike: The frequently mentioned return on investment and price to earning ratio are important financial ratios, aren't they?

Johnson: Yes. There are many financial ratios, but they can be grouped into two kinds. One is for the analysis of the corporation's solvency, and the other is for the analysis of the corporation's profitability. These ratios can be computed by using relative formulas.

Mike: The ratios worked out are to be compared with those of the previous years before some problems can be revealed, aren't they?

Johnson: Yes. Besides, it's necessary to compare these ratios with those of competitors in the same industry.

Unit 8 Interpretations of financial statements

Questions:

What is the ratio analysis approach?

Self-test Exercises

1. Decide whether the following statements are true or false according to the text.

(1) A firm with a current ratio of 2 would be in a healthy situation.

(2) A manufacturing company's stocks should always be included in calculating its liquidity.

(3) A bank which had lent money to a company would be happy if its times interest earned ratio rose.

(4) The higher the percentage of a company for gearing, the smaller is its long-term debt.

(5) A shareholder might consider selling his/her shares in a company if its figure for dividend cover fell.

2. Match the ratios listed in the text with their main functions.

Ratio	Main function
Current ratio	(i) Allows shareholders to judge their chance of receiving payments.
Quick ratio	(ii) Helps a company decides its debt collection policy.
Gearing	(iii) Shows if a business can pay its most urgent debts.
Times interest cover	(iv) Shows profits compared to all the company's capital.
Dividend cover	(v) Shows if funds are available to pay long-term debt costs.
Stock turnover	(vi) Shows equity capital of a company compared to loan capital.
Average collection period	(vii) Permits management to evaluate its use of assets.
Profit margin	(viii) Provides a more accurate picture of short-term debt strength.
Return on total assets	(ix) Shows profit compared to non-loan capital.
Return on owner's equity	(x) Shows profits compared to sales earnings.

3. Use points from both boxes A and B and link them together with "if" to make sentences which are true according to the text.

A		B
(a) Ratios provide useful information		(i) they are related to requirements.
(b) Ratios fail to make financial aspects clearer.		(ii) Excessive numbers of them are provided.
(c) Ratios are really effective	if	(iii) They are considered solutions in themselves.
(d) Ratios are misused		(iv) They are seen in an industry wide context.

参考译文

第一节 财务分析介绍

比率分析

一旦你理解一套财务报表是如何构造的,你就需要能够对它们进行分析,找出它们真正揭示的是什么。作为一名经理,解释和分析财务报表将能够使你对你公司今年的业绩与去年进行比较,将你公司与其他竞争者进行比较,并找出可以改进的弱点。

财务报表中纯粹的数字没有多大意义。例如,告诉你零售商店税前利润是1亿9千6百万美元是无用信息,除非把它与产生利润的营业额或集团公司中占用的资本联系起来。

比率分析是用于分析财务报表的一种有用工具。但是要使得比率有意义,它们必须与以前年度计算的相应比率进行比较,与公司所在行业比率进行比较。行业比率由各行业统计清算所编制。

比率把财务报表中包含的信息量,变成了可操作的形式。如果需要太多计算的话,这一目的就失去意义。你必须知道哪些比率组合能够满足你的需要。

流动性比率

作为经理,你首先关心的是保证公司短期的生存。公司能够偿还短期负债吗?

流动比率=流动资产/流动负债

该比率是将流动资产与流动负债进行比较,通常用来衡量短期清偿能力,如一家公司在其流动负债到期时能否立即偿还的能力。流动比率对于想借款或从其供应商处获得信贷的公司尤其重要,潜在的债权人用这一比率来衡量公司的流动性或偿还短期负债的能力。相对而言,小公司应拥有更高的流动比率来满足未预料的现金需求,小公司流动比率经验比值是2∶1。流动比率最好同行业水平进行比较。

速动比率(也叫酸性测试比率)=(流动资产-存货)/流动负债

该比率比流动比率对短期偿债能力的测试更加严格。它只考虑现金、有价证券(现金等价物)和应收账款,因为这几项被认为是流动资产中流动性最强的。速动比率小于1暗示需要依靠存货和其他流动资产来清偿短期债务。

资本结构

公司净资产可以通过所有者权益和长期负债共同筹得。杠杆比率通过计量股东缴款和贷入资金分析这一结构。零售商店没有长期负债,但是重要的比率是:

长期负债/净资产×100%

损益表为资本结构提供了另一个有用的分析角度。为了偿付长期负债的固定利息,在利润中有一个良性的安全边际吗?杠杆比率高的公司可能显示出耗尽利润来支付这一固定

Unit 8 Interpretations of financial statements

负担的信号。

已获利息倍数(TIE)=税前利润/利息费用

银行界人士使用已获利息倍数评估一家公司偿还债务的能力。银行界人士通常希望该比率等于或大于 2，表示企业每年获取的利润是利息费用的两倍或更多倍。如该比率为 1 或小于 1，就表明企业赚得的利润不足以偿还利息费用。

为了保证股利是安全的，股东希望将利润与应付股利进行比较：

股利报酬率=利润/应付股利

活动和效率比率

这些反映存货周转率和平均收款期的比率有助于管理者和外部人士判断一个公司管理资产的效率。销售额数字与各种资产投资额相比较。制造企业趋于显示一个缓慢的存货周转率。

平均收款期=应收账款/每天销售额

该比率用于衡量将平均销售额转换成现金的时间长短，这种衡量界定了应收账款与现金流量之间的关系。更长的平均收款期要求在应收账款上的投资更大，应收账款上的更大投资意味着能用于现金流出的现金更少。

存货周转率=销售额/存货

该比率用于衡量企业过去期间管理和销售存货的平均效率，如公司每期存货可以周转多少次，是变好还是变坏了。存货周转越快，公司管理资产的效率越高。但是，如果公司处于财务困境中，濒于破产存货周转率的突然增加可能表明公司从其供货商中拿不到产品。

获利能力比率

获利能力是一个主体赚取利润的能力，而赚取利润的能力取决于运营的有效性和效率，以及企业所拥有的资源。

投入资本报酬率((ROCE)衡量企业使用其资本的有效性。衡量企业总使用资产报酬率的公式是：息税前利润/(资产总额-流动负债)。它显示了投入企业资本的百分比回报率，表示出企业管理层使用资源获取利润的有效性。

有几种计算这个比率的替代方法，这取决于"利用的资本"的定义，也取决于使用者更喜欢使用税前利润还是税后利润。

净利润比率

净利润比率=净利润/销售额×100%

净利润比率即是净利润占销售额的百分比，表示每 1 元销售收入中净利润有多少。

销售毛利率

销售毛利率=毛利润/销售额×100%

销售毛利率表示了销售额和所售货物或所提供劳务直接成本之间的关系。这一比率应相对稳定。如果该比率持续降低，则很可能表示需要增加生产力，使盈利能力回升到以前水平。

销售毛利率和销售净利率间的区别表现出费用控制的效率。

每股盈余

普通股东有两种方式获得对股份有限公司投资的收益：

(1) 股利：表示实际分配给股东的收入。股利政策除了取决于年度利润外，还取决于多种因素。

(2) 留存利润：留存利润增加企业的公积和股票的股本价值。

每股盈余有助于评估普通股东对一个公司投资的全面业绩。它将普通股(不管股利大小)获得的利润与所发行的普通股数量联系起来。

市盈率

市盈率将股票的市场价格与每股盈余联系起来。这便于比较不同公司股票的业绩。

	2008	2009
市场价值		
每股盈余		
市盈率		

市盈率高表示对股票业绩的要求高。当兼并谣传激发出对公司股票的需求时，市盈率会快速上涨。

第二节　财务比率分析的局限性

财务比率分析的主要局限性有。

1) 比率的选择

选择进行分析的比率有一定难度。如，对于杠杆比率有不同的定义。第二个例子是评估资产的周转率。

2) 历史成本会计

绝大多数企业的财务报表都是基于历史成本概念来编制的，很少或是完全不考虑通货膨胀，这必然导致低估资产负债表上的资产。而且许多企业在其资产负债表上并不包括无形资产，如商誉。

3) 季节性波动

许多企业的经营活动水平是季节性变动的，如圣诞卡市场。因而，资产负债表上列示的资产和负债并不能代表全年的总体状况。

4) 时间滞后

大多数财务报表的使用者必须依靠经过审计后发布的财务资料。这些报表资料发布时已经过去了几个月的时间，此时的信息就过时了。

5) 不同类型的资产所有权

大多数企业开展经营要用到固定资产。一些企业选择购买所用到的固定资产，而另一些企业选择使用属于其他人的固定资产，并为此支付租金。

Unit 9 Cost Accounting and Management Accounting

Objectives

- Students should learn to identify the basic cost elements of manufacturing costs.
- Students should have a comprehension of the characteristics and the roles of management accounting.
- Students ought to know what the Cost-Volume-Profit analysis is?
- Students ought to make clear the difference between direct materials and indirect materials, direct labor and indirect labor.
- Students ought to know the main concepts of cost accounting.

Dialogue

1. The five main concepts in cost accounting

John: You were absent yesterday. Where have you been?
Mary: Oh, I was ill. I got a high fever.
John: How are you feeling now?
Mary: Much better. By the way, what did you learn yesterday?
John: We learned something about "cost accounting".
Mary: "Cost accounting", what is that?
John: Cost accounting is an essential specialty within the accounting field. The main objective of industry is to determine the selling price of the products or the cost of services that are furnished by a company.
Mary: I must have missed a lot.
John: Don't worry ! You can learn it yourself. Just make clear the five main concepts in cost accounting.
Mary: What are the five concepts?
John: They are: direct materials, indirect materials, direct labor, indirect labor and manufacturing overhead.
Mary: That's all I missed?
John: And the two principles of cost accounting systems: job-order cost accounting and

process cost accounting.

Mary: Thank you so much. I'll spend some time reading this part tonight.

John: If you get any questions, don't hesitate to ask me.

Mary: It's so kind of you.

译文：成本会计中的五个主要概念

约翰：你昨天没来，去哪了？

玛丽：噢，我病了，发高烧。

约翰：现在你感觉好点了？

玛丽：好多了。顺便问一下，你们昨天学什么了？

约翰：我们学了成本会计的一些知识。

玛丽：成本会计？那是什么？

约翰：成本会计是会计领域的一个专业。生产的重要目的是决定一个产品的市场价格或一个公司所提供服务的成本。

玛丽：我肯定落了很多知识。

约翰：别急，你可以自学，弄清楚成本会计的五个主要概念就行了。

玛丽：哪五个概念？

约翰：它们是：直接材料、间接材料、直接人工、间接人工和制造费用。

玛丽：就这些？

约翰：还有成本会计的两个原则：分批成本制度和分步成本会计制度。

玛丽：太谢谢了，今晚我再看看这部分。

约翰：你有什么问题就来问我吧。

玛丽：你真好。

2. product costs

Mary: Then what expenditure are the product costs composed of?

John: Mary, If we want to produce bread, what do we need First?

Mary: Flour.

John: Yes. Just like we need iron ore for producing steel and sheet steel for producing automobiles, the raw materials can become an integral part of the finished product. Therefore, such raw material costs are direct material costs.

Mary: What else do product costs include?

John: Direct labor costs. Direct labor costs encompass all labor costs for specific work performed on products. Besides these two kinds of direct costs, there is a diverse collection of expenses incurred in the workshop, which is called manufacturing overhead.

Mary: I think manufacturing overhead is indirect costs which is not traceable to specific products. Then how to calculate it?

John: Do you remember the matching principle we have learned? Indirect costs must be assigned to products by some allocation method.

Mary: You mean, at the end of one month, they are allocated to the various products made during this period according to a given allocation method?

John: Exactly.

译文：产品成本

玛丽：产品成本都包括哪些内容呢？

约翰：玛丽，如果我们想生产面包，首先需要什么呢？

玛丽：面粉。

约翰：是啊。就像炼钢需要铁矿，制造汽车需要钢板一样，原材料是构成产品实体的重要部分。所以，原材料成本就是直接材料成本。

玛丽：产品成本还包括哪些呢？

约翰：直接人工成本。直接人工成本包括所有的为生产产品而发生的特定人工成本。除了这两方面的直接成本之外，在工厂中还会产生各种杂项费用，被称为制造费用。

玛丽：制造费用是间接成本，不能追溯于某种特定产品，那么又该如何计算呢？

约翰：还记得我们学过的配给法则吗？间接成本必须按照一定的方法分配给产品。

玛丽：你是说，在月末，作为间接成本的制造费用将会根据一定的配给方法，分摊到在此期间生产出来的各种产品上吗？

约翰：完全正确。

Section 1   Cost Elements

In fact, manufacturing costs can be reclassified in many different ways depending on the final goal of a particular cost analysis. However, the most common and basic cost classification scheme associated with cost accounting is the grouping of manufacturing costs into three elements: direct material costs, direct labor costs, or indirect manufacturing costs (factory overhead). Direct costs are traceable to specific products, whereas indirect costs must be assigned to products by some allocation method.

1. Direct Material Costs

All manufactured products require basic raw material ingredients. The ingredient may be iron ore for producing steel, sheet steel for producing automobiles, or flour for producing bread. Direct materials are raw materials that become an integral part of the finished product and are conveniently and economically traceable to specific units of productive output. Therefore, such raw material costs are direct costs. The less significant raw materials and other production

supplies that cannot be conveniently or economically assigned to specific products are identified and accounted for as indirect materials. Indirect material costs are included as part of manufacturing (or factory) overhead costs.

2. Direct Labor Costs

Personnel connected with the manufacturing process include machine operators, maintenance people, managers and supervisors, support personnel, and other people performing the material handling, inspection, and storage functions. Because all these people are connected in some way with the production process, their wages and salaries must be accounted for as production costs of the product. Direct labor costs encompass all labor costs for specific work performed on products that are conveniently and economically traceable to end products. Labor costs for production-related activities that cannot be associated with, or are not conveniently and economically traceable to end products, are called indirect labor costs.

3. Manufacturing Overhead

The third manufacturing cost element serves as a catch-all for manufacturing costs that cannot be classified as direct materials or direct labor costs. Manufacturing (factory) overhead costs are a diverse collection of production-related costs that are not practically or conveniently traceable to end products. This same collection of costs has also been called factory overhead, factory burden, and indirect manufacturing costs. Examples of the major classifications of manufacturing overhead costs are listed below: indirect labor costs: life truck driver's wages, maintenance and inspection labor, engineering labor, machine helpers; indirect materials and supplies: nails, rivets, lubricants, small tools; other indirect factory costs: building maintenance, machinery and tool maintenance, property taxes, property insurance, pension costs, depreciation on plant and equipment.

4. Product and Period Costs

Product costs and period costs are commonly used terms in cost accounting analyses. These terms are linked closely with the manufacturing cost elements, combining the three elements under a single classification. Direct materials, direct labor, and manufacturing overhead costs all become part of a product's unit manufacturing cost. These three manufacturing cost elements collectively are called product costs. Product costs are those costs associated with the production of a product and are therefore inventoriable. Such costs, when converted into a product's unit cost, are used to establish values for ending Work in Process and Finished Goods Inventory balances on year-end financial statements.

Product costs are also un-expired costs because, as inventory balances, they are considered assets of the company. Assets represent unused resources of an organization. Period costs (expenses) are expired costs of an accounting period and represent dollars attached to resources

Unit 9 Cost Accounting and Management Accounting

used during the period. Any cost or expense item on an income statement is a period cost. Product costs become period costs when they are attached to units sold during the period. Operating expenses such as selling and administrative expenses are always classified as period costs. Period costs are always linked to services consumed during a period and are never used to determine product unit cost or to establish ending inventory balances.

Tips: Companies that use process cost systems include oil refineries, power plants, soft-drink bottlers, breweries, flour mills, and most "assembly-line" or "mass-production" manufacturing operations.

采用分步成本制的公司包括炼油、发电、软饮料瓶装、酿酒、食品加工和大部分"组装线"或"大量生产"的制造活动企业。

Section 2 Cost Accounting—A Concept Emphasis

There are many different concepts of cost in accounting, and the one which is relevant in any particular context depends very much on the purpose to be served by the cost accounting. In general, cost information is needed for three different purposes. The first is a financial accounting purpose, involving the measurement of costs as part of the process of income determination and asset valuation. The second is a cost accounting purpose, relating to planning and cost control. The third purpose in providing cost information is concerned with another managerial problem, that of formulating business policy and making operating decisions.

1. Cost Classifications for Income Measurement: Direct and Indirect Cost

A cost classification that relates to the traceability of costs to cost units is particularly useful for income measurement purposes. The cost unit is the unit of activity, the cost of which is being measured. There are several types of cost unit, such as particular job or product or batch of products, or a particular manufacturing process; or a department. The cost unit is largely determined by the nature of the manufacturing activity in which the enterprise is engaged.

Costs that are directly associated with a particular unit of activity are called direct costs. Those costs that are incurred by the factory for the benefit of production in general, and which can not be identified with individual units of activity, are known as indirect costs. The cost of labor applied to a particular product thus constitutes a direct cost, while the factory manager's salary is an example of an indirect cost.

Product costs and period costs. Accountants often distinguish between product costs and period costs. Product costs are those identified with goods purchased or produced for resale; they are also called inventoriable costs because they are initially identified as a part of the inventory on hand. In turn, these inventoriable costs become expenses in the form of cost of goods sold only when the inventory is sold. In contrast, period costs are noninventoriable costs; they are deducted as expenses during the current period without having been previously classified as costs of inventory.

2. Cost Classification for Planning and Control: Variable and Fixed Costs

Variable costs are defined as costs which vary directly and necessarily with changes in the level of output. They are also often assumed to vary more or less in proportion, so that average costs per unit of output remain relatively constant. Variable costs comprise prime costs and variable manufacturing overhead.

Fixed costs are those costs which are unaffected by changes in the level of production. Examples are factory rent and depreciation of machinery. A fixed cost may be said to be "fixed" only in relation to a given period of time and a given range of activity. Costs which are fixed in the short run when capacity is given may become variable in the longer run when capacity can be increased.

Some costs and expenses are partly fixed and partly variable, for example, machine repairs. Also, costs may be variable for some purposes and fixed for others. Generally, direct costs are variable, while manufacturing overhead may be either fixed or variable.

3. Controllable and Non-controllable Costs

The concept of controllable costs is used to establish responsibility for costs and performance at different management levels, and thus to facilitate the delegation of authority. Some costs are controllable at the factory-floor level, while other costs are controllable only at an executive-management level, perhaps on a discretionary basis, e.g. in the case of research and development expenditures. In the evaluation of efficiency, the only costs which should be taken into account are those which can be controlled by the person responsible for the department or activity under review. The other costs — the non-controllable costs — are irrelevant for purposes of fixing responsibility or assessing performance.

4. Cost Classification for Decision Making: Incremental and Sunk Cost

Incremental costs by definition relate to the additional costs of making a change, such as increasing the level of activity or adding a new product line. Incremental costs are sometimes regarded as synonymous with the economist's marginal costs, but a distinction should be drown between the two concepts. Marginal costs are costs at the margin, i.e. the costs of a single additional unit of production, whereas incremental costs can be the costs of additional batches of production, the additional costs resulting from changes in the pattern of production, or indeed the additional costs of any changes in policy. Marginal costs thus constitute a special case of incremental costs and their use in business decision making is restricted to areas where a single unit is of some significance. Incremental costs, like marginal costs, need to be considered in relation to a particular time interval, and for purposes of some decisions it is necessary to distinguish between long-run and short-run incremental costs.

Sunk costs comprise all those costs which remain the same irrespective of which alternative is chosen, and which are therefore not relevant to the decision in question.

In many situations, incremental costs may be the same as variable costs. But it is important not to confuse one concept with the other (nor sunk costs with fixed costs). For example, suppose one has a choice of continuing to sell one million units of a product in Shanghai rather than in Beijing. The variable manufacturing costs are unlikely to be affected by the decision, hence they are sunk costs and can be ignored. On the other hand, certain non-manufacturing costs, such as transport and advertising, may be incremental costs for purposes of this decision.

5. Avoidable and Unavoidable Costs

Avoidable costs and unavoidable costs may be considered to be special types of incremental and sunk costs, respectively. While incremental costs are associated with an increase in activities, the concept of unavoidable cost is relevant to a contraction of activities. Avoidable costs are costs that can be eliminated if activity is discontinued. Generally, it will be found that direct costs may often be avoided while allocated costs may not.

6. Opportunity Costs

Opportunity cost is the value of the sacrifice or opportunity forgone. For example, if a young man can earn $10,000 a year in a gainful employment, the opportunity cost to him of three years' study at a tertiary institution would appear to be $ 30,000. In business, the opportunity cost of a scarce resource may be defined simply as the earnings which may be derived from the best alternative use of the resource. For example, the opportunity cost of using funds for a particular purpose may be measured by reference to the highest interest which could be earned on those funds or by the highest return which could be obtained on alternative investments of similar risk. Similarly, the opportunity cost of processing partly-finished goods may be measured by reference to the proceeds from an immediate sale, which must be sacrificed in order to continue processing.

7. Future Costs

For purpose of decision making, the most relevant costs are future costs, because decisions generally relate to the future. Current costs also have relevance for many decisions but, by and large, past costs are irrelevant for decisions.

Examples of management's use of future costs may be found in a large number of areas, including cost control, long-range planning, budgeting, evaluation of capital projects and business decisions in general.

Section 3 Management Accounting

1. Introduction

Management accounting is about providing information to help managers run the businesses. Management accounting is not the same as financial accounting; it is a separate type of accounting activity. It is carried out by management accountants who need to have special abilities.

The business world consists of three broad groups of enterprises: primary producers, manufacturers and service providers. Primary producers carry out "extractive" activities such as mining, farming and fishing. Manufacturers take primary products, or the output of other manufacturers, and convert them into goods. Services are activities such as transport, education, banking, telecommunications, entertainment and health provision.

Businesses take inputs, such as materials, labor, equipment, land and money and convert them into products, such as oil, computers and medical treatment. All businesses need information about their past, present and future performance. Much of that information will be the same for all types of enterprise. However, what the business produces, and how it is produced, will also influence the information that a business requires. Good information must be fit for its purpose. That means the information must be reliable and sufficiently accurate for its intended purpose. The information must be provided timely. Late information is of little use. Good information must be economic. That means that the value of the information to the manager must be greater than its cost. Information costs will include the cost of obtaining data, analyzing it, interpreting it and presenting it as information to managers concerned with the provision of information.

This involves gathering and analyzing data to produce information. Much of this data, such as production quantities, working times, materials costs and selling prices, will be numerical. The data will be converted by management accounting techniques into management accounting information, which is in the desired form for its intended use. So management accountants must be numerate. They must also be able to set up and operate information gathering and analyzing systems.

Management accounting is also concerned with the interpretation of information, so the information which has been gathered must be converted into a form which has meaning. Therefore, management accountants must understand what the information they have gathered means. To do this they need to understand the way the business works, its production methods, its products and its markets.

The information produced is communicated to managers in the form of reports. These

Unit 9 Cost Accounting and Management Accounting

reports may be regular, such as monthly profit statements, or one-off reports responding to special requests from managers. Therefore, management accountants must be able to design reports and set up reporting systems. They must also be able to understand what it is that managers want to know.

2. The role of management accounting in business

Management accounting is an activity carried out within an organization. It is intended to provide information to assist the managers of the organization in four areas:

Planning. Information provided by management accounting is used by managers to help them to organize the future activities of the business. Planning information is forward looking. It consists of forecasts and estimates. These may be based on information about the business's past performance. A major area where management accounting information is used for planning is in the annual operating budget for a business. Therefore, management accountants must be forward looking, good at estimating and expert at budgeting.

Controlling. There are several ways in which management accounting information assists managers in controlling the operations of the business. One is by producing reports which compare the past quantities, costs and revenues for a period with the budgeted costs. This is known as budgetary control. Another type of reporting system, called standard costing, compares each individual product's actual costs and revenues with its planned costs and revenues. The management accountant must be able to identify and explain the causes of any differences between planned and actual costs to managers so that they can take any necessary action. So management accountants must possess good investigative skills. They must also be tactful and persuasive to gain the cooperation of their colleagues in other parts of the organization.

Decision-making. Producing information to assist managers in decision-making is a major role for management accounting. Decisions may be short term, such as: which products to make, how to make them, in what quantities they should be made, and at what price they should be sold. They may be long-term decisions, such as: whether to develop a new product, whether to invest in new equipment and if so, which equipment to choose, whether to expand a business or close it down, and whether to make a product or to buy it from outside. Management decisions can be improved if they are based on reliable and relevant information.

Appraising performance. Management accounting information can be used to assist managers in appraising the performance of individual managers, departments, products and enterprises. Appraisal information on departments and products may come from budgetary control or standard costing systems. A business's performance can also be analyzed by using ratios, such as the ratio between profits and sales or the ratio between profits and capital invested in the business. Management accountants must be able to interpret correctly the information which they produce for appraisal purposes if they are to help managers make the correct judgement on performance, if appraisal information is misleading, it could harm a business by encouraging unsuccessful managers and/or failing to recognize and encourage successful managers.

3. Common technical terms used in management accounting

Cost behavior. Cost behavior refers to the relationship between the level of output and costs, that is, how costs behave in relation to the level of output. It is possible to identify two extreme types of cost behavior: fixed and variable costs. A fixed cost does not vary with the level of output while a variable cost does vary with the level of output.

Break-even point. Break-even point is the level of activity at which there is neither a profit nor a loss. An alternative definition is "that level of revenue which exactly matches total costs". The break-even point can be stated in terms of units or as a money value. Therefore, the break-even point is the minimum quantity a business must sell, or the minimum revenue it must obtain, to survive.

Contribution ratio. Contribution is calculated by subtracting variable cost from the selling price. Contribution per unit divided by unit selling price is termed as contribution ratio.

Margin of safety. The margin of safety is the difference between the forecast turnover for a product (or group of products) and the break-even turnover. It is usually calculated as a ratio.

Margin of safety ratio=(forecast turnover-break-even turnover)÷Forecast turnover×100%

If the margin of safety for a forecast is very small, then the business may not even break-even.

Master budget. Master budget is the budget into which all subsidiary budgets are consolidated, normally comprising budgeted income statement, budgeted balance sheet and budgeted cash flow statement.

Variance. A variance is the difference between a planned, budgeted or standard cost and the actual cost incurred. The same comparisons may be made for revenues.

Internal rate of return. Internal rate of return is the annual percentage return achieved by a project, at which the sum of the discounted cash inflows over the life of the project is equal to the sum of the discounted cash outflows.

Section 4   Cost-Volume-Profit Analysis

Cost-Volume-Profit analysis expresses the relationships among a company's costs, volume of activity and income. Cost-Volume-Profit analysis is a key factor in many decisions, including choice of product lines, pricing of products, marketing strategy and utilization of productive facilities.

Unit 9 Cost Accounting and Management Accounting

Managers are constantly faced with decisions about selling prices, variable costs, and fixed costs. Basically, managers must decide how to acquire and utilize economic resources in light of some object. Unless they can make reasonably accurate predictions about cost and revenue levels, their decisions may yield undesirable or even disastrous results. These decisions are usually short-run: How many units should we manufacture? Should we change our price? Should we spend more on advertising? However, long-run decisions such as buying plant and equipment also hinge on predictions of the resulting cost-volume-profit relationships.

We obtain an overview by examining the interrelationships of changes in costs, volume, and profits, sometimes too narrowly described as break-even analysis. The break-even point is often only incidental in these studies. Instead, the focus is on the impact upon operate income or net income of various decisions that affect sales and costs. The break-even point is that point of activity (sales volume) where total revenues' and total expenses are equal; that is, there is neither profit nor loss.

Consider the following example:

A person plans to sell a toy rocket at the state fair. He may purchase these rockets at 50 cents each with the privilege of returning all unsold rockets. The booth rental is $200, payable in advance. The rockets will be sold at 90 cents each. How many rockets must be sold to break even?

The first solution method for computing the break-even point is the equation method. Every income statement may be expressed in equation form, as follows:

Sales−Variable Expenses−Fixed Expenses = Net Income or

Sales=Variable Expenses + Fixed Expenses + Net Income

This equation provides the most general and easy-to-remember approach to any break-even or profit-estimate situation. For the example above:

Let X = Number of units to be sold to break-even

$0.90X = 0.50X + 200 + 0$

$0.40X = 200 + 0$

$X = (200+0)/0.40$

$X = 500$ units (or $450 total sales at 90 cents)

A second solution method is the contribution-margin or marginal-income method. Contribution margin is equal to sales minus variable expenses. Sales and expenses are analyzed as follows:

1) Unit contribution margin to coverage of fixed expenses and desired net income = Unit Sales Price − Unit Variable Expense = 0.90−0.50 = 0.40

2) Break-even point in terms of units sold

= Fixed Expenses + Desired Net Income/Unit Contribution margin

= ($200+0) /0.40

= 500 units

Stop a moment and relate the contribution –margin method to the equation method.The key calculation was dividing $200 by 0.40.Look at the third line in the equation solution. It reads:

0.40X =200 + 0

X= (200 + 0) / 0.40

Giving us a general formula:

Break-even point in units

= Fixed Expenses + Desired net Income/Contribution Margin per unit

Both the contribution margin and the break-even point are altered by changes in unit variable costs. Thus, in the toy-rocket example, if the cost of a toy rocket is raised from 50 cents to 70 cents and the sales price is unchanged at 90 cents, the unit contribution falls from 40 cents to 20 cents and the break-even point increases from 500 to 1,000 units ($200 fixed expenses divided by 0.20). A decrease in rocket cost from 50 cents to 30 cents would change the unit contribution from 40 cents to 60 cents. The new break-even point would become 333 units ($ 200 fixed expenses divided by 0.60).

Variable costs are subject to various degrees of control at different volumes because of psychological as well as other factors. When business is booming, management tends to be preoccupied with the generation of volume "at all costs". When business is recessing, a sales force may be established to reach markets directly instead through slack, management tends to ride hard on costs. Decreases in volume are often accompanied by increases in selling expenses and lower selling prices; at the same time labor turnover falls, labor productivity changes, and raw material prices change. This is another illustration of the limitations of a break-even chart; conventional break-even charts assume proportional fluctuations of variable costs with volume. This implies adequate and uniform control over costs, whereas in practice such control is often erratic.

Fixed costs are not static year after year. They may be deliberately increased in order to obtain more profitable combinations of production and distribution; these affect the three major profit determinants: revenue, variable costs, and fixed expenses. For example, more complicated machinery may be bought so as to reduce unit variable costs. Increases in labor rates are likely to make it desirable for a firm to invest in labor-saving equipment.

In some cases, on the other hand, it may be wise to reduce fixed costs in order to obtain a more favorable combination. Thus, direct selling may be supplanted by the use of manufacturers' agents. A company producing stoves may find it desirable to dispose of its foundry if the resulting reduction in fixed costs would more than counterbalance increases in the variable costs of purchased castings over the expected volume range.

When a major change in fixed costs is proposed, management uses forecasts of the effect on the targeted net income and the contribution margin as a guide toward a wise decision. The

Unit 9 Cost Accounting and Management Accounting

management accountant makes continuing analyses of cost behavior and redetermines break-even points periodically. He keeps management informed of the cumulative effect of major and minor changes in the company's cost and revenue patterns.

应用专栏

Useful Expressions

cost accounting	成本会计
direct material	直接材料
indirect material	间接材料
direct labor	直接人工
indirect labor	间接人工
manufacturing overhead	制造费用
prime cost	主要成本
machine repairs	机器设备修理费
incremental cost	增量成本
sunk cost	沉入成本，历史成本
marginal cost	边际成本
opportunity cost	机会成本
future cost	未来成本
noninventoriable cost	非存货性成本
primary producers	初级产品制造者
cost behavior	成本习性
contribution ratio	贡献毛利率
margin of safety	安全边际
master budget	总预算
management accounting	管理会计
allocation rate	分配率
cost allocation	成本对象
cost tracing	成本汇集，成本追溯
direct method	直接分配法
payroll system	工资系统
reciprocal method	交互分配法
step-down method	顺序分配法

Cost-Volume-Profit Analysis　　　　　　本-量-利分析
Standardized Cost Accounting　　　　　标准成本会计

1. In fact, manufacturing costs can be reclassified in many different ways depending on the final goal of a particular cost analysis.

实务中，按照特定成本最终分析目标，制造成本能够用许多不同方法分类。

2. Direct materials include all materials of an integral part of the finished product and are easily traced to the finished product.

直接材料包括生产产品所有的、直接计入产品成本的材料。

3. Indirect materials are used in the manufacturing process but are not easily traced to special units or batches of production and are accounted for as factory overhead.

间接材料是用在生产过程中的一些成本，不是生产过程中某一环节或生产某一批产品直接计入的成本，而是维持整个工厂生产过程中的像水、电、房租一类的支出。

4. Direct labor represents the gross wages of personnel who worked directly on the production of goods.

直接人工是指给那些直接参与产品制造的员工的工资成本。

5. Indirect labor is used in the manufacturing process but is not applied to the finished product.

间接人工是指间接用于产品生产的人工的工资。

6. Manufacturing overhead consists of cost except direct material and direct labor, including indirect material, indirect labor, depreciation, electricity, fuel, insurance, insurance and property taxes.

生产经营费包括间接材料、间接人工、折旧、电、燃料、保险和财产税等费用，但不包括直接人工和直接材料的成本费。

7. Variable costs are defined as costs which vary directly and necessarily with changes in the level of output. They are also often assumed to vary more or less in proportion, so that average costs per unit of output remain relatively constant.

变动成本是指直接随着产量的变化而变化的成本，人们认为变动成本或多或少地与产量成正比例地变动，这样一来，单位产品的平均成本是相对稳定的。

8. Fixed costs are those costs which are unaffected by changes in the level of production. Examples are factory rent and depreciation of machinery.

固定成本是指不随产量变动而变动的成本，如企业的租金费用和折旧费用。

9. The concept of controllable costs is used to establish responsibility for costs and performance at different management levels, and thus to facilitate the delegation of authority.

可控制成本的概念常被用来确定成本责任以及各级管理人员的工作表现，以便于授权。

10. Management accounting is about providing information to help managers run the businesses. Management accounting is not the same as financial accounting; it is a separate

Unit 9 Cost Accounting and Management Accounting

type of accounting activity. It is carried out by management accountants who need to have special abilities.

管理会计就是向公司管理者提供管理信息的一门学科。管理会计不同于财务会计，它是一门独立的会计学科，是由具有较高能力的会计管理人员来从事的。

11. Management accounting is an activity carried out within an organization. It is intended to provide information to assist the managers of the organization in four areas: planning, controlling, decision-making and appraising performance.

管理会计是企业内部的一项活动，它可以为企业管理者提供以下四方面信息：计划、控制、决策和业绩评价。

12. Cost-Volume-Profit analysis expresses the relationships among a company's costs, volume of activity and income. Cost-Volume-Profit analysis is a key factor in many decisions, including choice of product lines, pricing of products, marketing strategy and utilization of productive facilities.

本量利分析是对公司经营和收入中的成本数量和利润之间的关系所进行的分析。本量利分析在诸如产品系列的选择、产品定价、营销策略，以及生产设施的利用等许多决策中都是关键的因素。

Additional Reading Material

Distinguish process costing from job order costing. Process costing is a system for assigning costs to goods that are produced in a continuous sequence of steps, or process. Process costing is used by companies that mass produce identical goods in large quantities. Job order costing is for companies that produce custom goods in relatively small quantities. In process costing systems, costs are accumulated by processing departments and flow from one department to another until the product is completed. In contrast, in job order systems, costs are accumulated on job cost records.

Record process costing transactions. Journal entries in a process costing system are like those in a job order system, with one key exception: a job order system typically uses one work in Process Inventory account, but a process costing system uses one such account for each processing department. Direct materials and conversion (direct labor and overhead) costs are debited to the Work in Process Inventory accounts of the individual processing departments in which the costs are incurred. As goods move from one department to the next, the Work in Process Inventory account of the receiving department is debited and the account of the transferring department is credited. After processing is completed, the cost of the goods moves with them into Finished Goods Inventory and Cost of Goods Sold.

Compute equivalent units of production. The main accounting task in process costing is to determine, for each department, the costs assigned to (1) units of product completed and transferred out during a production period (either into the next process or into finished goods inventory) and (2) ending inventory of work in process. A complication arises because goods in process may be in various stages of completion. To help them assign costs to the two categories of output units, accountants compute equivalent units of production—the amount of work expressed in terms of fully completed units of output. Equivalent units are computed for each input cost category.

Apply costs to units completed and to units in ending work in process inventory. Accounting for a department's costs is a five-step procedure. Firstly, the flow of production in physical (output) units is determined. Secondly, equivalent units of production are computed for units completed and transferred out and for ending work in process inventory. Thirdly, the total cost to account for is determined by adding the beginning balance of work in process to costs incurred during the current period. Fourth, unit costs are computed for each input category. And fifth, physical units are costs by multiplying equivalent units of production from step 2 by equivalent-unit costs from step 4.

Account for a second processing department by the FIFO method. FIFO, one of two methods that are widely used for process costing, focuses on current-period work. With this method, equivalent units of work performed in the current month are costs at current-month unit costs.

Account for a second processing department by the weighted-average method. The processing departments are summarized in monthly production cost reports. Manners the beginning of the month and the current month's work—with unit costs that are a weighted, average of current and prior-month costs. In both methods, the operations of comparing the actual costs in the reports with budgeted costs to evaluate processing.

Oral Practices

Directions: *Read the following dialogue and then answer the questions.*

Mary: Are you ready for the test tomorrow?

John: Oh, the test of Management accounting, a piece of cake!

Mary: Let's check each other what we've got in heart.

John: Good idea! You go first.

Mary: What are the seven stages of the decision-making process?

John: Identify objectives, search for alternative courses of action, gather information about alternatives, select alternatives courses of action, and implement the decisions, and … and …

Mary: Compare actual and planned outcomes.

John: Don't remind me ! And the last: respond to variances from plan.

Mary: Well done!

Unit 9 Cost Accounting and Management Accounting

John: It's your turn. What are the five functions of management in a company?

Mary: They are planning, controlling, organizing, communicating and motivating.

John: Good student! Another …

Mary: Oh, time for lunch. Good luck!

John: You, too.

Questions:

1. What are the seven stages of the decision-making process?
2. What are the five functions of management in a company?

Self-Test exercises

Stick-up Ltd, a manufacturer of adhesives, wants to account for factory overheads on a department basis. Production takes place in two departments—the mixing department, where the various raw materials are combined, and the bottling department where the product is packaged in special applicators. The plant operation is supported by two service departments. The store controls the receipt and issue of all materials, while the maintenance department ensures that all plant and equipment in the factory is operating efficiently.

The following information and statistics have been prepared for the year 2005.

Table 9-1 $

costs	total	mixing	bottling	maintenance	store
Indirect labor	95,000	33,600	30,400	13,000	18,000
Indirect materials	46,800	23,450	18,645	1,475	3,230
Depilation- plant	18,000	9,000	6,000	1,000	2,000
Rates	3,600				
Power	33,600				
Insurance—building	22,500				
—plant	10,500				
	230,000				
Other information:					
Area (m²)	4,500	1,500	2,000	400	600
Kilowatt hours	6,000	3,500	1,800	300	400
Value of plan	200,000	100,000	70,000	10,000	20,000
No.of material requisitions	5,000	2,000	1,000	2,000	
Maintenance hours	2,000	350	1,400		250
Direct labor costs	390,000	110,000	280,000		
Machine hours	25,000	20,000	5000		

> Calculate an overhead allocation rate for the two production departments on the following basis.
>
> Mixing department: $ per machine hour
>
> Bottling department: % direct labor costs

参考译文

第一节 成本要素

实务中，按照特定成本最终分析目标，制造成本能够用许多不同方法分类。然而与成本会计相关的最通用、最基本的方法是将制造成本集中起来分为三要素：直接材料成本、直接人工成本和间接制造成本(工厂间接费用)。直接成本可追溯于某种特定产品，而间接成本必须按照一定方法分配给产品。

(1) 直接材料成本。所有制成品需要基本的原材料成分。这些成分也许是炼钢所需的铁矿，生产汽车所需的钢板或生产面包所需要的面粉。直接材料是构成产品实体的原材料，并且是能够既方便又经济地计入特定单位的生产量中。因此，原材料是直接成本。非主要原材料和其他不能既方便又经济地分配给特定产品的生产辅料被认定计入间接材料成本。间接材料成本是制造成本的组成部分。

(2) 直接人工成本。与制造过程相关的员工包括机器操作人员、维修人员、管理人员和主管人员、辅助人员及其他从事原材料管理、检查和保管的人员。由于所有这些职员多少与生产过程有关，所以他们的工资和薪金必须作为产品的生产成本计入产品成本。直接人工成本包括所有的为生产产品的特定人工成本，并可以方便又经济地计入最终产品。生产活动中与最终产品没有联系的或不便于计入最终产品的人工成本称为间接人工成本。

(3) 制造费用。因为既不能划分为直接材料，也不能划分为直接人工成本，第三个制造成本要素为杂项费用。制造费用成本是与生产相关成本的杂项费用的集合，不能实际地或方便地计入最终产品。这种成本集合也称作工厂间接费用、制造间接费用和间接制造成本。制造费用成本的主要分类如下：间接人工成本：卡车司机的工资、维修及检验工人工资、工程人员工资和机械助理人员工资；间接材料和辅料：钉子、铆钉、润滑油和小型工具；其他间接制造成本：建筑物维修费、机器及工具维修费、财产税、财产保险费、退休费、厂房及设备资产折旧。

(4) 产品成本及期间成本。产品成本和期间成本是成本会计分析中的常用术语，这些概念与制造成本要素关系密切，将三个要素归为一类：直接材料、直接人工及制造费用成本，它们一起构成产品单位制造成本。这三个制造成本要素集中地被称做产品成本。产品成本是与产品生产相关，所以是可储存的。当其转变为产品单位成本时，这种成本在编制年终资产负债时可用于确定期末在制品和产成品的存货价值。

产品成本也是未耗成本，因为作为存货金额，它们被认为是公司的资产。资产表示一个经济组织未耗用的资源。期间成本(费用)是会计期间已耗成本，并表示归属当期内已耗用资源的价值，收益表中任何成本或费用项目都是期间成本。生产费用附加于当期已售单位产品时成为时间成本。经营费用，如销售费用和行政管理费用，总是划分为期间成本。期间成本总是与某一时期内所消耗的劳务相关联，而从不用于确定产品单位成本或确定期末存货余额。

第二节 成本会计——相关概念

会计中成本的概念有多种，哪一种能够适用于某种特殊情况，取决于成本会计的目的。一般说来，人们出于三个原因需要掌握成本资料。第一个原因是进行财务会计核算的需要，因为在确定利润和评估资产的过程中需要对成本加以计量；第二，是成本会计的需要，主要是为了进行成本计划和成本控制；提供成本资料的第三个原因涉及管理方面的问题，即为了制定企业的经营方针和做出经营决策。

1．**为计算利润而进行的成本分类：直接成本和间接成本**

按照追溯成本到各成本计算单位的方法进行成本分类，对于利润计算是非常有用的。所谓成本计算单位是指要按其计量经济活动的成本的单位，它可以有多种，如某项工作或产品，或一批产品，或者是一个产品加工步骤，或者是一个部门，都可以成为成本计算单位。成本计算单位取决于企业所从事的生产活动的性质。

与某种特定的成本计算单位直接相关的成本叫做直接成本。那些为企业的一般生产管理而发生的成本，不能确切地分清它是为哪种工作而发生的，这样的成本叫做间接成本。为生产某种产品而发生的劳动力的成本就属于一种直接成本，企业经理的工资就属于一种间接成本。

产品成本和期间成本。会计人员经常区分产品成本和期间成本。产品成本是指为销售而购进或制造的产品的成本，它也被称做存货性的成本，因为这种成本最初都是存货的一部分，当这些存货被售出的时候，这一部分存货性成本就以销售成本的形式转化为费用。与此相对应，期间成本是非存货性的成本，它们将直接作为当期费用予以扣除，而不必先将其归属为产品成本。

2．**为编制计划进行控制而作的成本分类：变动成本和固定成本**

变动成本是指直接随着产量的变化而变化的成本，人们认为变动成本或多或少地与产量成正比例地变动，这样一来，单位产品的平均成本是相对稳定的。变动成本包括主要成本和制造费用中的变动部分。

固定成本是指不随产量变动而变动的成本，如企业的租金费用和折旧费用。所谓固定费用，只是在一定的期间里，一定的业务范围内是固定的。有些成本，当产量一定时，在一段比较短的时期里，表现为固定成本，但从长期角度来看，当产量增加后，这些成本可以转化为变动成本。

有些成本和费用既有固定的部分，也有变动的部分，如机器设备的修理费用。某些成本在有些情况下是固定的，而在有些情况下则是变动的。一般说来，直接成本属于变动成本，制造费用既可以是固定成本也可以是变动成本。

3．可控制成本和不可控制成本

可控制成本的概念常被用来确定成本责任以及各级管理人员的工作表现，以便于授权。有些成本在企业的最低阶层是可以控制的，有些成本只在高级管理人员阶层是可控的，也就是取决于管理人员的决定，如研究与开发支出。评价效率时，应该加以考虑的成本只是那些被考核的有关部门或业务负责人可以控制的成本，其他成本——不可控制成本，对于确定人员的责任，评价他们的表现是不相关的。

4．为决策而进行的成本分类：增量成本和沉没成本

增量成本的含义是指经营活动发生某种变化，如业务量提高或增加一条新的产品线，所额外增加的成本。增量成本有时候被看做是经济学家们所说的边际成本的同义词，但实际上应该把这两个概念区分开来。边际成本是指一定变量所影响的成本变化，也就是增加一个单位的产量所带来的成本；而增量成本可以是指额外增加的一批产品的成本，由于生产格局的变化而增加的成本，或者是由于经营方针变化而增加的成本。所以，可以说边际成本是增量成本的一个特殊种类，它们在经济决策中的应用仅限于单位成本的变化具有十分重要意义的地方。增量成本必须与一定的期间结合起来研究，这一点与边际成本是一致的，在做某种决策的时候，区分短期增量成本和长期增量成本是很有必要的。

沉没成本是指那些不论在什么情况下都保持不变的成本，因而与决策没有关系。

在许多情况下，增量成本可能与变动成本相同，但正确区分这两个不同的概念是十分重要的，同时也要区分沉没成本和固定成本。举例来说，某人可以继续选择在上海而不是在北京销售一百万件产品的决策方案，在这里，制造费用中的变动成本不会受到这个决策的影响，因此属于沉没成本，可以忽略。另一方面，一些非制造成本，如运输费用和广告宣传费用，在这个决策中就会变成增量成本。

5．可避免成本和不可避免成本

可避免成本和不可避免成本可以被分别认为是特殊种类的增量成本和沉没成本。增量成本与经济业务量的增加有关，不可避免成本与经济活动的缩减有关。所谓可避免成本，是指如果中止某种经济活动就可以免于发生的成本。一般说来，直接成本多是可避免成本，而间接成本则属于不可避免成本。

6．机会成本

机会成本，是指放弃某种机会或做出某种牺牲的价值。举例来说，假如一位年轻人可以在一个岗位上每年赚 1 万美元，那么如果他选择在大学里学习 3 年，这一行动方案的机会成本就是 3 万美元。从商业角度说，一项紧缺资源的机会成本就是这项资源的最佳使用方案所能带来的收入。例如，按某种方式使用一笔资金的机会成本可以确定为这些资金可

以带来的最高的利息收入，或投资于另一种风险相似的项目所能带来的最高收入。同样，加工半成品的机会成本就是直接出售这些半成品的收入，如果选择继续加工这些半成品，那么就必须放弃销售半成品的收入。

7. 未来成本

做决策时，未来成本是最需要考虑的相关成本，因为决策多半与未来的事项有关。当期成本也常常与决策有关，但一般来说，在做决策时不需考虑历史成本。

管理人员在许多情况下都要用到未来成本的概念，包括成本控制、长期计划、预算、对建设项目的评估和一般的经济决策。

第三节 管理会计

1. 引言

管理会计就是向公司管理者提供管理信息的一门学科。管理会计不同于财务会计，它是一门独立的会计学科，由具有较高能力的会计管理人员来从事的。

社会上的经济组织可以分为以下三类：初级产品生产者、制造者和提供服务者。初级产品生产者也就是从事"开采"活动的企业，如采矿、农业和捕鱼等。制造企业就是将初级产品或其他加工过的产品进一步加工，生产出新产品的企业。服务企业就是提供运输、教育、银行、通信、娱乐和医疗服务的部门。

企业在经营中投入原材料、劳动力、机器设备、土地和现金等资产，然后通过生产过程制造出新的商品，如汽油、计算机和医疗设备等。所有的企业都需要了解关于企业过去、现在和将来的信息。大部分信息对于各种类型的企业都是适用的。然而，企业所需的信息将受到它所生产的产品和如何生产等因素的影响。因此，有价值的信息必须是那些能满足管理需要的信息，也就是说，信息必须可靠、充分和准确，而且信息的获得必须及时，过时的信息没有任何使用价值。最后，信息的获得必须符合成本效益原则，也就是说提供给管理者的信息所带来的收益应该大于它的成本。信息的成本包括获得信息、分析信息、解释信息以及将它提供给管理人员的成本。

管理会计是用于提供信息的，其活动包括收集和分析生产的有关数据。大多数信息(如产量、工时、材料费和售价)都是用数字表示的。管理会计将这些数据转化成有用的管理信息，并且这些数据会因用途的不同而采用不同的表现形式。因此，管理会计师必须善于利用数据，而且他们必须具有建立、应用收集和分析信息系统的能力。

管理会计还包括对信息的解释，即对收集的信息进行解释以了解经济活动的本质。因此，管理会计师必须明白他们所收集信息的内涵。为了做到这一点，他们必须了解企业的运作方式、生产产品的方式以及它的产品和产品市场的性质。

信息是以报告的形式传达给管理人员的。这些报告可以是常规的，如每月的利润表，也可以根据管理人员的需要做特别的报告。因此，管理会计师必须能够设计报告并且建立一套报告体系，而且他们必须清楚地了解管理人员的需要。

2. 管理会计在企业中的作用

管理会计是企业内部的一项活动，它可以为企业管理者提供以下四方面信息：

计划　管理会计提供的信息可以帮助管理人员规划未来的经济活动。应用于计划的信息应该具有前瞻性，它包括预测和估计，这种预测和估计是根据企业过去的经营成果做出的。管理会计应用于计划的一个重要领域即是企业每年的经营预算。因此，管理会计师必须面向未来，熟练掌握和运用估计与预算的技能。

控制　管理会计帮助管理者控制企业活动表现为以下几个方面：其一就是预算控制，即通过编制报告，将过去一个时期的产量、生产成本和收入与各自的预算数相比较，这一过程叫做预算控制。另一个控制系统是标准成本法控制系统，即将产品的单位产品的实际成本和收入，与单位标准成本和标准收入相比较。

这就要求管理会计师必须能发现并解释实际数与标准数之间产生差异的原因。因为只有这样，才能为管理人员下一步降低成本指明方向。因此，管理会计师必须具有敏锐的观察力，并且具有良好的沟通能力，与其他部门的工作人员协作，共同为降低成本做出努力。

决策　管理会计为管理者提供决策信息是其重要职能之一。它可应用于短期决策，如决策生产什么、如何生产以及产品的产量和售价等；也可应用于长期决策，如决策是否开发新产品、是否投资新设备和选择什么设备、是否应该扩大企业规模或应该关闭企业、是自制产品还是外购产品等。如果管理人员用于决策的信息是可靠、相关的，那么决策的效率就会大大提高。

业绩评价　管理会计可帮助管理者考核企业中每一个经理和每一个部门的经营业绩。对部门或产品的考核依据来自于预算数或标准成本数。企业的经营业绩也可以通过各种比率来评估，如使用销售利润率和投资报酬率等。如果管理会计师要帮助企业管理人员准确地评价企业的经营业绩，他必须能准确地解释那些用于评估业绩的信息。如果评价信息具有误导性，就可能因为奖励一个无所作为的管理者或因为没有奖励有突出贡献的管理人员而挫伤员工的积极性。

3. 管理会计中的常用术语

成本习性　成本习性是指成本与产量间的变动关系，也就是成本如何随产量的变动而变动。根据成本习性，成本可大致分为以下两类：固定成本和变动成本。固定成本不随产量变化而变化，而变动成本是指总成本随产量变化而变化的成本。

保本点　保本点是指企业处于既不盈利也不亏损状态下的销量。它也可以定义为："收入和总成本相等时的销量"。保本点可以用数量表示，也可以用金额表示。因此，保本点就是企业生存的最低销售量，是企业的最低销售额。

边际贡献率　边际贡献等于销售收入减去变动成本后的差额，单位边际贡献除以单位售价就是边际贡献率。

安全边际　安全边际等于产品的预计销售量减去保本销售量的差额。它也可以用安全边际率来表示，其计算公式如下：

安全边际率=(预计销售量−保本销售量)÷预计销售量×100%

如果预计的安全边际非常小,那么企业将面临不能保本的风险。

总预算 总预算是通过将所有明细预算汇总得来的,通常包括收入预算表、资产负债预算表和现金流量预算表。

差异 差异就是实际发生成本与计划成本、预算成本和标准成本间的差额。这种比较方法同样适用于收入。

内部收益率 内部收益率是使一个投资项目的未来现金流入现值等于未来现金流出现值的年收益率。

第四节 成本-数量-利润分析

本量利分析是对公司经营和收入中的成本数量和利润之间的关系所进行的分析。本量利分析在诸如产品系列的选择、产品定价、营销策略,以及生产设施的利用等许多决策中都是关键的因素。

企业管理者经常要进行关于销售价格、变动成本和固定成本的决策,从根本上说来,管理者必须针对某些目标来决定经济资源的获取和利用问题。除非他们能对成本与收入水平做出相当准确的预测,否则,他们的决策将会产生不良的甚至灾难性的后果。这些决策通常都是短期政策,如决定生产多少产品、要不要改变价格、该不该增加广告费等。不过,购建厂房设备等的长期决策也取决于成本-数量-利润关系的预测结果。

研究成本-数量-利润三者之间相互关系的过程,有时被过于狭隘地说成是盈亏平衡点分析。其实,盈亏平衡点往往只是这些研究中的一个方面,而重点应该是研究影响销售与成本的各种决策对营业或净收益的影响。盈亏平衡点是总收入与总成本恰好相等的业务量(销售量),也就是不盈不亏的保本点。下面举个例子来说明。

某人打算在本州商品交易会出售一种玩具火箭,这种玩具进价为每枚50美分(未售出的火箭可以退货)。售货摊位的租金为\$200,需要预付,玩具火箭按每枚90美分出售。该人必须销售多少枚才能盈亏平衡?

第一种计算盈亏平衡点的方法是方程法。任何一个收益表都可用以下方程来表达:

销售收入-变动费用-固定费用=净收益

销售收入=变动费用+固定费用+净收益

这些方程是求解盈亏平衡点或估算利润的最易记的一般公式。

根据本例数据:

令 X=达到盈亏平衡点的数量

$0.90X=0.50X+200+0$

$0.40X=200+0$

$X=(200+0)/0.40$

X=500 枚(或按每枚 90 美分计算,销售收入即为\$450)

第二种解法是边际贡献法,即边际收益法。边际贡献等于销售收入减去变动费用。销售收入与费用的情况分析如下：

1) 抵补固定费用并实现目标净收益的单位边际贡献

=单位售价-单位变动费用=0.90-0.50

= 0.40

2) 用销售量表示的盈亏平衡点

=固定费用+目标净收益/单位边际贡献=(200+0)/0.40=500 枚

现在把边际贡献法和方程法联系起来看，发现计算过程的关键是$200除以$0.40。回头再看一下按方程法计算的第三行，即：

0.40X=200+0

X=(200+0)/0.40

从这里可以推导出下列一般公式：

以数量表示的盈亏平衡点=固定费用+目标净收益/单位边际贡献

边际贡献和盈亏平衡点都随着单位变动成本的增减而变动，因此，在本例中，如果玩具火箭的成本从 50 美分提高到 70 美分，而售价不变，仍是 90 美分，那么单位边际贡献将从 40 美分降为 20 美分，盈亏平衡点销售量也将从 500 枚提高到 1 000 枚(固定费用$200 除以 20 美分)。如果这种玩具的成本从 50 美分降到 30 美分，那么单位边际贡献将从 40 美分增到 60 美分，而盈亏平衡点也将变为 333 枚(固定费用$200 除以 60 美分)。

由于心理因素以及其他因素，在不同销售水平下的变动成本会受到不同程度的影响。在经济繁荣期间，管理层往往不顾成本而使劲扩大生产。在经济衰退期间，管理层则将加紧控制成本。销售量往往随着销售费用的增加和售价的下降而减少下去；与此同时，劳工流动率下降，劳动生产率发生变化，原材料价格也发生变化。这从另一方面说明了盈亏平衡图的局限性。传统的盈亏平衡图假定变化成本和销售量成正比例变动，这意味着成本已经得到了充分的控制。可是，实际上这类控制常常是不稳定的。

固定成本并非年年都是不变的。它们可以被有意识地提高，以便更好地组合生产和分配，获得更多的利润。这样，就会影响决定利润的三个主要因素：收入、变动成本和固定成本。例如，企业可能购置高效的新机器去降低单位变动成本；工资率的提高，也可能促使企业对节省劳动力的设备进行投资。

另一方面，在某些情况下，为了使生产和销售更好地组合起来，降低固定成本也许是明智的。这样，也许就不采用直接销售而是采用代理人经销的办法了。炉具制造公司可能会发现，在一定的销售量范围内，如果将铸造设备处置掉而降低的固定成本大于外购铸件而提高的变动成本，则处置设备更为合算些。

当打算大幅度变动固定成本时，管理层需预测其对目标净收益和边际贡献的影响，以做出明智的决策。管理会计师要对成本性态进行经常的连续分析，定期重新确定盈亏平衡点，要向管理层报告本公司的成本和收入模式中大小变动的累计影响。

Unit 10 Auditing

Objectives

- Students ought to know the three kinds of auditing.
- Students ought to make clear the process of auditing.
- Students ought to make clear the four basic types of the audit report.
- Students ought to know the two reasons of auditing.
- Students ought to know the information of the engagement letter.

Dialogue

1. Audit Process

John: Hello! Mary. Are you free now?

Mary: Yes, I have nothing special. But why?

John: Oh, we will have an examination of auditing tomorrow. Let's have a revision, will you?

Mary: Good! I just want to do that. Let's begin then.

John: Ok. Do you remember the three kinds of auditing?

Mary: Yes. They are internal auditing, external auditing and governmental auditing.

John: Right. Then what information does an engagement letter include?

Mary: Let me think. It should include the following information: name of the client and its year-end date; financial statement to be examined and other reports to be prepared; identification of any limitations imposed by the client or the timing of the engagement that may affect the auditor's ability to gather sufficient competent evidential matter in support of the financial statements, and… and…

John: Don't worry. Let me go on. The next includes the type of opinion expected to be issued as a result of the audit work; the auditor's responsibility for the detection on errors and irregularities; obligations of the client's staff to prepare schedules and statements and assist in other aspects of the audit work and the audit fee and the manner of payment.

Mary: Oh, my God! You are so great!

John: Thank you. Now, let's review the audit process which includes six steps.

Mary: I will say the first three ones: 1) Review the client's system of internal control, and prepare a description of the system in the audit working papers. 2) Conduct tests to determine the reliability of the key internal control procedures. 3) Evaluate the effectiveness of the system of internal control in preventing material errors in the financial statements.

John: Good. The last three ones are: 4) Prepare a report to management containing recommendations for improving the system of the internal control. 5) Conduct comprehensive tests to substantiate specific account balance and perform other auditing procedures. 6) Form an opinion and issue the audit report.

Mary: Very good.

译文：审计程序

约翰：你好，玛丽！你现在有空吗？

玛丽：有空，没什么特别的事儿。为什么这样问？

约翰：噢，我们明天有个审计考试，我们一起复习一下吧，好吗？

玛丽：好，我正想复习呢，那我们现在就开始吧。

约翰：行。你记得审计的三种形式吗？

玛丽：记得。它们是内部审计、外部审计和政府审计。

约翰：正确。那么一份审计委托书应当包括哪些内容呢？

玛丽：让我想想。它应当包括以下内容：委托人名称及其会计年度截止日；需要审查的财务报表以及需要编制的其他报告；说明由于委托人或委托书上的时间安排所造成的可能影响审计师搜集足够充分的证据以证明财务报表公允性的能力的所有限制条件，还有……还有……

约翰：别急，我来接着说。还包括作为审计结果而发表的意见书预计将属于什么种类；审计师在发现错误和不法行为方面的责任；需由委托人的职员编制附表和报表并协助其他审计工作的义务以及审计费用和付款方式。

玛丽：噢，我的天，你真了不起！

约翰：谢谢。现在我们来复习审计程序的六个步骤吧。

玛丽：我来说前三个。1) 审查委托人的内部控制系统，并在审计工作底稿中编制对这一系统的说明书；2) 进行审计测试，借以确定关键性内部控制程序的可靠性；3) 评价内部控制系统在防止财务报表出现重大错误方面的有效性。

约翰：好。后面三个是：4) 向管理当局编送有关改进内部控制系统的建议报告；5) 进行综合测试，借以验证特定账户余额并实施其他审计程序；6) 形成审计意见并签发审计报告。

玛丽：很好。

2. Audit Report

Mary: Can you tell me the four types of the audit report?

John: Of course. They are unqualified opinion, qualified opinion, adverse opinion and

Unit 10 Auditing

disclaimer of opinion.

Mary: OK. What conclusions can make an auditor issue the unqualified opinion?

John: I think it should include three aspects. 1) The financial statements present fairly overall financial position, results of operations, and changes in financial position in conformity with GAAP or another comprehensive basis of accounting. 2) GAAP or the other comprehensive basis of accounting applied on a basis consistent with that of the proceeding period. 3) The financial statements have adequate information disclosure.

Mary: Right. What conclusions can make an auditor issue the qualified opinion?

John: I think it should include five aspects. 1) The scope of the auditor's examination was restricted by the circumstances of the engagement, condition of the client's records, or other reasons. 2) There is material uncertainty regarding the statements. 3) Disclosure is lacking. 4) An accounting principle or the method of its application is not in conformity with GAAP. 5) Accounting principles followed in the current period are not consistent with those in the proceeding period.

Mary: OK. When does an auditor issue an adverse opinion?

John: Issuance of an adverse opinion is a rare occurrence. When the financial statements taken overall are not fair presentations, an auditor issues an adverse opinion, but usually the auditor and the client are able to resolve the accounting problems that might mandate an adverse opinion through arbitration.

Mary: Then, when does an auditor issue disclaimer of opinion?

John: Disclaimers are issued for the following reasons. 1) The auditor is unable to apply procedures deemed necessary in an audit engagement and the effect is so pervasive that a qualified opinion is not appropriate. 2) An uncertainty regarding the financial statements is so pervasive that a qualified opinion is not appropriate. 3) The auditor has not audited the financial statements.

Mary: Your memory is so excellent.

John: You are also excellent. I think we will pass the examination.

Mary: I hope so.

译文：审计报告

玛丽： 你能告诉我审计报告的四种类型吗？

约翰： 当然可以。它们是：无保留意见，保留意见，否定意见和放弃发表意见。

玛丽： 好的。什么结论可以使审计师出具无保留意见书？

约翰： 我认为应当包括三个方面：1)财务报表公允地反映年公司的财务状况、经营成果及财务状况的变动情况，符合《公认会计原则》或其他类的会计综合基础。2)《公认会计原则》或其他类的会计综合基础是在与前期保持一致的基础上应

193

用的。3)财务报表具有充分的信息揭示。

玛丽：正确。什么结论可以使审计师出具保留意见书？

约翰：我认为应当包括五方面内容：1)审计师的审查范围受到委托书条件、委托人的会计记录条件或其他原因的限制。2)报表上存在着某种很大的不确定性。3)揭示不齐全。4)某项会计原则或其应用方法不符合《公认会计原则》。5)本期所遵循的会计原则未能与前期保持一致。

玛丽：好。什么时候审计师会出具否定意见报表？

约翰：出具否定意见书是十分罕见的。当财务报表作为一个整体未能做到公允反映时，审计师会出具否定意见报表。通常审计师和委托人通过仲裁，便能够解决可能导致否定意见的会计问题。

玛丽：什么时候审计师会发表放弃意见的报告？

约翰：放弃意见是基于以下的原因：1)审计师未能实施审计委托书中所阐明的程序，而且其影响甚广以致不便出具保留意见书。2)有关财务报表的不确定性甚广以致不便出具保留意见书。3)审计师未能对财务报表进行审计。

玛丽：你的记忆力真棒！

约翰：你也很出色。我想我们会通过考试的。

玛丽：希望如此。

Tips: One key justification for independent audits, as we have seen, is the economy that results from producing expert opinion-based judgments from limited but reliable evidential matter.

正如我们看到的，独立审计的一个关键理由是经济体系，它产生于根据有限但可靠证据得出的专家意见为基础的判断。

Section 1　Introduction of Modern Auditing

1. The definition of Modern Auditing

Modern Auditing is a systematic process of objectively obtaining and evaluating evidence regarding assertions about economic actions and events to ascertain that degree of correspondence between those assertions and established criteria and communicating the results to interested users.

It reveals that there are three aspects in the definition of the modern auditing. Firstly, auditing is a systematic process based on logic and reasoning. Secondly, during an examination of financial statements the auditing objectively obtains and evaluates evidence regarding assertion about economic actions and events embodied in the financial statements to ascertain the degree of correspondence between those assertions and established criteria which are generally accepted accounting principles in the audit of financial statements prepared by a company. Thirdly, the key aspect of the definition is that auditing involves communicating the results of the audit to the interested users. The auditor communicates the findings of the audit process by issuing an audit report in which the auditors give an opinion as to whether the assertions are reported in accordance with the established criteria.

The objectives of auditing vary depending on the needs of users of the audit report. Internal auditing, external auditing and governmental auditing all serve different objectives.

2. Internal Auditing

Internal auditing is defined as an independent appraisal function established within an organization to examine and evaluate its activities as a service to the organization. The objective of internal auditing is to assist members of the organization in the effective discharge of their responsibilities. Internal auditing furnishes them with analyses, appraisal, recommendations, counsel and information concerning the activities reviewed.

3. External Auditing

External auditing involves reporting on financial statements reported by management for external users or third parties which include stockholders, creditors, bankers, potential investors and federal, state and local regulatory agencies. External audits are performed by independent CPA firms. Independence is the backbone of external auditing.

4. Governmental Auditing

Governmental auditing covers a wide range of activities on the federal, state and local levels and numerous regulatory agencies. Governmental auditors not only examine financial statements but also determine whether government program objectives are met and whether certain government agencies and private enterprises comply with applicable laws and regulations.

5. Reasons of Auditing

Entities are audited by independent CPAs for numerous reasons. Some audits are needed because they are required by law. Companies regulated by Securities and Exchange Commission are required to have annual independent audits. Absentee ownership is another reason why audits are needed. Stockholders desire audits to determine management's stewardship of their assets. Some banks also require audits financial statements before granting loans. Likewise, when business firms are under consideration for mergers or sale, audits are desirable to properly ascertain the business's financial condition. Termination or death of a partner usually necessitates an audit to allocate assets in accordance with the partnership agreement. Also some suppliers require audited financial statements before they will grant a large amount of credit for sales of their products. At the same time, if the employees or management know they will be audited,

they will prevent and detect errors or irregularities, so audits can also have a preventive effect.

Section 2 the Process of Auditing

The CPA firm will examine the entity's accounting records, its system of internal control and the previous year's audit report according to its desire. If there was a previous audit, inquiries must be made of the processor auditor in accordance with Statement on Auditing Standards No. 7, which are issued by the Auditing Standards Board.

1. Two Types of Inquiries

The inquiries are basically of two types. Firstly, the successor auditor will make inquiries of the predecessor auditors to decide whether to accept the engagement. Thus, the successor auditor will make inquiries about the integrity of the entity's management and the reason for change in auditors. Secondly, if the successor auditor decides to accept the engagement, he or she will make inquiries of the predecessor auditor about matters, such as beginning accounting balances, which will facilitate the current audit.

2. The Engagement Letter

Once the client has engaged the CPA firm to perform the audit, the CPA firm will send an engagement letter confirming the arrangement for the audit. Obtaining an engagement letter signed by the chief executive officer and chief financial officer of the client is very important as the letter becomes the audit contract that describes the responsibilities of the auditor and the client.

The engagement letter should include the following information:

1) Name of the client and its year-end date.
2) Financial statement to be examined and other reports to be prepared.
3) Identification of any limitations imposed by the client or the timing of the engagement that may affect the auditor's ability to gather sufficient competent evidential matter in support of the financial statements.
4) The type of opinion expected to be issued as a result of the audit work.
5) The auditor's responsibility for the detection on errors and irregularities.
6) Obligations of the client's staff to prepare schedules and statements and assist in other aspects of the audit work.
7) The audit fee and the manner of payment.

3. The Audit Process

After receiving the engagement letter, the auditor will start the following audit process:

(1) Review the client's system of internal control, and prepare a description of the system in the audit working papers. A review of the client's system of internal control is logically a first step in very audit engagement. The nature, extent and timing of the audit work to be performed on a particular engagement depend largely on the effectiveness of the client's system of internal control in preventing material errors in the financial statements. Before the auditors can evaluate the effectiveness of the system, they need a knowledge and understanding of how it works.

(2) Conduct test to determine the reliabilities of the key internal control procedures. Audit tests to determine whether key internal control procedures have been operating effectively throughout the period under audit are called tests of compliance which measure the effectiveness of a particular control procedure. It does not substantiate the dollar amount of an account balance. The tests are essentially the tests of compliance.

(3) Evaluate the effectives of the system of internal control in preventing material errors in the financial statements. A major objective of internal control is to produce accurate and reliable accounting data. Auditors should make an intensive investigation in areas where internal control is weak. However they are justified to performing less intensive auditing work in area where internal controls are strong. This process of deciding on the matters to be emphasized during the audit, based on the evaluation of internal control, means that the auditors will modify their audit program by expending audit procedures in some areas and reducing them in orders.

(4) Prepare a report to management containing recommendations for improving the system of internal control. When serious deficiencies in internal control are discovered, the auditors should issue a recommendation letter to the client containing suggestions for overcoming the weakness. This internal control letter not only produces the client with valuable suggestions for improving internal control but also serves to minimize the liability of the auditors in the event that a major defalcation or other serious loss is later discovered.

(5) Conduct comprehensive tests to substantiate specific account balances and perform other auditing procedures. Tests designed to substantiate the fairness of a special financial statement item are termed substantive tests. Examples of substantive tests include confirmation of account receivable, observation of the taking of physical inventory and determination of an appropriate cutoff of transactions to be included in the year under audit. In addition to conducting substantive tests, the auditors will perform other audit procedures before completing the field work. For example, investigating related party transactions that may warrant special disclosure.

(6) Form an opinion and issue the audit report. Since the audit represents an acceptance of considerable responsibility by the CPA firm, a partner must first review the working papers from the engagement to ascertain that a thorough examination has been completed and to form an opinion on the financial statements. If the auditors are to issue anything other than an unqualified opinion of standard form, considerable care must go into the precise wording of the audit report. Consequently, the audit report is usually issued a week or more after the last day of fieldwork.

Section 3　Audit Report

The standard report consists of a scope paragraph and an opinion paragraph. The scope paragraph is a representation of the work performed by the auditor, which designates the statements and period covered. The opinion paragraph gives the auditor's opinion on the statements. Sometimes circumstances require that the auditor's report be a departure from a standard short-term report. Such reports will usually contain three paragraphs. The scope of the auditor's examination is given in the first paragraph. An explanation of why the auditor is departing from a standard report is set forth in the middle paragraph. The auditor's opinion or the reasons for disclaiming one, is included in the third paragraph. A long-form audit report usually contains scope and opinion paragraphs. However, these reports also contain analyses that are useful to management or to creditors.

Under certain specific conditions, there are four types of audit reports that may be issued by auditors. They are unqualified opinion, qualified opinion, adverse opinion and disclaimer of opinion.

1. Unqualified Opinion

An auditor may issue an unqualified opinion report when he or she has reached the following conclusions, based on an examination of the financial statements in accordance with accepted auditing standards:

1) The financial statements present fairly overall financial position, results of operations, and changes in financial position in conformity with GAAP or another comprehensive basis of accounting.

2) GAAP or the other comprehensive basis of accounting applied on a basis consistent with that of the proceeding period.

3) The financial statements have adequate information disclosure.

2. Qualified Opinion

An auditor may issue a qualified opinion report when he or she has complained with applicable accepted auditing standards regarding an examination of the financial statements and reached the conclusion that the financial statements present fairly overall in conformity with GAAP or other comprehensive basis of accounting, but there is an exception regarding a material item:

1) The scope of the auditor's examination was restricted by the circumstances of the engagement, condition of the client's records, or other reasons.

2) There is material uncertainty regarding the statements.

3) Disclosure is lacking.

4) An accounting principle or the method of its application is not in conformity with GAAP.

5) Accounting principles followed in the current period are not consistent with those in the proceeding period.

3. Adverse Opinion

An adverse opinion states that the financial statements taken overall are not fair presentations. Issuance of an adverse opinion is a rare occurrence. Usually the auditor and the client are able to resolve the accounting problems that might mandate an adverse opinion through arbitration. The auditor must have reached this opinion based on an examination in accordance with accepted auditing standards. An adverse opinion may result from lack of fairness in the application of accounting measurement or disclosure principles. The auditor's report must explain all of the substantive reasons for the opinion.

4. Disclaimer of Opinion

If the restriction on the auditor's ability to gather evidence is so pervasive that the auditor can't support an overall opinion on the financial statements, a disclaimer of opinion is warranted. When a disclaimer of opinion is issued, the auditor's report must disclose all of the substantive reasons for the disclaimer which is issued for the following reasons:

1) The auditor is unable to apply procedures deemed necessary in an audit engagement and the effect is so pervasive that a qualified opinion is not appropriate.

2) An uncertainty regarding the financial statements is so pervasive that a qualified opinion is not appropriate.

3) The auditor has not audited the financial statements.

应用专栏

Useful Expressions

auditing *n.*	审计，查账，审计学
examination of financial statements	财务报表审查
audit report / auditor's report	审计报告，审计师报告
internal auditing	内部审计
external auditing	外部审计
governmental auditing	政府审计
audit fee	审计费

audit process	审计程序，审计过程
system of internal control	内部控制系统
predecessor auditor	前任审计师
Statement of Auditing Standards	审计准则公告
the Auditing Standard Board	(美国)审计准则委员会
auditing objective	审计目标
successor auditor	后继审计师
engagement letter	审计委托书
audit contract	审计合同
audit working paper	审计工作底稿
test of compliance	符合性测试
audit program	审计计划
audit procedure	审计步骤
deficiency n.	亏空，缺乏
defalcation n.	盗用公款，亏空额
comprehensive test	综合性测试
substantive test	实质性测试
conformation of account receivable	应用账款的询证
taking of physical inventory	存货的实物盘存
cutoff of transactions	交易截止
field work	现场工作
related party transaction	有关当事人的交易
unqualified opinion	无保留意见书，无保留意见
adverse opinion	否定意见是，否定意见
short-term report	(审计)短式报告
long-term report	(审计)长式报告
disclaimer n.	放弃发表意见的(审计)报告
clean opinion	无保留意见
the general accepted auditing standards	公认审计准则
qualified audit report	有保留意见的审计报告
arbitration n.	仲裁
suspend vt.	中止，停止
impair vt.	损害，削弱

1. Auditing is an analytical process applied to everyday business situations.
   审计是应用于日常经营的分析性程序。
2. The auditor's evaluation of the control systems operating within the enterprise has a

direct influence on the scope of the examination he undertakes and the nature of the tests he conducts.

审计师对企业内部控制系统的评价对其审计检查的范围和审计测试的性质有直接影响。

Additional Reading Material

1. An audit report with an unqualified opinion

Audit report 1

To: The Board of Directors (or Shareholders) of ABC company Ltd.

We have audited the accompanying balance sheet of ABC Co., Ltd. as of December 31, 2003, and the related statements of income and cash flows for the year then ended. These financial statements are the responsibility of the Company's management. Our responsibility is to express an audit opinion on these financial statements based on our audit.

We conducted our audit in accordance with the Independent Auditing Standards for Certified Public Accountants. Those Standards require that we plan and perform the audit to obtain reasonable assurance about whether the financial statements are free of material misstatement. An audit includes examining, on a test basis, evidence supporting the amounts and disclosures in the financial statements. An audit also includes assessing the accounting principles used and significant estimates made by management, as well as evaluating the overall financial statement presentation. We believe that our audit provides a reasonable basis for our opinion.

In our opinion, the financial statements give a true and fair view(or are presented fairly, in all material respects,) of the financial position as of December 31, 2003, and the results of its operations and its cash flows for the years then ended in accordance with the requirements of both the Accounting Standard for Business Enterprises and other relevant financial and accounting laws and regulations promulgated by the States.

    Certified Public Accountant: Wang Yin
    Certified Public Accountant: Zhao Rui
**Certified Public Accountants(name and stamp of the firm)
Beijing, People's Republic of China
February 25, 2004

2. An audit report containing an unqualified opinion with an explanatory paragraph

Audit Report 2

To: The Board of Directors (or Shareholders) of ABC company Ltd.

We have audited the accompanying balance sheet of ABC Co., Ltd. as of December 31, 2003, and the related statements of income and cash flows for the year then ended. These financial statements are the responsibility of the Company's management. Our responsibility is to express an audit opinion on these financial statements based on our audit.

We conducted our audit in accordance with the Independent Auditing Standards for Certified Public Accountants. Those Standards require that we plan and perform the audit to obtain reasonable assurance about whether the financial statements are free of material misstatement. An audit includes examining, on a test basis, evidence supporting the amounts and disclosures in the financial statements. An audit also includes assessing the accounting principles used and significant estimates made by management, as well as evaluating the overall financial statement presentation. We believe that our audit provides a reasonable basis for our opinion.

In our opinion, the financial statements give a true and fair view(or are presented fairly, in all material respects,) of the financial position as of December 31, 2003, and the results of its operations and its cash flows for the years then ended in accordance with the requirements of both the Accounting Standard for Business Enterprises and other relevant financial and accounting laws and regulations promulgated by the States.

In the course of our audit, we have reminded the management that, due to the sharp price decline in the stock market since January 2004, an investment loss totaling RMB5,700,000 would be incurred if the short-term equity securities held by your Company were sold out on March 10.

     Certified Public Accountant: Wang Yin

     Certified Public Accountant: Zhao Rui

  **Certified Public Accountants (name and stamp of the firm)

Beijing, People's Republic of China

  February 25, 2004

3. An audit report containing a qualified opinion

Audit Report 3

To: The Board of Directors (or Shareholders)of ABC company Ltd.

We have audited the accompanying balance sheet of ABC Co., Ltd. as of December 31, 2003, and the related statements of income and cash flows for the year then ended. These financial statements are the responsibility of the Company's management. Our responsibility is to express an audit opinion on these financial statements based on our audit.

We conducted our audit in accordance with the Independent Auditing Standards for Certified Public Accountants. Those Standards require that we plan and perform the audit to obtain reasonable assurance about whether the financial statements are free of material misstatement. An audit includes examining, on a test basis, evidence supporting the amounts and disclosures in the financial statements. An audit also includes assessing the accounting principles used and significant estimates made by management, as well as evaluating the overall financial statement presentation. We believe that our audit provides a reasonable basis for our opinion.

The accompanying balance sheet at December 31, 2003 includes project service fees receivable of RMB17,309,667 and other long-term receivables of RMB160,599,155. These amounts are owing by one of the joint venture investors of the Company and certain business partners of that investor. As described in Notes 5 and 6 to the financial statements, there is uncertainty about the collectibility of these receivables. Because the ability of the debtors to repay these receivables is dependent upon the success of future operations of certain projects and upon the ability of the debtors to comply with the terms of their agreements with the Company, it is not possible to estimate the amount which ultimately will be collected. Provision for loss relating to the project service fees receivable has been made at approximately 3% of the year-end balance, and no provision is made for other long-term receivables.

In our opinion, except for the possible effects of the uncertainty about the collectibility of the project service fees and other long-term receivables, the financial statements referred above give a true and fair view(or are presented fairly, in all material respects,) of the financial position as of December 31, 2002, and the results of its operations and its cash flows for the years then ended in accordance with the requirements of both the Accounting Standard for Business Enterprises and other relevant financial and accounting laws and regulations promulgated by the States.

The accompanying financial statements have been prepared assuming that the Company will continue as a going concern. However, as explained in Note 10 to the financial statements, the Company has been unable to negotiate an extension of its borrowings with its foreign joint venture investor beyond December 31, 2004. Further, as described above, there is uncertainty about the collectibility of project service fees receivable and other long-term receivables. Because of this uncertainty, and without the continued financial support of the foreign investor, there is substantial doubt that the Company will be able to continue as a going concern beyond 2004. Consequently, adjustments may be required to the recorded asset amounts. The financial statements do not include any adjustments that might result from the outcome of this uncertainty.

    Certified Public Accountant: Wang Yin

    Certified Public Accountant: Zhao Rui

    **Certified Public Accountants (name and stamp of the firm)

Beijing, People's Republic of China

    February 25, 2004

4. An audit report containing an adverse opinion

Audit Report 4

To: The Board of Directors (or Shareholders) of ABC Company Ltd.

We have audited the accompanying balance sheet of ABC Co., Ltd. as of December 31, 2003, and the related statements of income and cash flows for the year then ended. These financial statements are the responsibility of the Company's management. Our responsibility is to express an audit opinion on these financial statements based on our audit.

We conducted our audit in accordance with the Independent Auditing Standards for Certified Public Accountants. Those Standards require that we plan and perform the audit to obtain reasonable assurance about whether the financial statements are free of material misstatement. An audit includes examining, on a test basis, evidence supporting the amounts and disclosures in the financial statements. An audit also includes assessing the accounting principles used and significant estimates made by management, as well as evaluating the overall financial statement presentation. We believe that our audit provides a reasonable basis for our opinion.

The inventory costing method as in Note XX and the valuation method for fixed assets as in Note XX do not follow the historical cost principle. This departure from the accounting standards has caused a RMBY XX decrease in the inventory value as well as a RMBY XX increase in the original value of fixed assets, which has a material impact on the correctness of the income determination.

In our opinion, due to the material impact of the matters mentioned above, the financial statements referred above give a true and fair view (or are presented fairly, in all material respects,) of the financial position as of December 31, 2003, and the results of its operations and its cash flows for the years then ended in accordance with the requirements of both the Accounting Standard for Business Enterprises and other relevant financial and accounting laws and regulations promulgated by the States.

  Certified Public Accountant: Wang Yin

  Certified Public Accountant: Zhao Rui

**Certified Public Accountants(name and stamp of the firm)

Beijing, People's Republic of China

February 25, 2004

5. An audit report containing a disclaimer of opinion

Audit Report 5

To: The Board of Directors (or Shareholders) of ABC Company Ltd.

We were engaged to audit the balance sheet of your Company as of December 31, 2003 and the related statements of income and cash flows for the year then ended. These financial statement are the responsibility of the Company's management.

According to our examination, most of the inventory purchases and product sales of your Company are, as disclosed in the accompanying Note XX, transactions between related parties. However, we were unable, as a result of the limits imposed by management, to perform the necessary audit procedures on those transactions. Thus we were unable to conclude whether these transactions were fair and reasonable.

Because of the inability to perform the necessary audit procedures on the related party transaction mentioned above and the impossibility to determine their impact on the financial statements as a whole, we are unable to express an audit opinion whether the financial statements referred to above comply with the requirements of both the Accounting Standard for Business Enterprises and other relevant financial and accounting laws and regulations promulgated by the States, or whether these financial statements present fairly the financial position as of December 31, 2003, and the results of its operations and its cash flows for the years then ended.

Certified Public Accountant: Wang Yin

Certified Public Accountant: Zhao Rui

**Certified Public Accountants(name and stamp of the firm)

Beijing, People's Republic of China

February 25, 2004

6. An audit report containing special purpose engagements

Audit Report 6

To: The Board of Directors (or Shareholders)of ABC Company Ltd.

We have audited the accompanying statement of expenditures of ABC Limited Beijing Representative Office (the "Office") for the year ended December 31, 2003 which has been prepared on the tax basis. This statement is the responsibility of the Office's management. Our responsibility is to express an opinion on this statement based on our audit.

We conducted our audit in accordance with the Independent Auditing Standards for Certified Public Accountants. Those Standards require that we plan and perform the audit to obtain reasonable assurance about whether the financial statements are free of material misstatement. An audit includes examining, on a test basis, evidence supporting the amounts and disclosures in the financial statements. An audit also includes assessing the accounting principles used and significant estimates made by management, as well as evaluating the overall financial statement presentation. We believe that our audit provides a reasonable basis for our opinion.

In our opinion, the statement of expenditures referred to above has been properly prepared on the tax basis, and presents fairly, in all material respects, the expenditures of the

Office for the year ended December 31, 2003.

This report is intended solely for the purpose of filing with the tax authorities and should not be used for any other purpose.

Certified Public Accountant: Wang Yin

Certified Public Accountant: Zhao Rui

**Certified Public Accountants (name and stamp of the firm)

Beijing, People's Republic of China

February 25, 2004

Oral Practices

Directions: *Read the following conversation and then answer the questions.*

A: Good morning, Manager Guo.

B: Good morning, Mr. Liu. Welcome to our company. How are you getting on with your work here?

A: Busy but smoothly. We have reviewed the company's operating activities, examined financial statements, checked the accounting records and supporting business patterns.

B: It's very kind of you to do so. Our primary concern is whether you could complete your audit work by the end of this month, since we are required to make a report to the board of directors. We urgently need your audit report.

A: Don't worry. Just as indicated in the audit engagement letter, the deadline for issue of the audit report is May 16. I think you are sure to have our audit report in time.

B: Will you please tell me something about the report?

A: Of course, our report contains two paragraph**s**: a scope paragraph and an opinion paragraph. The scope paragraph states the range of our examination, including the balance sheet, the statement of operations, and the statement of retained income for the accounting period.

B: This is called a complete examination, right?

A: Exactly.

B: Now, what's your opinion on the current state of our company's fiscal affairs?

A: We think all your accompanying balance sheet and statements present fairly, and they are in accordance with generally accepted accounting principles.

B: That is to say, our accounting records are consistent with the practices of the previous accounting period.

A: Yes. Here is the report.

B: Many thanks for your opinion. We'll pay greater attention to your suggestions so as to ensure things are running smoothly.

Questions:

1. What are the generally accepted accounting principles?
2. What information does an engagement letter include?

Self-test Exercises

Section 1

Supply the missing information in the following statements.

1. Auditing is a _____ process based on logic and reasoning.
2. In the audit of financial statements prepared by a company, the established criteria are generally accepted _____ principles.
3. In the audit _____, the auditor gives an opinion as to whether the assertions are reported in accordance with the established criteria.
4. Auditing involves _____ the results of the audit to the interested users.
5. _____ auditing, _____ auditing, and _____ auditing all serve different objectives.
6. The _____ of internal auditing is to assist members of the organization in the effective discharge of their responsibilities.
7. External auditing involves reporting on financial statements prepared by management for _____ users or _____ parties.
8. External Audits are performed by independent _____ firms.
9. _____ is the backbone of external auditing.
10. Stockholders desire audits to determine management's _____ of their assets.

Section 2

1. Supply the missing information in the following statements.

   (1) If there was a previous audit, inquiries must be made of the _____ auditor.

   (2) An engagement letter is the audit _____ that describes the responsibilities of the auditor and the client.

   (3) A review of the client's system of internal control is a _____ step in very audit engagement.

   (4) A compliance test measures the _____ of a particular control procedure.

   (5) Auditors should make an intensive investigation in areas for which internal control is _____.

   (6) When serious deficiencies in internal control are discovered, the auditors should issue a _____ letter to the client.

(7) Tests designed to substantiate the fairness of a special financial statement item are termed _____ tests.

(8) If the auditors are to issue anything other than an _____ opinion of standard form, considerable care must go into the precise wording of the audit report.

2. Which information should be included in an engagement letter?

a. name of the client and its year-end date

b. financial statement to be examined and other reports to be prepared

c. the audit fee and the manner of payment

d. the type of opinion expected to be issued as a result of the audit work

e. the auditor's responsibility for the detection on errors and irregularities

f. obligations of the client's staff to prepare schedules and statements and assist in other aspects of the audit work.

g. identification of any limitations imposed by the client or the timing of the engagement that may affect the auditor's ability to gather sufficient competent evidential matter in support of the financial statements

3. Please give out the correct order of an audit process.

a. to evaluate the effectives of the system of internal control in preventing material errors in the financial statements

b. to conduct comprehensive testes to substantiate specific account balances and perform other auditing procedures

c. to review the client's system of internal control, and prepare a description of the system in the audit working papers

d. to form an opinion and issue the audit report

e. to prepare a report to management containing recommendations for improving the system of internal control

f. to conduct tests to determine the reliabilities of the key internal control procedures

Section 3

1. Supply the missing information in the following statements.

(1) The standard report consists of a scope paragraph and an _____ paragraph.

(2) There are four types of audit reports. They are the unqualified opinion report, the qualified opinion report, the _____ opinion report and the _____ of opinion report.

(3) When a disclaimer of opinion is issued, the auditor's report must disclose all of the _____ reasons for the disclaimer.

2. Choose the best answer.

An auditor may issue _____ report when he or she has reached the following conclusions: 1) The financial statements present fairly overall financial position, results of operations, and changes in financial position in conformity with GAAP or other comprehensive basis of accounting. 2) GAAP or the other comprehensive basis of accounting applied on a basis consistent with that of the proceeding period. 3) The financial statements have adequate information disclosure.

    A. an unqualified opinion
    B. a qualified opinion
    C. an adverse opinion
    D. a disclaimer of opinion

3. Choose the best answer.

An auditor may issue _____ report when he or she has reached the conclusion that the financial statements present fairly overall in conformity with GAAP or other comprehensive basis of accounting, but there is an exception regarding a material item: 1) The scope of the auditor's examination was restricted by the circumstances of the engagement, condition of the client's records, or other reasons. 2) There is material uncertainty regarding the statements. 3) Disclosure is lacking. 4) An accounting principle or the method of its application is not in conformity with GAAP. 5) Accounting principles followed in the current period are not consistent with those in the proceeding period.

    A. an unqualified opinion
    B. a qualified opinion
    C. an adverse opinion
    D. a disclaimer of opinion

4. Choose the best answer.

When the restriction on the auditor's ability to gather evidence is so pervasive that the auditor can't support an overall opinion on the financial statements, _____ is issued.

    A. an unqualified opinion
    B. a qualified opinion
    C. an adverse opinion
    D. a disclaimer of opinion

5. Choose the best answer.

_____ is issued for scope restriction relating to a material item which is not so pervasive as to impair the ability to issue an overall opinion on the financial statements.

    A. An unqualified opinion
    B. A qualified opinion
    C. An adverse opinion
    D. A disclaimer of opinion

6. Choose the best answer.

Which of the following reasons can make an auditor issue a disclaimer of opinion? _____

A. The auditor is unable to apply procedures deemed necessary in an audit engagement and the effect is so pervasive that a qualified opinion is not appropriate.

B. An uncertainty regarding the financial statements is so pervasive that a qualified opinion is not appropriate.

C. The auditor has not audited the financial statements.

D. The financial statements have adequate information disclosure.

参考译文

第一节 现代审计介绍

1. 现代审计的定义

现代审计是客观地获取和评价对经济行为或事项所陈述的证据，并将结果传递给有关使用者的一种系统的程序，其目的在于确定这些陈述与公认标准之间的吻合程度，并将结果传递给有利益关系的使用者。

现代审计的定义包含三方面内容。

首先，审计是一种以逻辑和推理为依据的系统程序。

其次，在审查财务报表过程中，审计师客观地获取和评价陈述的证据，来确定这些陈述与公认标准之间的吻合程度。在对公司所编制的财务报表的审计中，这些公认标准就是公认会计原则。

第三，这个定义的关键方面是，审计要向有利益关系的使用者传递审计结果。审计师通过签发报告来传递审计过程中发现的情况，在审计报告中，审计师应表达出自己的观点，即这些陈述是否按公认标准进行报告。

审计目标因审计报告使用者的不同需求而不同。内部审计、外部审计和政府审计服务于不同的目标。

2. 内部审计

内部审计是指某一组织内部所设立的用以审计和评价其活动，进而作为向该组织提供服务的独立评价职能。内部审计的目的在于，通过向该组织的成员提供对所审查活动的分析、评价、建议、咨询和信息，来帮助他们有效地履行其职责。

3. 外部审计

外部审计是指管理当局向外部使用者或第三方当事人编制有关财务报表的报告。第三方当事人包括股东、债权人、银行家、潜在的投资者以及联邦州和地方立法机构。外部审计有独立的会计师事务所执行，独立性是外部审计的根基。

4. 政府审计

政府审计涉及联邦政府、州政府和地方政府以及许许多多的管理机构的一系列广泛活动。政府审计师不仅审查财务报表，并且审查政府计划的目标是否达到，政府机构和民间企业是否遵守适用的法律和规章制度。

5. 审计的原因

经济主体基于不同的原因接受独立的注册会计师的审计。经济主体要求审计，是由于法律的要求。由证券交易委员会管理的公司必须接受年度的独立会计审计。不参与管理的业主权是要求审计的另一个原因。股东希望进行审计，以确定管理当局对他们的资产的经管责任。

有些银行发放贷款前也要求企业提供审计后的财务报表。当企业考虑兼并或出售时，为了恰当地确定企业的财务状况，审计也是必需的。

停业或合伙人的死亡往往也要求审计，以便根据合伙协议分配资产。同样，有些供应商在为其出售的商品提供巨额赊账时，也要求提供经过审计的财务报表。同时，如果雇员和管理当局知道他们将受到审计，可能有助于他们防止和发现错误或不法行为，所以，审计还有防患于未然的作用。

第二节　审计的程序

依据主体的需求，注册会计师事务所会审计该主体的会计记录、内部控制系统和上一年的审计报告。如果原来有过审计，必须依据审计准则委员会发布的《第七号审计准则》向前任审计师进行查询。

1. 两种查询

查询基本上有两种。第一，后继审计师向前任审计师进行查询，以便决定是否接受委托。因此，后继审计师要向前任审计师查询该主体管理当局的诚实性以及更换审计师的原因。第二，如果后继审计师决定接受委托，他或她会向前任审计师查询诸如初期账户余额等问题，以便于进行此次审计。

2. 委托书

一旦客户委托某注册会计师事务所进行审计，该注册会计师事务所就会发出一份确定审计事宜的委托书。获得一份由委托人的最高经理人和主要财务负责人签名的委托书是十分重要的，因为这份委托书将成为说明审计师与委托人双方责任的一项审计契约。

委托书应当包括以下内容：

(1) 委托人名称及其会计年度截止日。

(2) 需要审查的财务报表以及需要编制的其他报告。

(3) 说明由于委托人或委托上的时间安排所造成的可能影响审计师搜集足够充分的证据，以证明财务报表公允性的能力的所有限制条件。

(4) 为审计结果而发表的意见书预计将属于什么种类。

(5) 审计师在发现错误和不法行为方面的责任。

(6) 需由委托人的职员编制附表和报表并协助其他审计工作的义务。

(7) 审计费用和付款方式。

3. 审计程序

接到委托书后，审计师将开始进行以下审计程序：

(1) 审查委托人的内部控制系统，并在审计工作底稿中编制对这一系统的说明书。按照逻辑，审查委托人的内部控制系统是每项审计委托业务的第一个步骤，从性质、范围和时间安排方面来讲，为某项委托而开展的审计工作，在很大程度上取决于委托人的内部控制系统对于防止财务报表出现重大错误方面的有效程度。审计师在评价内部控制系统的有效性之前，必须了解并掌握它是如何运行的。

(2) 进行审计测试，借以确定关键性内部控制程序的可靠性。为了确定关键的内部控制程序在整个审计期间是否有效运行而进行的审计测试，称作符合性测试。符合性测试衡量特定控制程序的有效性，却并不对账户的金额加以验证。这一步骤的检验实际上是符合性测试。

(3) 评价内部控制系统在防止财务报表出现重大错误方面的有效性。内部控制的一个主要目标是提供精确可靠的会计数据。会计师应当对内部控制的薄弱环节进行深入细致的调查，然而他们也有正当理由在内部控制较为扎实的方面开展不那么细致的审计工作。以内部控制的评价为基础来确定审计期间的侧重点这一程序，意味着审计师将通过在某些方面缩小审计程序，相应地制定其审计计划。

(4) 向管理当局编送有关改进内部控制系统的建议报告。当发现管理内部控制系统存在着严重缺陷时，审计师应当向委托人提交一份关于克服这些缺陷的建议书。这份建议书不仅向委托人提供了改进内部控制的宝贵建议，而且也有助于在事后发现重大的盗用公款或其他严重损失的事件时，尽可能减少审计师的责任。

(5) 进行综合测试，借以验证特定账户余额并实施其他审计程序。为验证财务报表的公允性而进行的测试，可称作实质性测试。实质性测试包括应收账的询证、存货实物盘点的监盘和对包括在审计年度的交易进行适当的截止划分。除了进行实质性测试外，审计师在完成现场工作之前，还必须完成其他审计程序，比如调查可能需要特别披露的当事人的交易。

(6) 形成审计意见并签发审计报告。由于审计报告代表着注册会计师事务所承担的相当大的责任，合伙人必须首先检查该项审计委托的工作底稿，以确保全面的审查已经完成，并对财务报表发表意见。如果审计师要签发的意见书是标准格式的无保留意见书,必须对审计报告的精确措辞加以斟酌,所以审计报告通常是在完成现场工作的一周后甚至更晚时候才签发。

第三节 审计报告

标准审计报告由范围段落和意见段落组成。范围段落是对审计师所开展工作的描述,具体地说明所审查的报表及其时段。而意见段落则表述了审计师对这些报表的意见。有时,一些特殊的情况要求审计师的报告背离标准的短式报告,这类报告通常包含三个段落。第一个段落表明审计师的审查范围,第二个段落解释审计师背离标准报告的原因,第三个段落发表审计师的意见或放弃发表意见的原因。长式审计报告通常也包含范围段落和意见段落,然而这种报告还包含对管理当局或债权人有所帮助的分析。

在某些特定条件下,审计师可能出具四种类型的审计报告。它们分别是无保留意见报告、保留意见报告、否定意见报告和放弃发表意见报告。

1. 无保留意见报告

当会计师根据公认会计原则对财务报表进行审查并得出下列结论时,他或她会出具无保留意见审计报告。

(1) 财务报表公允地反映年公司的财务状况、经营成果及财务状况的变动情况,符合《公认会计原则》或其他的会计综合基础。

(2)《公认会计原则》或其他的会计综合基础是在与前期保持一致的基础上应用的。

(3) 财务报表具有充分的信息揭示。

2. 保留意见报告

当会计师遵照适用于财务报表审查的公认审计准则,得出财务报表在整体上做了公允的表述,并且符合《公认会计原则》或其他会计综合基础的结论,但在某个重大项目上存在着例外的情况时,他或她会出具保留意见报告。

(1) 审计师的审查范围受到委托书条件、委托人的会计记录条件或其他原因的限制。

(2) 报表上存在着某种很大的不确定性。

(3) 揭示不齐全。

(4) 某项会计原则或其应用方法不符合《公认会计原则》。

(5) 本期所遵循的会计原则未能与前期保持一致。

3. 否定意见报告

否定意见报告说明财务报表作为一个整体未能做到公允反映。出具否定意见书是十分罕见的,通常审计师和委托人通过仲裁便能够解决可能导致否定意见的会计问题。审计师必须按照公认审计准则对财务报表进行审查,才能发表这种意见。否定意见可能由于在应用会计计量或揭示原则时缺乏公允性。审计师的报告必须说明发表这种意见的实质性原因。

4．放弃发表意见报告

如果审计师搜集证据的能力受到普遍限制，以致无法为发表对财务报表的整体意见提供证据时，他放弃发表意见就是正当的。在放弃发表意见的报告中，审计师必须披露放弃发表意见的所有实质性原因。审计师放弃发表意见可能由于以下原因：

(1) 审计师未能实施审计委托书中所阐明的程序，而且其影响甚广，以致不便出具保留意见书。

(2) 有关财务报表的不确定性甚广，以致不便出具保留意见书。

(3) 审计师未能对财务报表进行审计。

附录 A 常用词汇汇编

一、常用会计词汇大全

1. 会计与会计理论涉及英语词汇

会计 accounting
决策人 decision maker
投资人 investor
股东 shareholder
债权人 creditor
财务会计 financial accounting
管理会计 management accounting
成本会计 cost accounting
私业会计 private accounting
公众会计 public accounting
注册会计师 Certified Public Accountant(CPA)
国际会计准则委员会 IASC
美国注册会计师协会 AICPA
财务会计准则委员会 FASB
管理会计协会 IMA
美国会计学会 AAA
税务稽核署 IRS
独资企业 proprietorship
合伙人企业 partnership
公司 corporation
会计目标 accounting objectives
会计假设 accounting assumptions
会计要素 accounting elements
会计原则 accounting principles
会计实务过程 accounting procedures
财务报表 financial statements
财务分析 financial analysis
会计主体假设 separate-entity assumption
货币计量假设 unit-of-measure assumption

持续经营假设 continuity(going-concern) assumption
会计分期假设 time-period assumption
资产 asset
负债 liability
业主权益 owner's equity
收入 revenue
费用 expense
收益 income
亏损 loss
历史成本原则 cost principle
收入实现原则 revenue principle
配比原则 matching principle
全面披露原则 full-disclosure (reporting) principle
客观性原则 objective principle
一致性原则 consistent principle
可比性原则 comparability principle
重大性原则 materiality principle
稳健性原则 conservatism principle
权责发生制 accrual basis
现金收付制 cash basis
财务报告 financial report
流动资产 current assets
流动负债 current liabilities
长期负债 long-term liabilities
投入资本 contributed capital
留存收益 retained earning

2. 会计循环涉及英语词汇

会计循环 accounting procedure/cycle
会计信息系统 accounting information system
账户 ledger
会计科目 account
会计分录 entry
原始凭证 source document
日记账 journal
总分类账 general ledger
明细分类账 subsidiary ledger

试算平衡 trial balance
现金收款日记账 cash receipt journal
现金付款日记账 cash disbursements journal
销售日记账 sales journal
购货日记账 purchase journal
普通日记账 general journal
工作底稿 worksheet
调整分录 adjusting entries
结账 closing entries

3．现金与应收账款涉及英语词汇

现金 cash
银行存款 cash in bank
库存现金 cash on hand
流动资产 current assets
偿债基金 sinking fund
定额备用金 imprest petty cash
支票 check (cheque)
银行对账单 bank statement
银行存款调节表 bank reconciliation statement
在途存款 outstanding deposit
在途支票 outstanding check
应付凭单 vouchers payable
应收账款 accounts receivable
应收票据 notes receivable
起运点交货价 F.O.B shipping point
目的地交货价 F.O.B destination point
商业折扣 trade discount
现金折扣 cash discount
销售退回及折让 sales return and allowance
坏账费用 bad debt expense
备抵法 allowance method
备抵坏账 bad debt allowance
损益表法 income statement approach
资产负债表法 balance sheet approach
账龄分析法 aging analysis method
直接冲销法 direct write-off method

带息票据 interest bearing note
不带息票据 non-interest bearing note
出票人 maker
收款人 payee
本金 principal
利息率 interest rate
到期日 maturity date
本票 promissory note
贴现 discount
背书 endorse
拒付费 protest fee

4．存货涉及英语词汇

存货 inventory
商品存货 merchandise inventory
产成品存货 finished goods inventory
在产品存货 work in process inventory
原材料存货 raw materials inventory
起运地离岸价格 F.O.B shipping point
目的地抵岸价格 F.O.B destination
寄销 consignment
寄销人 consignor
承销人 consignee
定期盘存 periodic inventory
永续盘存 perpetual inventory
购货 purchase
购货折让和折扣 purchase allowance and discounts
存货盈余或短缺 inventory overages and shortages
分批认定法 specific identification
加权平均法 weighted average
先进先出法 first-in, first-out or FIFO
后进先出法 last-in, first-out or LIFO
移动平均法 moving average
成本或市价孰低法 lower of cost or market(LCM)
市价 market value
重置成本 replacement cost
可变现净值 net realizable value

上限 upper limit
下限 lower limit
毛利法 gross margin method
零售价格法 retail method
成本率 cost ratio

5．长期投资涉及英语词汇

长期投资 long-term investment
长期股票投资 investment on stocks
长期债券投资 investment on bonds
成本法 cost method
权益法 equity method
合并法 consolidation method
股利宣布日 declaration date
股权登记日 date of record
除息日 ex-dividend date
付息日 payment date
债券面值 face value, par value
债券折价 discount on bonds
债券溢价 premium on bonds
票面利率 contract interest rate, stated rate
市场利率 market interest ratio, effective rate
普通股 common stock
优先股 preferred stock
现金股利 cash dividends
股票股利 stock dividends
清算股利 liquidating dividends
到期日 maturity date
到期值 maturity value
直线摊销法 straight-Line method of amortization
实际利息摊销法 effective-interest method of amortization

6．固定资产涉及英语词汇

固定资产 plant assets or fixed assets
原值 original value
预计使用年限 expected useful life
预计残值 estimated residual value
折旧费用 depreciation expense

累计折旧 accumulated depreciation
账面价值 carrying value
应提折旧成本 depreciation cost
净值 net value
在建工程 construction-in-process
磨损 wear and tear
过时 obsolescence
直线法 straight-line method (SL)
工作量法 units-of-production method (UOP)
加速折旧法 accelerated depreciation method
双倍余额递减法 double-declining balance method (DDB)
年数总和法 sum-of-the-years-digits method (SYD)
以旧换新 trade in
经营租赁 operating lease
融资租赁 capital lease
廉价购买权 bargain purchase option (BPO)
资产负债表外筹资 off-balance-sheet financing
最低租赁付款额 minimum lease payments

7. 无形资产涉及英语词汇

无形资产 intangible assets
专利权 patents
商标权 trademarks, trade names
著作权 copyrights
特许权或专营权 franchises
商誉 goodwill
开办费 organization cost
租赁权 leasehold
摊销 amortization

8. 流动负债涉及英语词汇

负债 liability
流动负债 current liability
应付账款 account payable
应付票据 notes payable
贴现票据 discount notes
长期负债一年内到期部分 current maturities of long-term liabilities
应付股利 dividends payable

预收收益 prepayments by customers
存入保证金 refundable deposits
应付费用 accrual expense
增值税 value added tax
营业税 business tax
应付所得税 income tax payable
应付奖金 bonuses payable
产品质量担保负债 estimated liabilities under product warranties
赠品和兑换券 premiums, coupons and trading stamps
或有事项 contingency
或有负债 contingent
或有损失 loss contingencies
或有利得 gain contingencies
永久性差异 permanent difference
时间性差异 timing difference
应付税款法 taxes payable method
纳税影响会计法 tax effect accounting method
递延所得税负债法 deferred income tax liability method

9．长期负债涉及英语词汇

长期负债 long-term Liabilities
应付公司债券 bonds payable
有担保品的公司债券 secured bonds
抵押公司债券 mortgage bonds
保证公司债券 guaranteed bonds
信用公司债券 debenture bonds
一次还本公司债券 term bonds
分期还本公司债券 serial bonds
可转换公司债券 convertible bonds
可赎回公司债券 callable bonds
可要求公司债券 redeemable bonds
记名公司债券 registered bonds
无记名公司债券 coupon bonds
普通公司债券 ordinary bonds
收益公司债券 income bonds
名义利率，票面利率 nominal rate
实际利率 actual rate

有效利率 effective rate
溢价 premium
折价 discount
面值 par value
直线法 straight-line method
实际利率法 effective interest method
到期直接偿付 repayment at maturity
提前偿付 repayment at advance
偿债基金 sinking fund
长期应付票据 long-term notes payable
抵押借款 mortgage loan

10．财务报表涉及英语词汇

财务报表 financial statement
资产负债表 balance sheet
收益表 income statement
现金流量表 statement of cash flows
账户式 account form
报告式 report form
编制(报表) prepare
工作底稿 worksheet
多步式 multi-step
单步式 single-step
营运资金 working capital
全部资源概念 all-resources concept
直接交换业务 direct exchanges
正常营业活动 normal operating activities
财务活动 financing activities
投资活动 investing activities

11．财务报表分析涉及英语词汇

财务报表分析 analysis of financial statements
比较财务报表 comparative financial statements
趋势百分比 trend percentage
比率 ratios
普通股每股收益 earnings per share of common stock
股利收益率 dividend yield ratio
市盈率 price-earnings ratio(PE)

普通股每股账面价值 book value per share of common stock
资本报酬率 return on investment
总资产报酬率 return on total asset
债券收益率 yield rate on bonds
已获利息倍数 number of times interest earned
债券比率 debt ratio
优先股收益率 yield rate on preferred stock
营运资本 working capital
周转 turnover
存货周转率 inventory turnover
应收账款周转率 accounts receivable turnover
流动比率 current ratio
速动比率 quick ratio
酸性试验比率 acid test ratio

12．合并财务报表涉及英语词汇

合并财务报表 consolidated financial statements
吸收合并 merger
创立合并 consolidation
控股公司 parent company
附属公司 subsidiary company
少数股东权益 minority interest
权益联营合并 pooling of interest
购买合并 combination by purchase
权益法 equity method
成本法 cost method

13．物价变动中的会计计量涉及英语词汇

物价变动之会计 price-level changes accounting
一般物价水平会计 general price-level accounting
货币购买力会计 purchasing-power accounting
统一币值会计 constant dollar accounting
历史成本 historical cost
现行价值会计 current value accounting
现行成本 current cost
重置成本 replacement cost
物价指数 price-level index
国民生产总值物价指数 gross national product implicit price deflator (or GNP deflator)

消费物价指数 consumer price index (or CPI)
批发物价指数 wholesale price index
货币性资产 monetary assets
货币性负债 monetary liabilities
货币购买力损益 purchasing-power gains or losses
资产持有损益 holding gains or losses
未实现的资产持有损益 unrealized holding gains or losses
现行价值与统一币值会计 constant dollar and current cost accounting

二、财会常用职位

会计助理 accounting assistant
记账员 accounting clerk
会计部经理 accounting manager
会计部职员 accounting staff
会计主管 accounting supervisor
行政经理 administration manager
行政人员 administration staff
行政助理 administrative assistant
行政办事员 administrative clerk
广告工作人员 advertising staff
法律顾问 adviser
航空公司订座员 airlines sales representative
航空公司职员 airlines staff
应用工程师 application engineer
副经理 assistant manager
证券分析员 bond analyst
证券交易员 bond trader
业务主任 business controller
业务经理 business manager
采购员 buyer
出纳员 cashier
化学工程师 chemical engineer
土木工程师 civil engineer
文书打字兼秘书 clerk typist & secretary
职员/接待员 clerk/receptionist
计算机资料输入员 computer data input operator

计算机工程师 computer engineer
计算机处理操作员 computer processing operator
计算机系统部经理 computer system manager
广告文字撰稿人 copywriter
副总经理 deputy general manager
经济研究助理 economic research assistant
电气工程师 electrical engineer
工程技术员 engineering technician
英语教师 english instructor/teacher
外销部经理 export sales manager
外销部职员 export sales staff
外汇部职员 F.X. (foreign exchange)clerk
外汇部核算员 F.X. settlement clerk
财务主任 financial controller
财务报告人 financial reporter
财务经理 fund manager
审计长 general auditor
总经理助理 general manager assistant
总经理秘书 general manager's secretary
总经理 general manager/ president
计算机硬件工程师 hardware engineer
进口联络员 import liaison staff
进口部经理 import manager
保险公司理赔员 insurance actuary
国际销售员 international sales staff
口语翻译 interpreter
生产线主管 line supervisor
维修工程师 maintenance engineer
管理顾问 management consultant
公关部经理 manager for public relations
经理 manager
制造工程师 manufacturing engineer
生产员工 manufacturing worker
市场分析员 market analyst
市场开发部经理 market development manager
销售助理 marketing assistant
销售主管 marketing executive

市场销售部经理 marketing manager
市场调研部经理 marketing representative manager
销售代表 marketing representative
市场销售员 marketing staff
机械工程师 mechanical engineer
采矿工程师 mining engineer
音乐教师 music teacher
造船工程师 naval architect

三、常用银行英语词汇

账目编号 account number
存户 depositor
存款单 pay-in slip
存款单 a deposit form
自动存取机 a banding machine
存款 deposit
存款收据 deposit receipt
私人存款 private deposits
存单 certificate of deposit
存折 deposit book, passbook
信用卡 credit card
本金 principal
透支 overdraft, overdraw
双签 counter sign
背书 endorse
背书人 endorser
兑现 cash
兑付 honor a cheque
拒付 dishonor a cheque
止付 suspend payment
支票 cheque, check
支票本 cheque book
记名支票 order cheque
不记名支票 bearer cheque
横线支票 crossed cheque
空白支票 blank cheque

空头支票 rubber cheque
票根 cheque stub, counterfoil
现金支票 cash cheque
旅行支票 traveler's cheque
转账支票 cheque for transfer
未付支票 outstanding cheque
已付支票 canceled cheque
伪支票 forged cheque
银行家 banker
行长 president
储蓄银行 savings bank
大通银行 Chase Bank
花旗银行 National City Bank of New York
汇丰银行 Hongkong Shanghai Banking Corporation
麦加利银行 Chartered Bank of India, Australia and China
东方汇理银行 Banque de I'IndoChine
中央银行 central bank, national bank, banker's bank
发行币银行 bank of issue, bank of circulation
商业银行，储蓄信贷银行 commercial bank
储蓄信贷银行 member bank, credit bank
贴现银行 discount bank
汇兑银行 exchange bank
委托开证银行 requesting bank
开证银行 issuing bank, opening bank
通知银行 advising bank, notifying bank
议付银行 negotiation bank
保兑银行 confirming bank
付款银行 paying bank
代收银行 associate banker of collection
委托银行 consigned banker of collection
清算银行 clearing bank
本地银行 local bank
国内银行 domestic bank
国外银行 overseas bank
钱庄 unincorporated bank
银行分行 branch bank

信托储蓄银行 trustee savings bank
信托公司 trust company
金融信托公司 financial trust
信托投资公司 unit trust
银行的信托部 trust institution
银行的信用部 credit department
商业信贷公司(贴现公司) commercial credit company(discount company)
街道储蓄所 neighborhood savings bank, bank of deposit
合作银行 credit union
商业兴信所 credit bureau
无人银行 self-service bank
建设银行 construction bank
工商银行 industrial and commercial bank
交通银行 bank of communications
互助储蓄银行 mutual savings bank
邮局储蓄银行 post office savings bank
抵押银行 mortgage bank, building society
实业银行 industrial bank
家宅贷款银行 home loan bank
储备银行 reserve bank
特许银行 chartered bank
往来银行 corresponding bank
承兑银行 merchant bank, accepting bank
投资银行 investment bank
进出口银行 import and export bank (EXIMBANK)
合资银行 joint venture bank
钱庄 money shop, native bank
信用社 credit cooperatives
票据交换所 clearing house
公共会计 public accounting
商业会计 business accounting
成本会计 cost accounting
折旧会计 depreciation accounting
电脑化会计 computerized accounting
总账 general ledger
分户账 subsidiary ledger
现金出纳账 cash book

现金账 cash account
日记账，流水账 journal, day-book
坏账 bad debts
投资 investment
结余 surplus
游资 idle capital
经济周期 economic cycle
经济繁荣 economic boom
经济衰退 economic recession
经济萧条 economic depression
经济危机 economic crisis
经济复苏 economic recovery
通货膨胀 inflation
通货紧缩 deflation
货币贬值 devaluation
货币增值 revaluation
国际收支 international balance of payment
顺差 favourable balance
逆差 adverse balance
硬通货 hard currency
软通货 soft currency
国际货币制度 international monetary system
货币购买力 the purchasing power of money
货币流通量 money in circulation
纸币发行量 note issue
国家预算 national budget
国民生产总值 national gross product
公债 public bond
股票 stock, share
债券 debenture
国库券 treasury bill
债务链 debt chain
直接(对角)套汇 direct exchange
间接(三角)套汇 indirect exchange
套汇汇率 cross rate, arbitrage rate
外汇储备 foreign currency (exchange) reserve
外汇波动 foreign exchange fluctuation

外汇危机 foreign exchange crisis
贴现 discount
贴现率 discount rate, bank rate
黄金储备 gold reserve
金融市场 money (financial) market
股票交易所 stock exchange
经纪人 broker
佣金 commission
簿记 bookkeeping
簿记员 bookkeeper
申请单 an application form
对账单 bank statement
信用证 letter of credit
保险库 strong room, vault
等价税则 equitable tax system
签字式样 specimen signature
营业时间 banking hours, business hours

四、常用外贸英语词汇

1. 货运用语

货物 goods/freight/cargo
运输 transportation/transit/conveyance
运送 transport/carry/convey
运输业 transportation business/forwarding business/carrying trade
运输代理人 a forwarding agent
承运人 a freight agent/a carrier
船务代理人 a shipping agent
陆上运输 transportation by land
海上运输 transportation by sea
货物运输 goods traffic/freight traffic/carriage of freights/carriage of goods
货轮 cargo boat/freighter/cargo steamer/cargo carrier
火车 goods-train/freight-train
卡车 goods-van/goods wagon/freight car/truck
货运办公室 goods-office/freight-department
运费率 freight/freight rates/goods rate
运费 carriage charges/shipping expenses/express charges

车费　cartage/portage
运费预付　carriage prepaid/carriage paid
运费到付　carriage forward/freight collect
运费免除/免费　carriage free
协定运费　conference freight/freight rate
运费清单　freight account
托运单　way-bill/invoice
运送契约　contract for carriage
装运　shipment/loading
装上货轮　ship/load/take on a ship
装运费　shipping charges/shipping commission
装运单/载货单　shipping invoice
装运单据　shipping documents
大副收据　mate's receipt
装船单　shipping order
提货单　delivery order
装船通知　shipping advice
包裹收据　parcel receipt
准装货单　shipping permit
租船契约　charter party
租船人　charterer
程租船/航次租赁　voyage charter
期租船　time charter
允许装卸时间　lay days/laying days
工作日　working days
连续天数　running days/consecutive days
滞期费　demurrage
滞期日数　demurrage days
速遣费　despatch money
空舱费　dead freight
退关　short shipment/goods short shipped/goods shut out/shut-outs
赔偿保证书(信托收据)　letter of indemnity/trust receipt
装载　loading
卸货　unloading/discharging/landing
装运质量　shipping weight/in-take-weight
卸货质量　landing weight

压舱 ballasting
压舱货 in ballast
舱单 manifest
船泊登记证书 ship's certificate of registry
航海日记 ship's log
船员名册 muster-roll
(船员，乘客)健康证明 bill of health
光票 clean bill
不清洁提单 foul bill
有疑问提单 suspected bill

2. 交货条件

交货 delivery
轮船 steamship(缩写 S.S)
装运，装船 shipment
租船 charter (the chartered ship)
交货时间 time of delivery
定程租船 voyage charter
装运期限 time of shipment
定期租船 time charter
托运人(一般指出口商) shipper, consignor
收货人 consignee
班轮 regular shipping liner
驳船 lighter
舱位 shipping space
油轮 tanker
报关 clearance of goods
陆运收据 cargo receipt
提货 take delivery of goods
空运提单 airway bill
正本提单 original B/L
选择港(任意港) optional port
选港费 optional charges
选港费由买方负担 optional charges to be borne by the buyers/optional charges for buyers' account
一月份装船 shipment during January / January shipment

一月底装船 shipment not later than Jan.31st./shipment on or before Jan.31st
一/二月份装船 shipment during Jan./Feb./Jan./Feb. shipment
在……(时间)分两批装船 shipment during...in two lots
在……(时间)平均分两批装船 shipment during...in two equal lots
分三个月装运 in three monthly shipments
分三个月，每月平均装运 in three equal monthly shipments
立即装运 immediate shipments
即期装运 prompt shipments
收到信用证后 30 天内装运 shipments within 30 days after receipt of L/C
允许分批装船 partial shipment not allowed/partial shipment not permitted/partial shipment not unacceptable

3．外贸价格术语

价格术语 trade term (price term)
运费 freight
单价 price
码头费 wharfage
总值 total value
卸货费 landing charges
金额 amount
关税 customs duty
净价 net price
印花税 stamp duty
含佣价 price including commission
港口税 portdues
回佣 return commission
装运港 port of shipment
折扣 discount / allowance
卸货港 port of discharge
批发价 wholesale price
目的港 port of destination
零售价 retail price
进口许可证 import license
现货价格 spot price
出口许可证 export license
期货价格 forward price

现行价格(时价)　current price
国际市场价格　world (international)market price
离岸价(船上交货价)　FOB-free on board
成本加运费价(离岸加运费价)　C&F-cost and freight
到岸价(成本加运费、保险费价)　CIF- cost, insurance and freight

附录 B 会计报表汇编

1. The Balance Sheet(资产负债表)

The balance sheet

Asset		Liabilities and Equity	
Cash		Liabilities	
Accounts receivable		Bank loan	
Notes receivable		Accounts payable	
Inventory		Notes payable	
Total current assets		Total current liabilities	
Long-term investments		Long-term liabilities	
Equipment		Total liabilities	
Automobiles		Equity：	
Less accumulated depreciation		Owner capital	
Total fixed assets		Total equity	
Total assets		Total liabilities and equity	

资产负债表

资　产		负债和所有者权益	
现金		负债	
应收账款		银行贷款	
应收票据		应付账款	
存货		应付票据	
流动资产合计		流动负债合计	
长期投资		长期负债	
设备		负债合计	
汽车		所有者权益：	
减：累计折旧		实收资本	
固定资产合计		所有者权益合计	
资产合计		负债和所有者权益合计	

Case for ××× Corporation

Balance Sheet for
××× Corporation

millions of dollars

Description	Annual Period 2001	Annual Period 2002	Annual Period 2003	Annual Period 2004	Annual Period 2005
Cash and Cash Equivalents	990	950	901	998	870
Short Term Marketable Securities	10	15	12	6	11
Accounts Receivable	1,020	1,550	1,830	2,250	3,040
Inventory	1,005	1,360	1,650	1,900	2,060
Other Current Assets	870	1,150	1,370	1,650	1,530
Total Current Assets	3,895	5,025	5,763	6,804	7,511
Fixed Assets	14,006	17,605	21,826	26,950	28,100
Accumulated Depreciation	−1,280	−1,700	−2,100	−2,550	−3,010
Net Fixed Assets	12,726	15,905	19,726	24,400	25,090
Long term Investments	360	320	120	590	905
Investments in Other Companies	65	0	0	250	412
Intangibles and Other Assets	100	110	105	135	195
Total Non Current Assets	13,251	16,335	19,951	25,375	26,602
Total Assets	17,146	21,360	25,714	32,179	34,113
Accounts Payable	2,050	3,150	3,290	3,870	4,800
Short Term Borrowings	1,200	1,830	2,580	3,100	3,550
Short Term Portion of LT Debt	12	15	25	30	36
Other Current Liabilities	1,050	1,250	1,480	1,590	1,301
Total Current Liabilities	4,312	6,245	7,375	8,590	9,687
Long term Debt / Borrowings	1,160	1,750	2,600	3,600	3,950
Other Long term Liabilities	650	750	701	890	995
Total Non Current Liabilities	1,810	2,500	3,301	4,490	4,945
Total Liabilities	6,122	8,745	10,676	13,080	14,632
Preferred Equity	0	0	0	0	0
Common Equity	2,044	2,005	2,069	2,090	2,120
Additional Paid in Capital	5,013	4,900	5,159	5,626	5,628

Case for ××× Corporation   (Continued)

Retained Earnings	5,097	7,050	9,840	15,050	20,005
Adj for Foreign Currency Transl	275	120	−550	−2,147	−6,722
Treasury Stock	−1,405	−1,460	−1,480	−1,520	−1,550
Total Shareholder Equity	11,024	12,615	15,038	19,099	19,481
Total Liabilities & Equity	17,146	21,360	25,714	32,179	34,113
Check: Assets = Liabilities + Equity?	0	0	0	0	0
Comment =>	Balances	Balances	Balances	Balances	Balances

2. Income Statement(利润表)

The Multiple-step Income Statement

ITEM	
Sales	
Cost of goods sold	
Gross profit	
Operating expenses:	
Depreciation expense	
Other operating expenses	
Total operating expenses	
Income from operations	
Other income:	
Gain on sale of land	
Other expense:	
Interest expense	
Income before income tax	
Income tax expense	
Net income	

多步式利润表

项　目	
销售收入	
销货成本	
毛利	
营业费用：	
折旧费用	
其他的营业费用	
总营业费用	

续表

项　目	
营业利润	
其他收益：	
销售土地收入	
其他的费用：	
利息费用	
所得税前利润	
所得税费用	
净利润	

The Single-step Income Statement

ITEM	
Sales	
Gain on sale of land	
Total revenues	
Expenses	
Cost of merchandise sold	
Depreciation expense	
Other operating expenses	
Interest expense	
Income tax expense	
Total expenses	
Net income	

单步式利润表

项　目	
销售收入	
销售土地收入	
总收入	
费用	
商品销售成本	
折旧费用	
其他的营业费用	
利息费用	
所得税费用	
总费用	
净利润	

Case for ××× Corporation

Income Statement for

××× Corporation

millions of dollars

Description	Annual Period 2001	Annual Period 2002	Annual Period 2003	Annual Period 2004	Annual Period 2005
Net Sales	12,060	16,700	21,170	24,700	27,400
Other Operating Revenues	16	19	26	37	48
Total Revenues	12,076	16,719	21,196	24,737	27,448
Cost of Goods Sold	−4,950	−7,050	−8,233	−9,050	−10,150
Other Operating Expenses	−11	−13	−17	−22	−28
Total Direct Expenses	−4,961	−7,063	−8,250	−9,072	−10,178
Selling, General & Administrative	−3,300	−3,880	−4,637	−5,670	−7,120
Operating Income	3,815	5,776	8,309	9,995	10,150
Interest Expenses	−117	−122	−216	−282	−304
Foreign Exchange (Loss) Gain	0	0	0	0	0
Associated Company (Loss) Gain	0	0	−22	0	0
Other Non Operating (Loss) Gain	0	17	0	0	0
Income Tax Expense	−790	−1,005	−2,050	−2,105	−2,660
Reserve Charges	0	0	0	0	0
Income Before Extra Ord Items	2,908	4,666	6,021	7,608	7,186
Extra Ordinary Items (Loss) Gain	0	0	0	0	0
Tax Effects of Extraordinary Items	0	0	0	0	0
Minority Interests	17	302	219	303	515
Net Income	2,925	4,968	6,240	7,911	7,701

3. The Cash Flow Statement (现金流量表)

The Cash Flow Statement

ITEM			
Cash flows from operating activities:			
Net income			
Add: Depreciation			
Decrease in inventories			
Increase in accrued expenses			

The Cash Flow Statement (Continued)

Deduct: Increase in account receivable			
Decrease in accounts payable			
Decrease in income tax payable			
Gain on sale of land			
Net cash flow from operating activities			
Cash flow from investing activities:			
Cash from sale of land			
Less: Cash paid to purchase land			
Cash paid for purchase of building			
Net cash flow from investing activities			
Cash flow from financing activities:			
Cash received from sale of common stock			
Less: Cash paid to retire bonds payable			
Cash paid to dividends			
Net cash flow from financing activities			
Increase in cash			
Cash at the beginning of the year			
Cash at the end of the year			

现金流量表

项 目			
经营活动的现金流量：			
净利润			
加：折旧			
存货的减少			
应计费用的增加			
减：应收账款的增加			
应付账款的减少			
应付所得税的减少			
销售土地收入			
经营活动的净现金流量			
投资活动的现金流量：			
销售土地的现金			
减：购买土地的现金			
购买房屋建筑物的现金			

投资活动的净现金流量					
筹资活动的现金流量：					
普通股股东投入的现金					
减：现金支付的债券利息					
现金支付的股利					
筹资活动的净现金流量					
现金流量净增加额					
年初现金流量					
年末现金流量					

Case for ×××Corporation

Cash Flow Statement for
××× Corporation

millions of dollars

Description	Annual Period 2001	Annual Period 2002	Annual Period 2003	Annual Period 2004	Annual Period 2005
Net Income	2,925	4,968	6,240	7,911	7,701
Depreciation and Amortization	310	420	400	450	460
(Increase) Decrease Defer Taxes	−2	11	11	−8	−11
(Gain) Loss on Sale of Assets	−55	0	45	0	0
(Increase) Decrease Current Assets	−162	−1,130	−738	−1,041	−707
Increase (Decrease) Current Liab	206	1,933	1,130	1,215	1,097
Cash Flow from Operations	3,222	6,202	7,088	8,527	8,540
Capital Expenditures	−1,455	−2,750	−3,880	−5,220	−4,108
Acquisition in Other Co's	−135	0	0	0	0
Proceeds from Sales of Assets	112	35	0	150	182
Purchases of Investments	−712	−1,979	−1,801	−2,314	−2,609
Sale of Investments	162	129	330	221	50
Other Investment Activities	33	−166	61	−12	0
Cash Provided (Used) from Investments	−1,995	−4,731	−5,290	−7,175	−6,485
Proceeds from Borrowings	1,070	1,044	1,460	1,880	1,105
Payments on Borrowings	−1,112	−650	−898	−801	−961
Dividends Paid to Shareholders	−1,330	−1,918	−2,461	−2,354	−2,329
Proceeds from Minority Interest	5	12	7	7	8
Issue Stock / Exercise Options	195	1	45	13	6

Case for ×× × Corporation(Continued)

Purchase / Retire Common Stock	0	0	0	0	0
Other Financing Activities	−75	0	0	0	−12
Cash Provided (Used) from Financing	−1,247	−1,511	−1,847	−1,255	−2,183
Increase (Decrease) to Cash	−20	−40	−49	97	−128
Beginning Cash Balance	1,010	990	950	901	998
Ending Cash Balance	990	950	901	998	870
Check: Should agree to Balance Sheet	0	0	0	0	0
Comment =>	Balances	Balances	Balances	Balances	Balances

4. Statement of Marketing Expenses (销售费用明细表)

STATEMENT OF MARKETING EXPENSES

STATEMENT OF MARKETING EXPENSES			FROM AJI-02	
For the year ended JULY.31,2006			MONETARY UNIT:YUAN	
ITEM	LINE NO.	THIS YEAR'S PLAN	THIS MONTH'S ACTUAL	LAST YEAR'S ACTUAL
Salaries and wages				
Depreciation				
Repairs				
Supplies consumed				
Amortization of low				
Cost and short lived articles				
Office expenses				
Travelling				
Commission				
Consignment handing fee				
Transportation				
Loading and unloading				
Packaging				
Insurance				
Advertising				
Rental				
Sales service fee				
Micellaneous				
TOTAL				

销售费用明细表

销售费用明细表			会外工 02 表附表 5	
			单位：元	
项 目	行 次	本年计划	本月实际	上年实际
工资				
折旧费				
修理费				
物料消耗				
低值易耗品摊销				
办公费				
差旅费				
销售佣金				
代销手续费				
运输费				
装卸费				
包装费				
保险费				
广告费				
租赁费				
销售服务费				
其他				
合计				

5. Statement of Profit Appropiation (利润分配表)

STATEMENT OF PROFIT APPROPIATION

STATEMENT OF PROFIT APPROPIATION		FROM AJI-02	
For the year ended DEC.31,2006		MONETARY UNIT:YUAN	
ITEM	LINE NO.	THIS YEAR'S ACTUAL	LAST YEAR'S ACTUAL
Net income			
Less：Staff and workers'bonus and welfare fund			
Reserve fund			
Enterprise expantion fund			
Profit reinvestment			
Add：Undistributable profits at beginning of year			
Recovery accumulated losses			

Statement of Profit Appropiation (Continued)

Profit available for distribution to owners			
Less: Dividends declared			
Including: Chinese investment			
Foreign investment			
Profits capitalized on return of investment			
Undistributed profits at end of year			

利润分配表　　　　　　　　　　　　　　　　　　　元

项　目	行　次	本年实际	上年实际
净利润			
减：职工奖励及福利基金			
储备基金：			
企业发展基金			
利润转作投资			
加：年初未分配利润			
已弥补亏损			
可供分配的利润			
减：已分配股利			
其中：中方股利			
外方股利			
利润归还投资			
年末未分配利润			

6. Statement of General and Administrative Expenses (管理费用明细表)

STATEMENT OF GENERAL AND ADMINISTRATIVE EXPENSES

STATEMENT OF GENERAL AND ADMINISTRATIVE EXPENSES			FROM AJI-02	
For the year ended JULY.31,2006			MONETARY UNIT: YUAN	
ITEM	LINE NO.	THIS YEAR'S PLAN	THIS MONTH'S ACTUAL	LAST YEAR'S ACTUAL
Company expenses				
Including: Salaries and wages				
Depreciation				
Repairs				
Supplies consumed				

Statement of General and Administrative Expenses (Continued)

STATEMENT OF GENERAL AND ADMINISTRATIVE EXPENSES For the year ended JULY.31,2006			FROM AJI-02 MONETARY UNIT: YUAN	
ITEM	LINE NO.	THIS YEAR'S PLAN	THIS MONTH'S ACTUAL	LAST YEAR'S ACTUAL
Amortization of low value articles				
Labor protection				
Office expenses				
Travelling				
Transportation				
Insurance				
Taxi expenses				
Labor union dues				
Board of directors' expenses				
Consulting fees				
Litigation fees				
Entertainment fees				
Taxes				
Land occupancy fees				
Technology transfer fee				
Amortization of intangible assets				
Amortization of other assets				
Staff and workers' training expenses				
Research and development expenses				
Bad debts				
Inventory shortage(less overage)				
Delegates Expenses				
Gasoline				
Communication Expenses				
Others				
TOTAL				

管理费用明细表

管理费用明细表			会外工 02 表附表	
年 月 日			单位：元	
项 目	行 次	本年计划	本月实际	上年实际
公司经费				
其中：工资				
折旧费				
修理费				
物料损耗				
低值易耗品摊销				
劳动保护费				
办公费				
差旅费				
运输费				
保险费				
交通费				
工会经费				
董事会费				
顾问费				
诉讼费				
交际应酬费				
税金				
场地使用费				
技术转让费				
无形资产摊销				
其他资产摊销				
职工培训费				
研究开发费				
坏账损失				
存货盘亏(减盘盈)				
外籍人员费				
汽油				
通信费				
其他				
合计				

7. Statement of Manufacturing Expenses(制造费用明细表)

STATEMENT OF MANUFACTURING EXPENSES

STATEMENT OF MANUFACTURING EXPENSES		FROM AJI-02	
For the year ended JULY 31,2006		MONETARY UNIT：YUAN	
ITEM	LINE NO.	THIS YEAR'S PLAN	THIS MONTH'S ACTUAL	LAST YEAR'S ACTUAL
Salaries and wages				
Depreciation				
Repairs				
Supplies consumed				
Amortization of low				
Worker insurance expense				
Labor protection				
Water abdelectricity				
Office expenses				
Entertainment				
Travelling				
Transportation				
Insurance				
Rental				
Design and drawing				
Experiment and inspection				
Environment protecton				
20 Bar steam				
4 Bar steam				
Cooling water				
Nitrogen				
Compressed air				
Control air				
Process water				
Waste water				
Demineralized water				
Fuel gas				
Micellaneous				
TOTAL				

制造费用明细表

制造费用明细表				
年 月 日				单位：元
项目	行次	本年计划	本月实际	上年实际
工资				
折旧费				
修理费				
物料消耗				
低值易耗品摊销				
劳动保护费				
水电费				
办公费				
交际应酬费				
差旅费				
运输费				
保险费				
租赁费				
设计制图费				
试验检验费				
环境保护费				
蒸汽 2MPa				
蒸汽 0.4MPa				
循环水				
氮气				
压缩空气				
仪表空气				
沉淀水				
污水				
脱盐水				
煤气				
其他				
合计				

附录 C 财务比率术语英文详解

Accounts Payable/Sales: Accounts payable divided by annual sales, measuring the speed with which a company pays vendors relative to sales. Numbers higher than typical industry ratios suggest that the company is using suppliers to float operations.

Assets/Sales: Total assets divided by net sales, indicating whether a company is handling too high a volume of sales in relation to investment. Very low percentages relative to industry norms might indicate overly conservative sales efforts or poor sales management.

Current Liabilities/Inventory: Current liabilities divided by inventory: A high ratio, relative to industry norms, suggests over-reliance on unsold goods to finance operations.

Current Liabilities/Net Worth: Current liabilities divided by net worth, reflecting a level of security for creditors. The larger the ratio relative to industry norms, the less security there is for creditors.

Current Ratio: Current assets divided by current liabilities, measuring current assets available to cover current liabilities, a test of near-term solvency. The ratio indicates to what extent cash on hand and disposable assets are enough to pay off near term liabilities.

Fixed Assets/Net Worth: Fixed assets divided by net worth. High ratios relative to the industry can indicate low working capital or high levels of debt.

Gross Profit/Sales: Pre-tax profits divided by annual sales. This is the profit ratio before product and sales costs, as well as taxes. This ratio can indicate the "play" in other expenses which could be adjusted to increase the net profit margin.

Net Profit/Sales: After tax profits divided by annual sales. This is the key profit ratio, indicating how much is put in the company's pocket for each $100 of sales.

Quick Ratio: Cash plus accounts receivable, divided by current liabilities, indicating liquid assets available to cover current debt. Also known as the acid ratio. This is a harsher version of the current ratio, which balances short-term liabilities against cash and liquid instruments.

Return on Assets: Net after tax profit divided by total assets, a critical indicator of profitability. Companies which use their assets efficiently will tend to show a ratio higher than the industry norm.

Return on Net Worth: Net after tax profit divided by net worth, which is the "final measure" of profitability to evaluate overall return. This ratio measures return relative to investment in the company. Put another way, return on net worth indicates how well a company leverages the investment in it.

Return on Sales: Net after tax profit divided by annual net sales, indicating the level of profit from each dollar of sales. This ratio can be used as a predictor of the company's ability to withstand changes in prices or market conditions.

Sales/Inventory: Annual net sales divided by inventory value. This gives a picture of how quickly inventory turns over. Ratios below the industry norm suggest high levels of inventory. High ratios could indicate product levels insufficient to satisfy demand in a timely manner.

Sales/Net Working Capital: Sales divided by net working capital (current assets minus current liabilities). Ratios higher than industry norms may indicate a strain on available liquid assets, while low ratios may suggest too much liquidity.

Total Liabilities/Net Worth: Total liabilities divided by net worth. This ratio helps to clarify the impact of long-term debt, which can be seen by comparing this ratio with current liabilities: net worth.

附录 D 企业会计准则——基本准则中英文对照

Accounting Standard for Business Enterprises: Basic Standard

Chapter I General Provisions

Article 1 In accordance with The Accounting Law of the People's Republic of China and other relevant laws and regulations, this Standard is formulated to prescribe the recognition, measurement and reporting activities of enterprises for accounting purposes and to ensure the quality of accounting information.

Article 2 This Standard shall apply to enterprises (including companies) established within the People's Republic of China.

Article 3 Accounting Standards for Business Enterprises include the Basic Standard and Specific Standards. Specific Standards shall be formulated in accordance with this Standard.

Article 4 An enterprise shall prepare financial reports. The objective of financial reports is to provide accounting information about the financial position, operating results and cash flows, etc. of the enterprise to the users of the financial reports, in order to show results of the management's stewardship, and assist users of financial reports to make economic decisions.

Users of financial reports include investors, creditors, the government and its relevant departments as well as the public.

Article 5 An enterprise shall recognize, measure and report transactions or events that the enterprise itself has occurred.

Article 6 In performing recognition, measurement and reporting for accounting purposes, an enterprise shall be assumed to be a going concern.

Article 7 An enterprise shall close the accounts and prepare financial reports for each separate accounting period.

Accounting periods are divided into annual periods (yearly) and interim periods. An interim period is a reporting period shorter than a full accounting year.

Article 8 Accounting measurement shall be based on unit of currency.

Article 9 Recognition, measurement and reporting for accounting purposes shall be on an accrual basis.

Article 10 An enterprise shall determine the accounting elements based on the economic characteristics of the transactions or events. Accounting elements include assets, liabilities, owner's equity, revenue, expenses and profit.

Article 11 An enterprise shall apply the double entry method (i.e. debit and credit) for bookkeeping purposes.

Chapter 2 Qualitative Requirements of Accounting Information

Article 12 An enterprise shall recognize, measure and report for accounting purposes transactions or events that have actually occurred, to faithfully represent the accounting elements which satisfy recognition and measurement requirements and other relevant information, and ensure the accounting information is true, reliable and complete.

Article 13 Accounting information provided by an enterprise shall be relevant to the needs of the users of financial reports in making economic decisions, by helping them evaluate or forecast the past, present or future events of the enterprise.

Article 14 Accounting information provided by an enterprise shall be clear and explicable, so that it is readily understandable and useable to the users of financial reports.

Article 15 Accounting information provided by enterprises shall be comparable. An enterprise shall adopt consistent accounting policies for same or similar transactions or events that occurred in different periods and shall not change the policies arbitrarily. If a change is required or needed, details of the change shall be explained in the notes.

Different enterprises shall adopt prescribed accounting policies to account for same or similar transactions or events to ensure accounting information is comparable and prepared on a consistent basis.

Article 16 An enterprise shall recognize, measure and report transactions or events based on their substance, and not merely based on their legal form.

Article 17 Accounting information provided by an enterprise shall reflect all important transactions or events that relate to its financial position, operating result and cash flows.

Article 18 An enterprise shall exercise prudence in recognition, measurement and reporting of transactions or events. It shall not overstate assets or income nor understate liabilities or expenses.

Article 19 An enterprise shall recognize, measure and report transactions or events occurred in a timely manner and shall neither bring forward nor defer the accounting.

Chapter 3   Assets

Article 20   An asset is a resource that is owned or controlled by an enterprise as a result of past transactions or events and is expected to generate economic benefits to the enterprise.

"Past transactions or events" mentioned in preceding paragraph include acquisition, production, construction or other transactions or events. Transactions or events expected to occur in the future do not give rise to assets.

"Owned or controlled by an enterprise" is the right to enjoy the ownership of a particular resource or, although the enterprise may not have the ownership of a particular resource, it can control the resource.

"Expected to generate economic benefits to the enterprise" is the potential to bring inflows of cash and cash equivalents, directly or indirectly, to the enterprise.

Article 21   A resource that satisfies the definition of an asset set out in Article 20 in this standard shall be recognized as an asset when both of the following conditions are met:

(a) It is probable that the economic benefits associated with that resource will flow to the enterprise;

(b) The cost or value of that resource can be measured reliably.

Article 22   An item that satisfies the definition and recognition criteria of an asset shall be included in the balance sheet. An item that satisfies the definition of an asset but fails to meet the recognition criteria shall not be included in the balance sheet.

Chapter 4   Liabilities

Article 23   A liability is a present obligation arising from past transactions or events which are expected to give rise to an outflow of economic benefits from the enterprise. A present obligation is a duty committed by the enterprise under current circumstances. Obligations that will result from the occurrence of future transactions or events are not present obligations and shall not be recognized as liabilities.

Article 24   An obligation that satisfies the definition of a liability set out in Article23 in this standard shall be recognized as a liability when both of the following conditions are met:

(a) It is probable there will be an outflow of economic benefits associated with that obligation from the enterprise; and

(b) The amount of the outflow of economic benefits in the future can be measured reliably.

Article 25 An item that satisfies the definition and recognition criteria of a liability shall be included in the balance sheet. An item that satisfies the definition of a liability but fails to meet the recognition criteria shall not be included in the balance sheet.

Chapter 5 Owner's Equity

Article 26 Owner's equity is the residual interest in the assets of an enterprise after deducting all its liabilities.

Owner's equity of a company is also known as shareholders' equity.

Article 27 Owner's equity comprises capital contributed by owners, gains and losses directly recognized in owner's equity, retained earnings, etc. Gains and losses directly recognized in owner's equity are those gains or losses that shall not be recognized in profit or loss of the current period but will result in changes (increases or decreases) in owner's equity, other than those relating to contributions from, or appropriations of profit to, equity participants.

Gains are inflows of economic benefits that do not arise in the course of ordinary activities resulting in increases in owner's equity, other than those relating to contributions from owners.

Losses are outflows of economic benefits that do not arise in the course of ordinary activities resulting in decreases in owner's equity, other than those relating to appropriations of profit to owners.

Article 28 The amount of owner's equity is determined by the measurement of assets and liabilities.

Article 29 An item of owner's equity shall be included in the balance sheet.

Chapter 6 Revenue

Article 30 Revenue is the gross inflow of economic benefits derived from the course of ordinary activities that result in increases in equity, other than those relating to contributions from owners.

Article 31 Revenue is recognized only when it is probable that economic benefits will flow to the enterprise, which will result in an increase in assets or decrease in liabilities and the amount of the inflow of economic benefits can be measured reliably.

Article 32 An item that satisfies the definition and recognition criteria of revenue shall be included in the income statement.

Chapter 7 Expenses

Article 33 Expenses are the gross outflow of economic benefits resulted from the course of ordinary activities that result in decreases in owner's equity, other than those relating to appropriations of profits to owners.

Article 34 Expenses are recognized only when it is probable there will be outflow of economic benefits from the enterprise which result in a reduction of its assets or an increase in liabilities and the amount of the outflow of economic benefits can be measured reliably.

Article 35 Directly attributable costs, such as product costs, labour costs, etc. incurred by an enterprise in the process of production of goods or rendering of services shall be recognized as cost of goods sold or services provided and are charged to profit or loss in the period in which the revenue generated from the related products or services are recognized. Where an expenditure incurred does not generate economic benefits, or where the economic benefits derived from an expenditure do not satisfy, or cease to satisfy, the recognition criteria of an asset, the expenditure shall be expensed when incurred and included in profit or loss of the current period.

Transactions or events occurred which lead to the assumption of a liability without recognition of an asset shall be expensed when incurred and included in profit or loss of the current period.

Article 36 An item that satisfies the definition and recognition criteria of expenses shall be included in the income statement.

Chapter 8 Profit

Article 37 Profit is the operating result of an enterprise over a specific accounting period. Profit includes the net amount of revenue after deducting expenses, gains and losses directly recognized in profit of the current period, etc.

Article 38 Gains and losses directly recognized in profit of the current period are those gains and losses that shall be recognized in profit or loss directly which result in changes (increases or decreases) to owner's equity, other than those relating to contributions from, or appropriations of profit to, owners.

Article 39 The amount of profit is determined by the measurement of the amounts of revenue and expenses, gains and losses directly recognized in profit or loss in the current period.

Article 40 An item of profit shall be included in the income statement.

Chapter 9　Accounting Measurement

Article 41　In recording accounting elements that meet the recognition criteria in the accounting books and records and presenting them in the accounting statements and the notes (hereinafter together known as "financial statements"), an enterprise shall measure the accounting elements in accordance with the prescribed accounting measurement bases.

Article 42　Accounting measurement bases mainly comprise:

(1) Historical cost: Assets are recorded at the amount of cash or cash equivalents paid or the fair value of the consideration given to acquire them at the time of their acquisition. Liabilities are recorded at the amount of proceeds or assets received in exchange for the present obligation, or the amount payable under contract for assuming the present obligation, or at the amount of cash or cash equivalents expected to be paid to satisfy the liability in the normal course of business.

(2) Replacement cost: Assets are carried at the amount of cash or cash equivalents that would have to be paid if a same or similar asset was acquired currently. Liabilities are carried at the amount of cash or cash equivalents that would be currently required to settle the obligation.

(3) Net realizable value: Assets are carried at the amount of cash or cash equivalents that could be obtained by selling the asset in the ordinary course of business, less the estimated costs of completion, the estimated selling costs and related tax payments.

(4) Present value: Assets are carried at the present discounted value of the future net cash inflows that the item is expected to generate from its continuing use and ultimate disposal. Liabilities are carried at the present discounted value of the future net cash outflows that are expected to be required to settle the liabilities within the expected settlement period.

(5) Fair value: Assets and liabilities are carried at the amount for which an asset could be exchanged, or a liability settled, between knowledgeable, willing parties in an arm's length transaction.

Article 43　An enterprise shall generally adopt historical cost as the measurement basis for accounting elements. If the accounting elements are measured at replacement cost, net realizable value, present value or fair value, the enterprise shall ensure such amounts can be obtained and reliably measured.

Chapter 10　Financial Reports

Article 44　A financial report is a document published by an enterprise to provide accounting information to reflect its financial position on a specific date and its operating results and cash flows for a particular accounting period, etc. A financial report includes accounting statements and notes and other information or data that shall be disclosed in financial reports. Accounting statements shall at least comprise a balance sheet, an income statement and a cash flow statement.

A small enterprise need not include a cash flow statement when it prepares financial statements.

Article 45   A balance sheet is an accounting statement that reflects the financial position of an enterprise at a specific date.

Article 46   An income statement is an accounting statement that reflects the operating results of an enterprise for a certain accounting period.

Article 47   A cash flow statement is an accounting statement that reflects the inflows and outflows of cash and cash equivalents of an enterprise for a certain accounting period.

Article 48   Notes to the accounting statements are further explanations of items presented in the accounting statements, and explanations of items not presented in the accounting statements, etc.

Chapter 11   Supplementary Provisions

Article 49   The Ministry of Finance is responsible for the interpretation of this Standard.

Article 50   This Standard becomes effective as from January 1. 2007

参 考 译 文

企业会计准则——基本准则

第一章   总则

第一条   为了规范企业会计确认、计量和报告行为，保证会计信息质量，根据《中华人民共和国会计法》和其他有关法律、行政法规，制定本准则。

第二条   本准则适用于在中华人民共和国境内设立的企业(包括公司，下同)。

第三条   企业会计准则包括基本准则和具体准则，具体准则的制定应当遵循本准则。

第四条   企业应当编制财务会计报告(又称财务报告，下同)。财务会计报告的目标是向财务会计报告使用者提供与企业财务状况、经营成果和现金流量等有关的会计信息，反映企业管理层受托责任履行情况，有助于财务会计报告使用者作出经济决策。

财务会计报告使用者包括投资者、债权人、政府及其有关部门和社会公众等。

第五条　企业应当对其本身发生的交易或者事项进行会计确认、计量和报告。

第六条　企业会计确认、计量和报告应当以持续经营为前提。

第七条　企业应当划分会计期间，分期结算账目和编制财务会计报告。

会计期间分为年度和中期。中期是指短于一个完整的会计年度的报告期间。

第八条　企业会计应当以货币计量。

第九条　企业应当以权责发生制为基础进行会计确认、计量和报告。

第十条　企业应当按照交易或者事项的经济特征确定会计要素。会计要素包括资产、负债、所有者权益、收入、费用和利润。

第十一条　企业应当采用借贷记账法记账。

第二章　会计信息质量要求

第十二条　企业应当以实际发生的交易或者事项为依据进行会计确认、计量和报告，如实反映符合确认和计量要求的各项会计要素及其他相关信息，保证会计信息真实可靠、内容完整。

第十三条　企业提供的会计信息应当与财务会计报告使用者的经济决策需要相关，有助于财务会计报告使用者对企业过去、现在或者未来的情况作出评价或者预测。

第十四条　企业提供的会计信息应当清晰明了，便于财务会计报告使用者理解和使用。

第十五条　企业提供的会计信息应当具有可比性。

同一企业不同时期发生的相同或者相似的交易或者事项，应当采用一致的会计政策，不得随意变更。确需变更的，应当在附注中说明。

不同企业发生的相同或者相似的交易或者事项，应当采用规定的会计政策，确保会计信息口径一致、相互可比。

第十六条　企业应当按照交易或者事项的经济实质进行会计确认、计量和报告，不应仅以交易或者事项的法律形式为依据。

第十七条　企业提供的会计信息应当反映与企业财务状况、经营成果和现金流量等有关的所有重要交易或者事项。

第十八条　企业对交易或者事项进行会计确认、计量和报告应当保持应有的谨慎，不应高估资产或者收益、低估负债或者费用。

第十九条　企业对于已经发生的交易或者事项，应当及时进行会计确认、计量和报告，不得提前或者延后。

第三章　资产

第二十条　资产是指企业过去的交易或者事项形成的、由企业拥有或者控制的、预期会给企业带来经济利益的资源。

前款所指的企业过去的交易或者事项包括购买、生产、建造行为或其他交易或者事项。

预期在未来发生的交易或者事项不形成资产。

由企业拥有或者控制，是指企业享有某项资源的所有权，或者虽然不享有某项资源的所有权，但该资源能被企业所控制。

预期会给企业带来经济利益，是指直接或者间接导致现金和现金等价物流入企业的潜力。

第二十一条　符合本准则第二十条规定的资产定义的资源，在同时满足以下条件时，确认为资产：

(一)与该资源有关的经济利益很可能流入企业；

(二)该资源的成本或者价值能够可靠地计量。

第二十二条　符合资产定义和资产确认条件的项目，应当列入资产负债表；符合资产定义、但不符合资产确认条件的项目，不应当列入资产负债表。

第四章　负债

第二十三条　负债是指企业过去的交易或者事项形成的，预期会导致经济利益流出企业的现时义务。

现时义务是指企业在现行条件下已承担的义务。未来发生的交易或者事项形成的义务，不属于现时义务，不应当确认为负债。

第二十四条　符合本准则第二十三条规定的负债定义的义务，在同时满足以下条件时，确认为负债：

(一)与该义务有关的经济利益很可能流出企业；

(二)未来流出的经济利益的金额能够可靠地计量。

第二十五条　符合负债定义和负债确认条件的项目，应当列入资产负债表；符合负债定义，但不符合负债确认条件的项目，不应当列入资产负债表。

第五章　所有者权益

第二十六条　所有者权益是指企业资产扣除负债后由所有者享有的剩余权益。

公司的所有者权益又称为股东权益。

第二十七条　所有者权益的来源包括所有者投入的资本，直接计入所有者权益的利得和损失、留存收益等。

直接计入所有者权益的利得和损失，是指不应计入当期损益、会导致所有者权益发生增减变动的、与所有者投入资本或者向所有者分配利润无关的利得或者损失。

利得是指由企业非日常活动所形成的、会导致所有者权益增加的、与所有者投入资本无关的经济利益的流入。

损失是指由企业非日常活动所发生的、会导致所有者权益减少的、与向所有者分配利润无关的经济利益的流出。

第二十八条　所有者权益金额取决于资产和负债的计量。
第二十九条　所有者权益项目应当列入资产负债表。

第六章　收入

第三十条　收入是指企业在日常活动中形成的、会导致所有者权益增加的、与所有者投入资本无关的经济利益的总流入。

第三十一条　收入只有在经济利益很可能流入从而导致企业资产增加或者负债减少，且经济利益的流入额能够可靠计量时才能予以确认。

第三十二条　符合收入定义和收入确认条件的项目，应当列入利润表。

第七章　费用

第三十三条　费用是指企业在日常活动中发生的、会导致所有者权益减少的、与向所有者分配利润无关的经济利益的总流出。

第三十四条　费用只有在经济利益很可能流出从而导致企业资产减少或者负债增加，且经济利益的流出额能够可靠计量时才能予以确认。

第三十五条　企业为生产产品、提供劳务等发生的可归属于产品成本、劳务成本等的费用，应当在确认产品销售收入、劳务收入等时，将已销售产品、已提供劳务的成本等计入当期损益。

企业发生的支出不产生经济利益的，或者即使能够产生经济利益但不符合或者不再符合资产确认条件的，应当在发生时确认为费用，计入当期损益。

企业发生的交易或者事项导致其承担了一项负债而又不确认为一项资产的，应当在发生时确认为费用，计入当期损益。

第三十六条　符合费用定义和费用确认条件的项目，应当列入利润表。

第八章　利润

第三十七条　利润是指企业在一定会计期间的经营成果。利润包括收入减去费用后的净额、直接计入当期利润的利得和损失等。

第三十八条　直接计入当期利润的利得和损失，是指应当计入当期损益、会导致所有者权益发生增减变动的，与所有者投入资本或者向所有者分配利润无关的利得或者损失。

第三十九条　利润金额取决于收入和费用、直接计入当期利润的利得和损失金额的计量。

第四十条　利润项目应当列入利润表。

第九章 会计计量

第四十一条 企业在将符合确认条件的会计要素登记入账并列报于会计报表及其附注(又称财务报表，下同)时，应当按照规定的会计计量属性进行计量，确定其金额。

第四十二条 会计计量属性主要包括：

(一)历史成本。在历史成本计量下，资产按照购置时支付的现金或者现金等价物的金额，或者按照购置资产时所付出的对价的公允价值计量。负债按照因承担现时义务而实际收到的款项或者资产的金额，或者承担现时义务的合同金额，或者按照日常活动中为偿还负债预期需要支付的现金或者现金等价物的金额计量。

(二)重置成本。在重置成本计量下，资产按照现在购买相同或者相似资产所需支付的现金或者现金等价物的金额计量。负债按照现在偿付该项债务所需支付的现金或者现金等价物的金额计量。

(三)可变现净值。在可变现净值计量下，资产按照其正常对外销售所能收到现金或者现金等价物的金额扣减该资产至完工时估计将要发生的成本、估计的销售费用以及相关税费后的金额计量。

(四)现值。在现值计量下，资产按照预计从其持续使用和最终处置中所产生的未来净现金流入量的折现金额计量。负债按照预计期限内需要偿还的未来净现金流出量的折现金额计量。

(五)公允价值。在公允价值计量下，资产和负债按照在公平交易中，熟悉情况的交易双方自愿进行资产交换或者债务清偿的金额计量。

第四十三条 企业在对会计要素进行计量时，一般应当采用历史成本，采用重置成本、可变现净值、现值、公允价值计量的，应当保证所确定的会计要素金额能够取得并可靠计量。

第十章 财务会计报告

第四十四条 财务会计报告是指企业对外提供的反映企业某一特定日期的财务状况和某一会计期间的经营成果、现金流量等会计信息的文件。

财务会计报告包括会计报表及其附注和其他应当在财务会计报告中披露的相关信息和资料。会计报表至少应当包括资产负债表、利润表、现金流量表等报表。

小企业编制的会计报表可以不包括现金流量表。

第四十五条 资产负债表是指反映企业在某一特定日期的财务状况的会计报表。

第四十六条 利润表是指反映企业在一定会计期间的经营成果的会计报表。

第四十七条 现金流量表是指反映企业在一定会计期间的现金和现金等价物流入和流出的会计报表。

第四十八条 附注是指对在会计报表中列示项目所作的进一步说明，以及对未能在这

些报表中列示项目的说明等。

第十一章 附则

第四十九条 本准则由财政部负责解释。

第五十条 本准则自 2007 年 1 月 1 日起施行。

附录 E　原版英文求职信：应聘会计师事务所

WALTER C. WASHINGTON
_____

300 PORTER Way

Clearview, OR 13728

Home：(313)577-5512

OFFICE：(313)988-4432

August 19, 2005

Mr. Cleon C. Carter

Manager of Corporate Accounting

General Electronics Company

800 Cleveland Way

Greenville, NC 18472

Dear Mr. Carter,

　　I am writing to apply for the position of Cost Accountant in your Corporate Accounting Department. I feel that I have excellent qualifications for this position, and would appreciate your careful consideration of the enclosed resume.

　　A 1990 graduate of Villanova University with a B.S. in Accounting, I have over 7 years of employment in the Accounting profession. This includes some 4 years as an Auditor with Price Waterhouse and another 3 years as a Cost Accountant with the Burlington Corporation. I have received excellent professional training and, throughout my career, as copies of past performance evaluations will attest, I have consistently attained the highest ratings possible.

　　Current annual compensation is $65,000, and I would expect a competitive increase in keeping with my qualifications and experience level.

　　Although open to relocation, my preference is for the Southeast. Other locations may be of interest dependent upon the specifics of the opportunity.

　　If you feel that your Corporate Accounting Department could benefit from the Contributions of a seasoned, knowledgeable Cost Accountant, I would appreciate hearing from you. I can be reached during normal business hours at (418) 335-7335.

　　Thank you for your consideration, and I look forward to hearing from you.

Sincerely yours,

Walter C Washington

Enclosure

参考答案

Unit 1

Section 2 & Section 3

1. assets, liabilities, owner's equity, revenue, expenses, profits
2. debts
3. assets
4. revenue-producing
5. excess
6. assets, liabilities, owner's equity
7. left, right
8. debit, credit
9. debited
10. debits

Section 4

1. 3
2. 4, 5
3. 如下所示。

Accounts Payable	(202)
Accounts Receivable	(102)
Capital	(301)
Cash	(101)
Drawing	(302)
Equipment	(107)
Service Income	(401)
Miscellaneous Expense	(509)
Notes Payable	(201)
Rent Expense	(501)

4. 略。

Section 5

1. journal

2. special journal

3. adjusting and closing

4. NOT posted

5. 略。

6.

	Sales Journal	General Journal	Cash Journal	Purchases Journal
(a)	√			
(b)			√	
(c)			√	
(d)				√
(e)		√		

Unit 2

Section 2

1. (1)B (2)C (3)A (4)D   2. B   3. B   4. C   5. C

6.

Transaction 1

Assets	=	Liabilities	+	Owner's equity	Rev.	−	Exp.	=	Net Inc.	Cash Flow
(200)	=		+	(200)		−	200	=	(200)	

Transaction 2

Assets	=	Liabilities	+	Owner's equity	Rev.	−	Exp.	=	Net Inc.	Cash Flow
3,000	=		+	3,000	3,000	−		=	3,000	

Transaction 3

Assets	=	Liabilities	+	Owner's equity	Rev.	−	Exp.	=	Net Inc.	Cash Flow
(100)	=		+	(100)		−	(100)	=	100	

Assets		=	Liabilities	+	Owner's equity	Rev.	−	Exp.	=	Net Inc.	Cash Flow	
100	(100)	=		+			−		=		100	OA

Transaction 4

	Account titles	debit	credit
Transaction 1	Bad debts expense Allowance for bad debts	$200	$200
Transaction 2	Accounts receivable	$3,000	

265

	Sales revenue		$3,000
Transaction 3	Allowance for bad debts	$100	
	Bad debts expense		$100
	Cash	$100	
	Accounts receivable		$100
Transaction 4	Sales revenue	$3,000	
	Bad debts expense		$100
	Retained earnings		$2,900

Section 3

1. D   2. ending inventory =345.88   3. ending inventory =325   4. the cost of goods=254,000   5. B   6. B   7. B

Section 4

1. marketable securities   2. stock , debentures   3. 略。

Unit 3

Section 1

1. property, plant, equipment

2. land, offices, buildings, factories, warehouses

3. fixed assets, intangible assets, deferred assets

4. purchase, self-construction

5. cost

6. purchase price, related taxes, additional costs

7. delivery and handling costs, installation costs, professional fees

8. professional fees, building permit fee

9. fair value of the asset given up

10. abandoning costs

Section 2

1. depreciable amount

2. disposal of the asset

3. the straight-line method, the units of production method

4. The straight-line method

5. the units of production method

6. the original cost

7. The depreciation amount of these years are the same under the straight-line method, it is (36,000−2000)/5=6800 yuan

8. Step 1: (18,000−1,000)/250,000= ￥0.068/a hole

　　Step 2: Year 2001: 30,000×0.068=￥2,040

　　　　　Year 2002: 40,000×0.068=￥2,720

　　　　　Year 2003: 75,000×0.068=￥5,100

9.

Year	Original/￥	Beginning Accumulated Depreciation/￥	Beginning Book Value/￥	×	Double Straight-line Rate/%	=	Annual Depreciation Expense/￥
2001	12,000	0	12,000	×	40	=	4,800
2002	12,000	4,800	72,00	×	40	=	2,880
2003	12,000	7,680	4,320	×	40	=	1,728
2004	12,000	9,408	2,592	×	40	=	1,036.80
2005	12,000	10,444.80	1555.20			=	555.20
总计							11,000

10.

Year	Original Cost/￥	Depreciation Base/￥	×	Depreciation Fraction	=	Annual Depreciation Expense/￥
2005	68,000	68,000−5,000	×	6/21	=	18,000
2006	68,000	68,000−5,000	×	5/21	=	15,000
2007	68,000	68,000−5,000	×	4/21	=	12000
2008	68,000	68,000−5,000	×	3/21	=	9,000
2009	68,000	68,000−5,000	×	2/21	=	6,000
2010	68,000	68,000−5,000	×	1/21	=	3,000
SYD 21	Total Depreciation Expense					63,000

Section 3

1. identifiable non-monetary asset

2. recognition

3. indefinite

4. huge benefits

5. patents, trademarks, copyrights, franchises and licenses, Internet domain names, construction permits

6. goodwill, brands, publishing titles

7. cost

8. amortization

9. profit and loss

10. contract, document

Section 4

1. Long-term assets refer to those that have high economic values and whose useful lives are more than one accounting period.

2. Fixed assets are tangible assets which have the following two main characteristics: Firstly, they are held for use in the production or supply of goods or services, for rental to others, or for administrative purposes. Secondly, they have useful lives more than one accounting year.

3. An tangible assets refers to the assets that one can touch and include natural resources, buildings, machines and so on.

4. An intangible assets can be defined as any identifiable non-monetary assets without physical substance which is owned or controlled by an enterprise.

5. The so-called useful life refers to the period over which an asset is expected to be available for use by an enterprise or the number of units of production or service expected to be obtained from the asset by an enterprise.

6. Depreciation is defined as the accounting process of systematically allocating the depreciable amount of a fixed asset over its useful life by a selected depreciation method.

7. The depreciable amount is the original cost of a fixed asset minus its estimated net residual value and accumulated impairment losses.

8. The estimated net residual value refers to the estimated amount that an enterprise would currently obtain from disposal of the asset, after deducting the estimated costs of disposal.

9. Amortization refers to the regular recognition of an expense over a period of its economic usefulness.

10. Goodwill refers to the added value of an enterprise or a business that is due to favorable factors such as reputation, location, efficiency, popularity and valuable relationship with customers. It belongs to the intangible asset with a marketable money valuable.

Section 5

1. F. Fixed assets are tangible assets.

2. F. Goodwill belongs to intangible assets.

3. T.

4. F. Equipment such as machinery, furniture, tools should be depreciated.

5. T.

6. T.

7. F. Bonds and stocks are not classified as intangible assets but as investments.

8. T.

9. T.

10. F. If the expected useful life and estimated net residual value are quite different from their previous estimate, they shall be revised accordingly.

Section 6

1. Long-term assets are valuable resources which can produce revenue to the businesses or enterprises. So they are very important for their development.

2. The cost of a purchased fixed asset includes the purchase price, related taxes, and other expenditures such as delivery and handling costs, installation costs, professional fees, etc.

3. The most common types of fixed assets include land, offices, factories, warehouses, machinery, furniture, tools, etc.

4. Patents, copyrights, franchises and licenses, and trademarks are the most common types of intangible assets.

5. They are the Straight-Line Method, the Units of Production Method, the Double Declining Balance Method, and the Sum-of-the-Years-Digits Method. The simplest method might be the Straight-Line method.

Unit 4

Section 1

1. unearned revenue   2. accounts payable   3. notes payable
4. the shareholders (owners)   5. a future event occurs   6. long-term

7.
(1) Cash $60,000
       Notes payable $60,000
(2) Interest expense $4,800
       Interest payable $4,800
(3) Notes payable $60,000
    Interest expense $4,800
       cash $64,800

Section 2

1. B

2.
(1) Cash   1,960,000
    Discount on bonds payable   40,000
          Bonds payable   2,000,000

Assets		=	Liabilities	+	Owner's equity	Rev.	−	Exp.	=	Net Inc.	Cash Flow
1,960,000	40,000	=	2,000,000	+			−		=		1,960,000 FA

(2) Paid semi-annual interest on $2,000,000 of 9 %, 10-year bonds.

    Bond interest expense   90,000

        Cash   90,000

Assets	=	Lia.	+	Owner's equity	Rev.	−	Exp.	=	Net Inc.	Cash Flow
(90,000)	=		+	(90,000)		−	90,000	=	(90,000)	(90,000) FA

(3) Amortized discount for six months on 10-year bond issue ($40,000÷20 = $2,000).

    Bond interest expense   2,000

        Discount on Bonds Payable   2,000

Assets	=	Liabilities	+	Owner's equity	Rev.	−	Exp.	=	Net Inc.	Cash Flow
	=	2,000	+	(2,000)		−	2,000	=	(2,000)	

Unit 5

Section 1,2

1. shareholders' equity

2. preferred stock, common stock

3. par value

4. outstanding

5. cash dividends, stock dividend

6. stock dividend

7. appropriation of retained earnings

8. Retained Earnings

9. statement of retained earnings

Section 3,4

1. T 2. T 3. T 4. F 5. F 6. T 7. T 8. F 9. F 10. F 11. T 12. T

Section 5,6

1. C 2. B 3. D 4. B 5. C 6. D 7. D 8. C 9. C 10. B

Unit 6

1. (1) A (2) D
2. (1) F (2) T (3) F (4) F (5) T (6) T (7) T (8) F

Unit 7

Section 1

略。

Section 2

略。
略。

Section 3

1. D 2. D 3. C

Unit 8

1.
(1) T (2) F (3) T (4) F (5) F
2.
Current ratio	(iii)
Quick ratio	(viii)
Gearing	(vi)
Times interest cover	(v)
Dividend cover	(i)
Stock turnover	(vii)
Average collection period	(ii)
Profit margin	(x)
Return on total assets	(iv)
Return on owner's equity	(ix)

3. (i) (d), (ii) (b), (iii) (a), (iv) (c)

Unit 9

The first step is to allocate the indirect costs to departments.

Rates—basis of allocation : area		
Mixing	(1,500÷4,500)×$3,600	$1200
Bottling	(2,000÷4,500)×$3,600	1,600
Maintenance	(400÷4,500)×$3,600	320
Stores	(600÷4,500)×$3,600	480
		$3,600
Power—basis of allocation: kilowatt hours		
Mixing	(3,500÷6,000)×$33,600	$19,600
Bottling	(1,800÷6,000)×$33,600	10,080
Maintenance	(300÷6,000)×$33,600	1,680
Stores	(400÷6,000)×$33,600	2,240
		$33,600
Insurance (buildings) —basis of allocation : area		
Mixing	(1,500÷4,500)×$22,500	$7,500
Bottling	(2,000÷4,500)×$22,500	10000
Maintenance	(400÷4,500)×$22,500	2000
Stores	(600÷4,500)×$22,500	3000
		$22,500
Insurance (plant) —basis of allocation : value of plant		
Mixing	(100,000÷200,000)×$10,500	$5,250
Bottling	(70,000÷200,000)×$10,500	3,675
Maintenance	(10,000÷200,000)×$10,500	525
Stores	(20,000÷200,000)×$10,500	1,050
		$10,500

The allocated indirect costs are shown in the follow table.

Allocated Indirect Costs
Departmental Overhead Distribution Sheet

Costs (Fixed/Variable)	Total	Mixing	Bottling	Maintenance	Stores
Indirect labor	95,000	33,600	30,400	13,000	18,000
Indirect materials	46,800	23,450	18,645	1,475	3,230
Depreciation—plant	18,000	9,000	6,000	1,000	2,000
Rates	3,600	1,200	1,600	320	480

续表

Power	33,600	19,600	10,080	1,680	2,240
Insurance—buildings	22,500	7,500	10,000	2,000	3,000
—plant	10,500	5,250	3,675	525	1,050
Total	230,000	99,600	80,400	20,000	30,000

Unit 10

Section 1

1. systematic

2. accounting

3. report

4. communicating

5. Internal, external, governmental

6. objective

7. external, third

8. CPA

9. Independence

10. stewardship

Section 2

1.
(1) processor (2) contract (3) first (4) effectiveness (5) weak (6) recommendation (7) substantive (8) unqualified

2. abcdefg

3. cfaebd

Section 3

1.
(1) opinion (2) adverse, disclaimer (3) substantive

2. A

3. B

4. D

5. B

6. A B C

参 考 文 献

1. 冷永杰. 会计专业英语. 北京: 机械工业出版社, 2003
2. 郝绍伦. 会计英语导航. 北京: 中国科学技术大学出版社, 2003
3. 张晓敏. 会计英语. 重庆: 重庆大学出版社, 2004
4. 于久洪. 会计英语. 北京: 人民大学出版社, 2005
5. 孟焰. 会计英语. 北京: 经济科学出版社, 2005
6. 常勋. 会计专业英语. 上海: 立信会计出版社, 2006
7. 李惠. 会计专业英语. 北京: 高等教育出版社, 2006
8. 中华人民共和国财政部. 企业会计准则. 北京: 经济科学出版社, 2006
9. 陈雪翎. 会计英语. 北京: 高等教育出版社, 2006
10. 陈汉东, 乐泓, 田小山. 实用会计英语. 长沙: 湖南人民出版社, 2008
11. 孙坤. 会计英语. 大连: 东北财经大学出版社, 2008
12. 许秉岩. 西方会计英语. 北京: 清华大学出版社, 1998
13. 黄世忠等. 会计英语教程. 厦门: 厦门大学出版社, 2004
14. 郭梅, 郭丽芳. 实用会计英语. 北京: 机械工业出版社, 2007
15. 孙雪静, 王荣花. 会计英语. 北京: 外文出版社, 2007